SOCIAL AND ECONOMIC NETWORKS IN EARLY MASSACHUSETTS

MARSHA L. HAMILTON

SOCIAL AND ECONOMIC NETWORKS IN EARLY MASSACHUSETTS

Atlantic Connections

THE PENNSYLVANIA STATE UNIVERSITY PRESS
UNIVERSITY PARK, PENNSYLVANIA

Library of Congress Cataloging-in-Publication Data

Hamilton, Marsha L., 1961–
Social and economic networks in early Massachusetts :
Atlantic connections / Marsha L. Hamilton.
p.   cm.
Summary: "An examination of the non-English communities
of early Massachusetts"—Provided by publisher.
Includes bibliographical references and index.
ISBN 978-0-271-03551-2 (cloth : alk. paper)
1. Massachusetts—Social life and customs—To 1775.
2. Social networks—Massachusetts—History.
3. Community life—Massachusetts—History.
4. Ethnicity—Massachusetts—History.
5. Massachusetts—Ethnic relations.
6. Massachusetts—Economic conditions.
I. Title.

F67.H23 2009
974.4'02—dc22
2009003686

It is the policy of The Pennsylvania State University Press to
use acid-free paper. This book is printed on Natures Natural,
containing 50% post-consumer waste, and meets the
minimum requirements of American National Standard for
Information Sciences—Permanence of Paper for
Printed Library Material, ANSI z39.48–1992.

For

MY MOTHER

AND

IN MEMORY OF MY FATHER

Contents

Acknowledgments

As with most books, this work could not have been completed without a great deal of help and support. First of all, my thanks go to Ned Landsman, my adviser at SUNY Stony Brook, who read many drafts of this manuscript over the years. I am grateful for his high standard of scholarship and intellectual generosity, two traits that have influenced me and shaped this project from the beginning. Many other friends and colleagues read drafts of this work and their comments have contributed much to my thoughts on the issues presented. My thanks to Robert Cray, Dianne Creagh, John Fea, Kevin Gumienny, Donna Rilling, Diane Robinson-Dunn, Steve Fuchs, Susanna Taipale, and Nancy Tomes. The anonymous readers for Penn State Press also offered many comments that greatly improved the manuscript. As usual, however, all errors are my own.

My colleagues in the Department of History at the University of South Alabama (USA) deserve many thanks for creating a wonderful environment in which to work. Clarence Mohr, chair of the department, has always been supportive with advice, encouragement, and funds for research travel. The members of the department over the past five years—Betty Brandon, Martha Jane Brazy, Rich Brown, Don DeVore, Bob Faust, Woody Hannum, Larry Holmes, Bob Houston, Mara Kozelsky, Mollie Lewis, Lenny Macaluso, Mel McKiven, Harry Miller, Mike Monheit, Joe Nigota, Dan Rogers, Michele Strong, Mike Thomason, John Turner, and Rebecca Williams—have provided encouragement and friendship, making work (both teaching and writing) a thoroughly enjoyable activity.

Several institutions also supported this project. In 1999–2000, the Massachusetts Historical Society awarded me a W. B. H. Dowse Fellowship for research in their collections. I also received a Summer Professional Development Grant from the College of Arts and Sciences at USA and a grant from the University of South Alabama Research Council that allowed me to travel to Glasgow and Edinburgh in 2005 for further research. The completion of the book would not have been possible without these funds.

The staffs of the Massachusetts Archives, the Massachusetts Historical Society, the Baker Library at Harvard University, the Philips Library at the Peabody Essex Museum, the New England Historic Genealogy Society, the Archives and Special Collections at the Mitchell Library (Glasgow), and at the National Archives of Scotland (Edinburgh) also deserve many thanks for their help. Quotations and citations from collections held by the Massachusetts Historical Society and the Baker Library at Harvard appear by permission of these institutions. I also thank the librarians at USA, especially the interlibrary loan staff for their help over the years.

Portions of several chapters were published in two articles: "Alternative Communities in Early Massachusetts," *Historical Journal of Massachusetts* 32, no. 2 (2004): 153–73; and "The Irish and the Formation of British Communities in Early Massachusetts," in *The Irish in the Atlantic World*, ed. David T. Gleeson (Columbia: University of South Carolina Press, forthcoming). I thank the publishers for allowing me to use parts of these essays in this book. I would also like to thank the participants in the conference "The Irish in the Atlantic World," sponsored by the Program in the Carolina Lowcountry and Atlantic World at the College of Charleston (spring 2007), for their comments on this paper and article. The questions and comments by David Gleeson, Patrick Griffin, Brad Wood, Kerby Miller, Nicholas Canny, and Thomas Truxes gave me new insight into the Irish experience in early America. I also presented portions of this material at the International Seminar on the History of the Atlantic World (Working Paper 02–11) at Harvard University, the Post-graduate Seminar in American History at Cambridge University, and the Post-graduate Seminar in American History at Oxford University. The comments of the seminar participants helped shape the focus of the book.

Finally, I would like to thank my family for their unwavering support and encouragement. Even when I doubted that this project would ever be completed, they never did.

A Note on Spelling and Dates

In general, spelling and dates are rendered here as written in the original documents, although superscriptions and abbreviations have been brought down and spelled out, and the Old English thorn and Latin spelling characteristics (*I* for *J*, *U* for *V*) have been changed to modern forms. In addition, I have standardized the spelling of proper names, using the spelling that occurs most frequently in the documents. Names do not necessarily conform to modern spelling, but each person's name is spelled the same throughout the book. I have also used double-dating for the period between January 1 and March 25, when the new year began under the Gregorian calendar in use in the seventeenth-century English colonies.

INTRODUCTION:

BRITISH AND ATLANTIC NETWORKS IN EARLY MASSACHUSETTS

In November 1693, the choleric governor of Massachusetts, Sir William Phips, witnessed an altercation on Boston's waterfront. Upon inquiry, he was told by Benjamin Faneuil, a Huguenot merchant who had arrived in the Bay Colony in 1689, that Jahleel Brenton, the customs collector, had ordered the seizure of a trading shallop from Port Royal, Nova Scotia, and all of its goods. Faneuil claimed that the seizure was based solely on the fact that the master and his crew were French, which he saw as unfair—but if true, it would put the master in violation of the Navigation Acts. Brenton and his deputies seemed to have strong legal grounds for the seizure. Nevertheless, an angry Phips exclaimed, "They are as good or better Englishmen then the Collector is, & let him seize them if he dare, if he doth I will break his head." Brenton's deputies prudently decided not to pursue their orders.[1]

Many issues lay behind this exchange. Phips had a quick temper; he was in fact recalled from office in 1694 in part because of his public beating of a captain in the Royal Navy. He had been involved in many earlier disputes with Brenton, largely over political power and the right to seize the goods of, and thereby profit from, violators of the trade laws. Phips was also trying to win support for his governorship among merchants and elites in Massachusetts and from royal officials in England. He hoped to expand trade with Acadia to consolidate his power in that region, as well as to please merchants and uphold the claim of English control over the territory. Enfolding Port Royal into New

England's orbit would secure Phips's economic and political interests, and so political intrigues and rivalries were deeply entwined in this incident.[2]

Phips's comments also acknowledged, perhaps unconsciously, the changes that had taken place in Massachusetts society by the end of the seventeenth century. The commerce of coastal communities such as Boston and Salem had attracted merchants and sailors from throughout the Atlantic world within a dozen years of their settlement. Trade with England, of course, had sustained the colony in its earliest years, familiarizing sailors with the region and its potential products. By the early 1640s, however, Boston merchants sent wood and foodstuffs to the West Indies, Spain, and the Spanish and Portuguese islands in the Atlantic. The early 1640s also saw an overture by the French in Acadia to open trade with Massachusetts.[3] By 1645, the General Court had ordered "that all ships that come for trading onely from other parts shall have free access to our harbors, & quiet riding there, & free to leave or depart without any molestation by us, they paying all such duties & charges required by law in the country as others do."[4] Thus fifteen years after settlement, Massachusetts leaders declared the colony open to trade from the wide Atlantic world.

Along with merchants and sailors, Massachusetts also became home to laborers and Protestant refugees from Europe. As early as the 1640s and 1650s, non-Puritan laborers had been brought to Massachusetts from Wales, Scotland, and Ireland.[5] Some of these laborers, such as ironworkers, possessed badly needed skills, but most were unskilled, filling a continuing need for general labor in the colony. Africans and "Spanish" Indians from South America also appeared in the colony, joining local Native Americans as a small part of the labor force in the late 1630s. In addition, after the revocation of the Edict of Nantes in 1685, many French Protestant merchants, including Benjamin Faneuil and his brothers, came to New England. Huguenots, as fellow Calvinists, had religious doctrines compatible with Puritan beliefs. Their attachment to ceremony and the celebration of Christmas, however, rankled orthodox Puritans at times.[6]

Such immigrants to Massachusetts brought important skills and contacts to the region. A chronic labor shortage existed in the colony throughout the first few decades; Puritan immigrants alone could not fill the need for skilled and unskilled workers. Ironworking in particular was not an industry that attracted many "godly" laborers, yet the Saugus ironworks and its non-Puritan workforce played an important role in the development of the local economy while also bringing diversity to the population.[7] Later in the century, merchants from Scotland and France brought new trade networks to the colony. Scots had long enjoyed close ties to the Dutch, for instance, who dominated the carrying trade throughout Europe and the Atlantic. Scottish resident factors in the

Netherlands tapped into Dutch overseas commerce, giving the English partners of Scottish merchants in New England access to these extensive commercial circles.[8] Non-English and non-Puritan residents thus broadened the range of economic activity, both locally and in the Atlantic world, in ways not possible by relying only on godly connections.

Non-English and non-Puritan laborers, merchants, and mariners lived throughout the region and, if they were settled residents and of European descent, could trade and hold property as equals with English colonials. In addition, the legal rights of some non-English settlers were defined in English law. Many French Protestants fled first to England and applied for naturalization or denization there, giving them at least partial rights of citizens in England and its colonies. Scots born after 1603, the year of James VI of Scotland's accession to the throne of England, had been considered citizens of England and its colonies since 1608, a result of the legal ruling in Calvin's Case, which declared that allegiance adhered to the sovereign, not the nation, and thus subjects of the monarch held rights in all the territories of that ruler. Scots and English, then, had reciprocal rights in England, Scotland, and their colonies. The Irish had rights in the English colonies due to their status as conquered subjects. According to Sir Edward Coke, the leading legal theorist in seventeenth-century England, although the Scots and Irish came by their rights in different ways, they could operate in the English colonies as legal subjects of England.[9] In Massachusetts, therefore, as long as they lived and worked in accordance with the established laws and customs of the colony, Scots and Irish were, for the most part, "as good Englishmen." Some men, such as William Phips, could even envision incorporating the French-speaking residents of a French colony into the English colonial world.

This apparent equality with English residents in Massachusetts, however, did not necessarily extend to the franchise. Before 1647, freemen, those residents entitled to vote, had to be members of a Congregational church. The law was changed in 1647, allowing non-freemen to participate in town affairs, although with some significant restrictions. Non–church members had to be approved by the freemen of the town in order to gain the right to vote in local elections. The restoration of Charles II prompted further reforms, and in 1664, non–Congregational church members could become freemen and participate fully in colony affairs. Property restrictions attached to this law limited participation to wealthy families (primarily those of newly arrived merchants). In general, then, most of the residents discussed here only qualified to participate in town affairs. Only those few who joined the Congregational church, mostly merchants, gained full citizenship in Massachusetts during the Old Charter period. Nevertheless, many non-Puritan settlers did take part in local affairs, and colony voting restrictions did not hamper their acquisition of property or participation in commerce.[10]

Even with legal and property rights, these non-English settlers did not become cultural "Englishmen." Many continued to see themselves as Scottish, Irish, or French, and perpetuated customs and traditions from home, while also constructing new identities that reflected their roles as colonials. Such residents added to the diversity and complexity of early Massachusetts society, and the communities and networks that they developed gave them roots in the colony and also brought the Bay Colony into a wider Atlantic world. These newcomers helped turn Massachusetts, among the most English of all the colonies, into an increasingly "British" space. In short, by the end of the seventeenth century, Massachusetts began to resemble societies in other parts of North America, composed of peoples from Britain—England, Scotland, and the Channel Islands—Ireland, and Continental Europe, and whose economies and politics were increasingly tied to England.

Scholars have long known that seventeenth-century Massachusetts, and New England in general, was not simply composed of English Puritans.[11] Incomplete records, however, mean that accurate population statistics cannot be compiled for this period. It must also be recognized that occupational and religious "outsiders" compounded national and ethnic diversity, further complicating the picture. Therefore, a full accounting of diversity is not feasible, but a brief account of some of the primary groups of non-Puritans will give a sense of the mix of peoples present in early Massachusetts. An additional complication is that the numbers of non-English and non-Puritan residents increased over the course of the century; there were more in 1690 than in 1640. Yet, even as speculative as the numbers of these settlers may be, it is clear that "Puritan" Massachusetts had accommodated many non-Puritans since the beginning of European settlement.

Daniel Vickers notes at least four hundred seafaring families in Salem and Marblehead by 1690, and Richard Gildrie estimates that seamen or men of unknown occupation made up 46 percent of the two waterfront wards in Salem in 1690. Although the individuals counted in these estimates overlap, nonetheless families of fishers, sailors, and dockworkers composed a large proportion of the coastal population, particularly when these figures are extrapolated to the much larger port of Boston. These maritime workers were largely English and Jersey Islanders, but most cannot be associated with a Congregational church. Because complete records do not exist for most early churches, and those that do survive rarely mention people who attended regularly but were not members, we cannot be certain about church affiliation. As Christine Heyrman points out, however, two of the primary fishing ports in the colony, Gloucester and Marblehead, did not establish Congregational churches until 1664 and 1684, respectively. It would also have been difficult for maritime workers to attend services regularly. In addition, because fishermen and sailors lived much of their lives on the water, unable to properly observe the Sabbath and not under the watch of ministers and neighbors, they were believed to be under greater temptations with fewer restraints than land-based residents.[12] Thus these families, regardless of nationality, were considered outsiders by their Puritan neighbors.

Merchants and their families are equally difficult to pin down. Although by the end of the century many merchants from old Puritan families still conducted business, new English, Scottish, French, and Channel Island commercial families had joined them. Men such as Richard Wharton, John Borland, Benjamin Faneuil, and Philip English had close connections to fellow merchants in their home countries, and they married New England women, thus creating an interlocking network of commercial families throughout the English Atlantic world. These marriages between established families and new immigrants make a clear distinction between old and new mercantile families hard to discern. Yet when considering only unmarried merchants and those who moved to Essex and Suffolk counties with families already, non-Puritan and non-English commercial families numbered in the hundreds by the 1690s.[13]

Many other non-Puritan immigrants arrived in New England during the last half of the seventeenth century. Several hundred Huguenot refugees settled in an agricultural community near Worcester, and French merchants gravitated to the port village of Boston, where they had long-standing ties to the town's commercial community. Many other French Protestants, merchants and farmers alike, went to Plymouth and Rhode Island. Huguenots in Rhode Island faced violence and severe discrimination, partly due to an ongoing land dispute between Connecticut and Rhode Island. When these families were forced out of their new homes, many resettled in Massachusetts and New York.[14]

In addition, between five hundred and seven hundred Scottish, Irish, and Jersey laborers came to the coastal counties of Massachusetts in the third quarter of the century. In the early 1650s, Scots captured by the English at the battles of Dunbar and Worcester were deported to all the colonies. New England received several hundred, mostly sent over by John Becx, a principal investor in the Company of Undertakers of the Ironworks in New England. Becx and the Undertakers were searching for a cheap labor force for the Saugus ironworks, and when the English government allowed them to acquire more men than were necessary for the company's immediate needs, they sold the excess captives to local landowners and craftsmen. Many Scots also went to sawmills in New Hampshire and southern Maine. Irish captives began to appear in Massachusetts around the same time as the Scots. The majority of these men and women went to the Chesapeake colonies and the West Indies, but many ended up in the northern colonies. Laborers from the Channel Islands began to arrive in the late 1660s and early 1670s, brought to Massachusetts by Jersey merchants to work in the fish trade and as household servants. These laborers were concentrated in Essex County towns, although a few also appeared in Boston and Springfield.[15]

Along with non-Puritans of European descent, approximately eight hundred Africans lived in Massachusetts by 1700.[16] Africans appear in the records of Massachusetts from a very early date. William Wood, in his 1634 pamphlet *New England's Prospect*, notes the presence of at least one African, and John Josselyn, in the first of his two voyages to New England, describes his encounters with three Africans owned by Samuel Maverick of Noddles Island in 1639. In addition, Emanuel Downing wrote to his brother-in-law John Winthrop in 1645 that a war with the Narragansett Indians would provide captives to exchange for African slaves in the West Indies, which he believed would greatly benefit Massachusetts. Thus, some Massachusetts residents saw African slavery as a positive solution to the general labor shortage in the colony. Blacks apparently were treated much like European servants in the early years; for example, in 1641, a "Negro maid" of Israel Stoughton of Dorchester became a church member. This status changed by the mid-1650s, when blacks and Indians were barred from training with the militias, although non-English European servants continued to be trusted with weapons. By the end of the century, many of the leading families and merchants in Boston and Salem owned African slaves. Samuel Sewall, the prominent Puritan merchant, judge, and diarist, discusses many Africans in Boston throughout his diary. Even though Africans composed less than 2 percent of the population of Massachusetts by 1700, they were not an uncommon sight on the streets of the larger towns.[17]

Hundreds of Christian Native Americans also lived within the colony's boundaries, along with thousands of "wild" Indians on the margins of English settlements. Devastating plagues in the mid-1610s decimated the Indian population in eastern Massachusetts, and so settlers in Plymouth in the 1620s and the Bay Colony in the 1630s faced fewer immediate threats from Native Americans than did their counterparts in the Chesapeake. Plymouth's attacks on the Indians at Wessagusset in 1623 and the Pequot War undertaken by Massachusetts in 1636–37 caused local Indians to realize that the English were warlike aggressors. Many Indians therefore tried to maintain a peaceful coexistence with these unpredictable strangers. Puritans initially made few attempts to convert the

Indians, aside from the efforts of minister John Eliot of Roxbury and Thomas Mayhew, Jr., of Martha's Vineyard, even though this was cited as a reason to establish the colony. Nevertheless, by the third quarter of the seventeenth century, Massachusetts had established fourteen "praying towns" of Christian Indians. Many Massachusetts settlers never quite trusted the sincerity of these conversions, however, and Christian Indians were badly mistreated during King Philip's War in 1675–76. Native Americans, then, Christian or not, were always seen as outsiders in Massachusetts society.[18]

This occupational, national, and ethnic diversity was compounded by religious differences. Although Congregationalism was the established church structure, by the 1660s Essex County claimed a small but highly visible core of Quaker converts. Quakers had appeared in Massachusetts in the late 1650s, only a few years after the sect had formed in Wales and western England. A product of poverty in these areas and the social and religious upheaval of the civil war years, the anticlerical and individualistic tendencies inherent in Quakerism posed a threat to the educated ministry and Congregational tenets of Puritanism. The early radicalism of the sect also threatened to undermine the established churches of Massachusetts. Thus when English Quakers appeared in the colony, they were quickly ushered out and warned not to return. Local adherents of the new religion, many of whom converted from orthodox Puritanism, were hauled before the Essex County court, fined, and forbidden to meet for religious services outside the local churches. Persecution continued for the next several years; Essex County Quakers were imprisoned, whipped, and banished until 1659, when Massachusetts executed two "traveling Friends." In 1661, Mary Dyer, a longtime resident of Massachusetts who converted to Quakerism early, and William Leddra, an English Quaker, were also executed. After these deaths, and with the knowledge that further persecution of Quakers would not be tolerated by the newly restored Stuart monarchy, Massachusetts leaders grudgingly accepted the presence of Quakers, although they attempted to keep the sect from attracting new converts. The radicalism of early Quakers gradually diminished through the seventeenth century, and although Massachusetts Quakers slowly became more accepted in society, they always remained slightly suspect in the eyes of their Puritan neighbors.[19]

Baptist congregations also began to appear throughout the region, establishing their first church in Charlestown in 1665. Although not welcome in Massachusetts, Baptists suffered less persecution than did Quakers. Many early Baptists were members in good standing of Congregational churches who had developed questions about the efficacy of infant baptism. In many ways, Baptists simply took traditional Calvinist beliefs to their logical extreme, and thus many traditional Puritans viewed them as legitimate. Dissention over the Halfway Covenant of 1662, wherein children of Congregational church members were brought under church discipline even though they had not experienced conversion, also made Baptist practices more acceptable. Thus, although not fully trusted, Baptists were not as outcast as other religious dissidents in early Massachusetts.[20]

The lines between English and non-English, and Puritan and non-Puritan cannot always be clearly drawn. The categories of occupation, nationality, ethnicity, and religion frequently overlapped. Most religious dissidents were English, for example, and many Scots and Huguenots practiced religions not widely divergent from Puritanism. Yet both of the latter groups were clearly outsiders in terms of nationality and therefore slightly suspect, at least for a few years after their initial immigration. "Praying Indians" were rarely trusted, in spite of their religious conversion and attempts to live in agricultural villages as prescribed by the Puritan leadership. Settlers in marginal occupations, such as fishermen and ironworkers, came from many national and ethnic groups. How and why these peoples settled into the larger community and became accepted by it differs from group to group. A complex society derives from many roots, and describing the development of that society cannot be attributed simply to religious or national compatibility. Some French settlers were welcomed because of their religion, whereas some English settlers were not welcomed, also due to their religion. Praying Indians should have been accepted because of their religion but, due to their ethnicity, they were not. The Scots and Irish legally had rights in the English colonies as subjects of the Stuart kings but were not necessarily trusted as residents of Massachusetts. Skilled workers and general laborers were almost always accepted as residents regardless of nationality (excluding, of course, Africans and Native Americans) because the colony needed them economically. Again, clear distinctions cannot be drawn; accommodation came from a convergence of reasons. Therefore, by the end of the seventeenth century, Massachusetts society cannot be described simply in terms of English and Puritan.[21]

Not all "strangers"—a term used to describe new or temporary residents, people not yet known to the larger community—affected the development of society. Many left the colony, either voluntarily or through banishment, and thus did not play a role in its development. Thomas Morton of Merrymount, whose May Day revels and competition in the fur trade vexed Plymouth leaders, and Samuel Gorton, whose religious beliefs undermined the emerging doctrine of Massachusetts, were captured and sent to England by the Puritan governments of these colonies. Both men tried to undermine the colonies once back in England but were not very successful at implementing changes.[22] Anne Hutchinson and Roger Williams created dissention in Massachusetts and took many followers with them to new settlements in Rhode Island, yet after their banishments they played little role in Massachusetts.[23] Robert Child—medical doctor, scientist, and friend of John Winthrop, Jr.—also threatened to undermine the "New England Way," as well as the authority of the magistrates, by arguing for a more Presbyterian style of church governance and threatening to appeal his case to England. Once again, after leaving the colony, Child had little influence on its development, although he remained in contact with Winthrop and was an investor in the Saugus ironworks in the early 1640s and other ventures undertaken by Winthrop.[24]

Many non-Puritan Europeans, however, especially economic migrants, did remain in the colony—moving from strangers to settled residents—but their contributions to the development of Massachusetts society have rarely been considered.[25] These inhabitants generally have been seen as either marginal to the colony or as assimilating into the dominant Puritan society. Clifford Shipton stated in 1936 "that the bulk of the immigrants before 1687 were absorbed into the Puritan society, a conclusion supported by the lists of church members." More recently, Stephen Innes argues that unruly ironworkers at the Saugus ironworks in the 1640s and 1650s were soon "tamed" by Puritan discipline. David Thomas Konig contends that the "Scots and the Irish occasionally clashed with the English population, but they migrated there in such small numbers that their adjustment was relatively easy."[26] In his study of the Huguenot emigration to North America, Jon Butler asserts that "Boston's relative homogeneity in religion and nationality may have smothered the small refugee population's cohesion and sustained resistance to conformity."[27] The one ethnic group acknowledged to have retained their customs and community within Puritan-dominated Massachusetts was Jersey Islanders, whom Konig places in opposition to their English neighbors. Although Jerseyans did enter into many disputes with their neighbors and resorted to legal action quickly to resolve personal and commercial problems, these issues can obscure the extent to which they participated in Massachusetts society.[28]

The standard dichotomy of marginalization or assimilation does not adequately explain the role of non-English and non-Puritan residents in early Massachusetts society. Some blended into Puritan-dominated communities fairly quickly, whereas others kept their distance to a greater or lesser extent. English and Welsh ironworkers fall at one end of this spectrum, and Jersey Islanders fall at the other end. The earliest ironworkers frequently married into middling families and obtained land, but Jersey immigrants married among themselves and retained a distinctive language and culture throughout the seventeenth century. Members of both groups, however, participated in community affairs and considered Massachusetts their home. Non-Puritans, as with the more frequently studied Puritan settlers, participated in several communities of interest based on religion, nationality, craft, trade, and place of residence, and identified themselves by these associations as the context warranted.

To assert the existence of such interlocking social ties does not imply that non-Puritan and non-English communities developed quickly, easily, or without friction. Although early Massachusetts leaders envisioned a settlement dominated by the godly, they quickly realized that they needed strangers. During the 1630s, Puritans who settled in New England knew that they could not isolate themselves from the world. Many migrants saw themselves as the "saving remnant" who would bring reformed religion back to England after God's wrath had cleansed the land. Puritans in New England thus watched events in England and Europe closely, and considered themselves part of the international community of reformed Protestants. Puritan ideology also insisted that the godly must struggle with temptation rather than hide from it; believers needed to remain engaged with the world.

Engagement cannot be equated, however, with tolerance. The leaders of Massachusetts tried to control who settled in their colony, and expelled heterodox settlers who refused to accept the developing status quo, such as Roger Williams and Anne Hutchinson, both of whom refused to muzzle their ideas for the sake of conformity.[29] Nathaniel Ward put this idea most succinctly in 1647 by writing, "Familists, Antinomians, Anabaptists, and other such Enthusiasts, shall have free Liberty to keep away from us." Other dissenters, such as William Pynchon of Springfield, were reprimanded for their beliefs only after publishing pamphlets that contradicted orthodox beliefs. Pynchon's tract *The Meritorious Price of Our Redemption* argues against Trinitarian Christianity, asserting that Christ was human rather than part of the godhead. The Massachusetts General Court deemed the pamphlet heretical and ordered that it be burned. Pynchon left the colony voluntarily in 1652 rather than retract his pamphlet and submit to official censure. Many others whose opinions fell within an acceptable range of ideas never faced public humiliation.[30] Political dissenters, such as Robert Child and his supporters, also troubled the colony, as did unruly servants and laborers. Yet religious dissenters helped define orthodoxy, whereas servants and laborers, godly and not, contributed to economic development. In many ways, strangers and dissenters shaped early Massachusetts.

Thus, by the end of the seventeenth century, a complex society had developed in Massachusetts that was neither strictly Puritan nor English. Non-English and non-Puritan laborers and servants, although lacking political authority, had contributed to the construction of the social web, and merchants brought overseas contacts spanning the Atlantic.[31] Although there was less ethnic and racial diversity than in New York, Pennsylvania, or Virginia, Massachusetts society began to resemble those in other parts of the emerging British Atlantic world.

This study began, as have so many other books, as a paper in a graduate research seminar. At that time, I became fascinated by the presence of the Scots and Irish in early Massachusetts and wondered why Scottish and Irish prisoners—men and women captured and forcibly deported from their homelands—stayed in Massachusetts. Many, of course, did not have the resources to leave after their terms of service, and the question became how they adapted to life in Massachusetts. I found that, like other early modern people, they developed communities and social networks that provided stability and opportunity in an English colony. Social relationships were more fluid than is normally associated with this period, even in a fairly homogeneous colony like Massachusetts. Early modern people coped with unfamiliar situations by forming networks and communities of interest that connected them to one another and to the larger world, rather than walling themselves off. Such communities can be found throughout the Atlantic world anyplace where "strangers" moved into a settled population. Although these networks have generally been associated with merchants, this study shows that smaller, more localized communities developed as well. These social networks were also the basis for the expansion of Atlantic commerce and communication.

The men and women presented in this book were identified through primary and secondary sources. I developed lists of non-English and non-Puritan residents by searching through court records for Essex and Suffolk counties; the published volumes as well as the documents in the Phillips Library, Peabody Essex Museum, the Massachusetts Archives, and the Massachusetts Historical Society; and individual town records within these counties. Salem and Boston have the most extensive records available; I also examined the Middlesex County records at the Massachusetts Archives, although they are not as well indexed as those for Essex and Suffolk counties, and so were much more difficult to search thoroughly. I found names as well through the Ironworks Papers in the Baker Library at Harvard University and membership lists of the Scots' Charitable Society (scs). Individual town histories produced in the late nineteenth and early twentieth centuries were also very useful. The only ship passenger list that exists is for the Scottish prisoners deported to Massachusetts in 1652 after the Battle of Worcester. I did not use surname analysis, although I checked in the indexes and finding aids every name that sounded as though it had a Scottish, Irish, or French derivation.[32] I also kept notes on residents closely associated with known strangers, although I did not include that person or family in this study unless I could positively identify them as non-Puritan or non-English.

The book is divided into five chapters and a conclusion that each examine different groups of settlers: ironworkers, farmers and agricultural laborers, and merchants. The first chapter lays out the historiographical and contextual background for the topic. After that, the book moves to case studies of specific groups of settlers. Because British communities developed out of the need for labor, the second chapter examines laborers and their networks, focusing primarily on the Saugus ironworkers. The earliest ironworkers came from England and Wales, recruited by John Winthrop, Jr., and the Undertakers of the Ironworks in New England. Most brought necessary skills to the colony and so were accepted, even though Massachusetts authorities were wary of their poor reputations. As the costs of running the ironworks increased, the Undertakers acquired Scottish captives. These men were largely unskilled, but also provided an important labor force in the region. Outsiders in several different ways, these ironworkers bonded with one another, maintaining relationships even as they moved around Massachusetts.

The third chapter looks at agricultural laborers as they developed communities in the commercial farming districts of northern Essex County. These residents were more grounded in a place than were the ironworkers, yet they did not develop traditional village communities. They lived on the margins of settled villages and enjoyed wide-ranging connections to other non-Puritan residents in the county. Similar communities appear to have existed in Suffolk and Middlesex counties, but the court records are far less complete than those in Essex County, making it much more difficult to trace such settlers in these areas.

The fourth chapter explores transatlantic commercial networks developed by merchants after the Restoration. English, Scottish, French, and Jersey merchants began to expand their ties throughout the Atlantic world, operating within British and Atlantic networks. These merchants frequently traded with countrymen, yet certainly not exclusively. Although these networks are better known than those developed by laborers and farmers, they were very similar in connecting people through nationality, profession, and kinship (although the commercial networks did cover greater distances, involve more people, and wield greater political and economic clout).[33]

The fifth chapter looks more closely at the ways in which non-English residents of Massachusetts kept their national identities and perpetuated traditional cultures as part of a developing British culture. Explicitly national organizations, such as the Scots' Charitable Society or the French Church in Boston, were ways to associate with one's heritage and, at the same time, construct new "national" identities in the colonies. Other residents continued to follow traditional patterns of subsistence, such as living on small plots of land and grazing livestock, and moving from place to place as opportunities shifted. Such patterns added to the diversity of Massachusetts and, when combined through kinship and social ties, allowed new traditions and new identities to develop. This chapter also examines the friction between English residents and their non-English neighbors.

The conclusion moves the British and Atlantic networks discussed in the previous chapters into the eighteenth century, examining the social and political consequences of these communities. We find that organizations indicating high social status in Massachusetts, such as the Ancient and Honorable Artillery Company, included members of many backgrounds. At the same time, loyalties to non-English identities had not decreased. The Scots' Charitable Society continued, with many second- and third-generation members who were born in Massachusetts and were also members of the Artillery Company. The elite members of the scs also actively recruited new immigrants and laborers to their ranks. Politically, non-Puritan residents of Massachusetts were represented throughout the spectrum. Some men supported closer dependence on England, favoring royal government and courting royal patronage, and some supported the continuance of local control. Many apparently remained aloof from political wrangles. In other words, Massachusetts society was becoming British in the eighteenth-century meaning of the term as citizens of Britain, and developing the provincial identity that has been so thoroughly explored by scholars in recent years. But this identity did not develop solely from English political and economic agitation, but also out of the multiple identities that had developed in British communities of the seventeenth century.

One

THE IDEA OF COMMUNITY IN
EARLY MASSACHUSETTS

Community has long been a favorite topic for historians of early New England. Since the seventeenth century, scholars of the region have equated communities with towns, and commitment to the community with land ownership and church membership. The focus on town and religion helped to solidify the image of New England as a homogeneous region in terms of religion, social ethos, political beliefs, and ethnicity. This image began with Puritan ministers and was picked up by later historians who saw New England as the primary culture hearth for the United States, as well as those who looked for consensus in American history. In this framework, dissent and difference in early New England were anomalies that generally led to expulsion and a recommitment to harmony within Puritan communities. Since the 1960s, however, the emphasis on diversity and contention has spawned new ways to look at community and social relationships, allowing historians to see that a certain level of dissent could be tolerated even in the most homogeneous communities as long as it did not threaten basic social institutions.

The outpouring of scholarship in the last forty years on diversity in early Massachusetts has drawn attention to the many divisions within Puritan society. Historians now recognize that religious ideals were not monolithic—the New England Way developed out of confrontation and accommodation with dissenters such as Roger Williams, Anne Hutchinson, and Samuel Gorton, as well as from discussions between New England ministers and their counterparts in England.[1] The leaders of the colony differed among themselves about the treatment of dissenters, as illustrated by the frequent disputes between John Winthrop and Thomas Dudley over the punishment of Williams and Hutchinson, the rights of freemen and deputies, and the use of authority by magistrates.[2] Colony leaders also disagreed about how closely the settlement should be connected to Atlantic trade and communication networks.[3] Colonists even held different ideas about both their relationship to England and the authority that the English government and church should wield over the settlement. The zealous and rather rash actions of John Endicott in 1634, for example, when he mutilated the English flag by ripping off the cross of St. George and declaring it idolatry, exposed these fears.[4]

Nevertheless, the idea of community still frequently conjures images of an idealized small town, perceived by many people as the bastion of American values, whose origins lay in Puritan New England. Although adherence to Congregational principles bound together many, if not most, of the region's early settlers, scholars of early Massachusetts know that neither the physical geography nor the personal relationships implied by the image of the "New England town" provide accurate characterizations of the time or place. The homogeneous image of the colony was largely constructed by second- and third-generation Congregational ministers trying to build unity in a rapidly changing society, thereby strengthening their own social and political status, and later by nineteenth-century historians to assert the prominence of Anglo-Americans against an influx of immigrants from southern and central Europe and in the face of a rapidly industrializing economy. Even the mental image formed when thinking of seventeenth-century New England—white churches with high steeples on village commons surrounded by white saltbox houses with green shutters—resulted from nineteenth-century beautification efforts to create a New England that had never existed.[5]

The New England community studies that began to be published in the 1960s, and that have remained a staple in northeastern historiography ever since, focus on towns and villages, dividing the region into localities that can be studied separately and where social interactions can be quantified. Although these studies reshaped our conception of early modern societies, many historians have started to use more flexible definitions of community, where community is seen as "a social network characterized by a distinctive kind of human interaction."[6] More recently, scholars have focused on the idea of "communities of interest," which refers to the bonds between people based on shared ideology, experiences, or goals. Although communities of interest can exist in a geographically defined space, they frequently transcend such boundaries. In her study of eastern Long Island, which was politically connected to Massachusetts and Connecticut in the seventeenth century, Faren Siminoff argues that as early as the 1630s, "community and identity were already being renegotiated" in New England, based on common goals and interests rather than nationality or locality. This new concept of community arose from the mixing of peoples in the Atlantic world and was based on a "voluntary cleaving to collectively asserted goals." While noting that not all inhabitants of southern New England accepted this definition of community, enough did that it "became a hallmark of Atlantic American life" and shaped colonists' relations with one another and with England.[7]

Towns, in New England parlance, are fairly large geographic units. Initially a town contained one village, but as the first settlement grew in population and leaders started dividing land farther away from the center, more villages developed. Residents of new settlements frequently petitioned the General Court to become separate towns so that they could control the distribution of land and form their own churches. This hiving process of town formation created new networks among Massachusetts residents. Even within the standard conception of the New England town, whether the phrase describes the legally defined land area or the actual settlement, residents had many ties to other towns and villages.[8] Official settlements, as defined by the General Court, existed in relationship to other towns, counties, and the colony, and neighborhoods within these settlements exhibited the same connections to the local communities. Non-Puritan residents who lived in marginal areas or on the outskirts of villages developed strong ties among themselves and within the larger society, yet these social and kinship networks did not necessarily correspond to a specific geographical or political unit. Many Scots, for example, maintained close ties with Scots who lived several towns away, as shown through bequests in wills or membership in the Scots' Charitable Society.[9]

Non-Puritan settlers, those who arrived in the colony voluntarily or involuntarily, primarily as economic migrants, also developed strong ties with their Puritan neighbors. They lived near, rented land from, and worked for these more settled inhabitants, in addition to participating in town affairs and forming local social and labor networks. Clear lines demarcating Puritan from non-Puritan neighborhoods and networks cannot be drawn since the lives of townspeople were so intertwined, yet membership in different networks can be seen among these residents. In other words, townspeople knew what bound various networks together, whether that was religion, ethnicity, labor, or neighborhood, while also recognizing differences among themselves. These networks existed simultaneously, sometimes in conflict, at other times in harmony. This overlap in communities, or networks, contributed to the complexity and stability of early Massachusetts society. Religion was a very important bond among many settlers, tying them to one another and to coreligionists in England, but other kinds of networks also brought people in the colony together.

Another important aspect in the construction of early modern communities was kinship. Social and commercial networks developed through kin relationships, which were extensive and frequently fictive. Cousinship in particular was a vague term that covered many kinds of relationships, and even people related only through the remarriage of stepparents could claim the obligations that kinship involved. These networks expanded rapidly, enmeshing people in social webs.[10] In Massachusetts, intermarriage among English, Scottish, Irish, and Jersey residents, and later Huguenot émigrés, meant that purely national identities did not dominate. Although many historians see exogamous marriage as evidence of weak ethnic ties, such marriages were unavoidable in non-English communities and tended to expand community networks.[11] The sons of Scottish men and Irish- or Englishwomen were eligible to join the Scots' Charitable Society, for example, and many Huguenot merchants supported the Calvinist French-liturgy church in Boston but attended the Anglican King's Chapel.[12] English, Scottish, and French merchants formed partnerships with one another, many of which were based on familial relationships, and traded to England, Scotland, France, the Netherlands, and their colonies, deciding on ports of call based on available products and conditions of trade rather than national interests. Religion also drew together settlers of many nationalities. Despite differences in church governance, many reformed Protestants saw themselves as part of an international movement. Thus the communities that developed in late seventeenth-century Massachusetts crossed many national, political, religious, and economic boundaries.[13]

By the turn of the eighteenth century, then, Massachusetts residents had constructed communities that transcended traditional geographical boundaries. They also had developed multiple identities based on their many communities of interest. Historians have studied the close connections that developed between England and its North American colonies in the eighteenth century, illuminating the intellectual processes through which colonists began to see themselves as British. The growth of British, or provincial, identity has been linked to many factors: the increase in trade between the colonies and British outports, such as Glasgow, Londonderry, and Bristol; the intellectual and religious connections provided by the Enlightenment and Great Awakening that gave colonists a sense of participation in the public marketplace of ideas; and the political changes of the late seventeenth century that assured colonists that they lived in an "empire of liberty" in which they played an important role. This idea of Britishness allowed colonists to aspire to "the same rights and privileges" as other citizens of the British empire.[14]

Although scholars have grounded the development of this provincial British identity in the eighteenth century, the process began in the policies instituted by

James VI of Scotland upon his accession to the English throne in 1603. James deliberately styled himself "King of Great Britain" as one means of unifying his kingdoms, and thus supported policies that would enhance the concept of "Great Britain."[15] In Britain his attempts to create a British identity met with limited success, but the concept had an important effect on England's earliest attempts to create colonies, as Nicholas Canny has demonstrated for Ireland.

In Ireland, "British" refers primarily to Scottish and English tenants on large estates in the English plantations. These farmers displaced Gaelic Irish as the English attempted to gain control over Ireland during the late sixteenth and early seventeenth centuries.[16] Establishing such Scottish and English communities was a conscious policy of James VI and I, and settlers eventually came to identify themselves as British. As Canny notes, James wanted to foster loyalty to the political changes that had taken place with the union of the crowns in 1603 and so encouraged his Scottish and English subjects to participate equally in ventures throughout his domain. In particular, James believed that Scots and English could share influence in the settlement of Ireland, where he envisioned Scottish and English tenants inhabiting estates in common, displacing the Irish. Although both Scots and English did settle in Ireland, Scottish landlords favored Scottish tenants and kept close contacts with home and with other Scots in Ireland. On many estates, contrary to Crown policy, Irish subtenants outnumbered Scottish and English tenants. Yet overall, the English, who held the best lands and controlled the government and church, dominated society. Scots frequently were relegated to land on the frontier, serving as a buffer between English estates and the lands of the "wild Irish." English law also prevailed in the plantation, and so Scottish landlords were forced to hire English lawyers in London and Dublin to safeguard their estates. Thus British communities did develop, but in slightly different forms than those envisioned by James, who desired mixed English and Scottish communities with fewer Irish tenants.[17]

The Scots were subordinate to the English in Ulster, but they attempted to form Scottish communities within the larger English-dominated society. Scottish proprietors obtained Scottish tenants whenever possible, married Scottish women, and maintained strong ties to Scotland. The result in Ulster was "a hybrid society of Scots, Irish, and English, with the balance decidedly in favor of the Scots, and it existed side by side with other micro-communities where the ethnic balance was more English or Irish depending on the nationality of the proprietors." Canny also argues that the Scots and Irish were expected to fill certain roles within the plantation in return for English acceptance of these "sub-communities," and that the mixed British community of Ulster resulted from a need for labor that could not be filled solely by English migrants.[18]

Canny asserts that British communities similar to those in Ireland developed in the Atlantic world after 1660, when the later Stuart monarchs needed the participation of Scots and Irish to settle and hold their overseas plantations, akin to their function under James VI and I. He writes, "The presence of Scots and Irish in English trans-oceanic settlements was usually in a menial, although sometimes numerically significant, capacity."[19] This description holds true for Massachusetts and New England in general—Scots and Irish were not leaders or instrumental in settling new regions—yet in Massachusetts the development of British communities began among settlers in the lower levels of society in the late 1640s and early 1650s, earlier than Canny posits for the Atlantic world as a whole. These communities developed out of the need for labor in the 1640s that brought many Scottish, Irish, and English servants and laborers to the colony, both voluntarily and involuntarily.

Unlike Ireland, in Massachusetts the development of British communities was not particularly self-conscious, nor initially was it rooted in labor. The earliest Puritan leaders wanted to attract godly settlers of any nationality—a desire related to their participation in the reformed Protestant international—to plant the lands left vacant by the waves of epidemic disease that devastated Native American communities in the 1610s. The Massachusetts General Court, for instance, encouraged the immigration of Scottish minister John Livingstone and his congregation from Ulster in 1634, and later agreed to set aside tracts of land for settlement by other groups of Scots who wrote to inquire about opportunities in the Bay Colony. Livingstone and his congregation set sail but were turned back by a hurricane. The other inquiries by Scots also did not result in settlements, probably due to political changes in Scotland at the time rather than discouragement from the General Court.[20] Similarly, in 1635, Massachusetts governor John Winthrop rejoiced when his son John was diverted by a storm to Ireland during a voyage from England to Massachusetts and thus had the opportunity to visit the estate of Sir John Clotworthy. Clotworthy and several of his tenants were considering a remove to Massachusetts and John Winthrop, Jr.'s visit was seen as a God-given opportunity to provide firsthand information to potential immigrants.[21] Thus the goal in the early decades of settlement was to create in Massachusetts a community of like-minded believers despite nationality, and not, as in Ireland, a British community that supported the political goals of the Scottish king of England. Also unlike planters in Ireland, Massachusetts settlers never referred to themselves as "British" in the seventeenth century. Yet British communities did form, and through the joint effort of English, Scots, Irish, Welsh, Channel Island, and other residents, Massachusetts had developed into a "British" space by the turn of the century.

The concept of Britishness has a long history. Recently, scholars have unraveled the complex identities constructed by early modern peoples. Colin Kidd has explored the ethnic, religious, and political mythologies used by various peoples in the Atlantic archipelago to create national identities, which changed over time in response to clashes among many political entities. English writers, for example, managed to incorporate Romans, Danes, and Normans—all invaders of the islands—with ancient Britons and the Anglo-Saxon core of English identity. One argument claimed that the seventeenth- and eighteenth-century English nation inherited the best legal and cultural traits of each, forming a hybrid ethnicity. In the eighteenth and early nineteenth centuries, as the concept of Britain as a nation of liberty developed, the Anglo-Saxon heritage began to predominate, serving as the root of the British attachment to liberty. Similarly, the medieval Scottish kingdom derived from the ancient state of Dalriada in the western highlands and gradually incorporated Scots, Picts, Northumbrians, and Britons from the River Clyde region. Scottish nationalists used this Dalriadic origin to support their claims for the long-standing independence of Scotland. Yet by the 1500s, Lowlanders co-opted this Scottish identity and used it to marginalize Highlanders and their culture, strengthening Lowland hold on power and authority in the nation and over the definition of Scottishness.[22]

Linda Colley and Kathleen Wilson have also examined the construction of British- and Englishness during the eighteenth and early nineteenth centuries. Both historians point to the development of empire itself as one key to understanding identity, whether one looks at it through a framework of wars and captivity, religion, gender, or culture. As the peoples of Britain and Ireland moved outward from their small territorial base, they had to rethink the meaning of nationhood, asking if national identity was territorial and political, if it was based in moral character or well-defined family lineage, or if identity was innate or immutable. Ideas about the origins of national identity were not mutually exclusive, however, and Britons pulled from many strands of history and religion to develop their beliefs.[23]

Another aspect of identity important to seventeenth-century Puritans was their participation in the international reformed Protestant movement. English Calvinists saw themselves as part of a great tide of reformed Christianity that would sweep away the heresies and human-inspired corruptions that had infected the "true" church. From the Marian exiles of the mid-sixteenth century, through the supporters of the battles of Dutch and French Protestants during the reign of Elizabeth, to those who opposed the pro-Spanish policies of James I, English Calvinists had been closely involved in the struggles of Continental Protestants against Catholics and other "heretics." This religious mission, which many believed would bring about the millennium, the thousand-year reign of Christ on Earth, bound English Puritans together and transcended national borders by giving them a common mission with European Calvinists. Puritans who settled in Massachusetts in the 1630s brought this sense of reformed communion with them, and their contact with Native Americans amplified this sense of mission. One of the justifications for leaving England, of course, was the conversion of Native Americans, which, many Puritans believed, when completed would help usher in the millennium. This identification with international Protestantism made easier the incorporation of other Calvinists, such as Scots Presbyterians and French Huguenots, into Massachusetts society.[24]

A common adherence to Calvinist doctrine, however, did not completely override nationalist issues. The arrival of several hundred Scots Presbyterians as prisoners of war in the early 1650s caused great concern among many English settlers of Massachusetts, as did the later migration of Huguenots after the revocation of the Edict of Nantes. In short, common religious ideology did not necessarily trump long-standing national enmities. This also illustrates the overlap of social and religious networks in Massachusetts. For example, Scottish Presbyterians who arrived as prisoners of war may well have attended their local Congregational church, but few apparently joined those churches, and even those Scots who did join churches (usually later in the century) still identified themselves as Scottish. Religion and nationality/ethnicity interacted in complicated ways. Calvinism did not create a homogeneous population; alternate interpretations of religious ideology and differences in nationality created fissures, even within a common Protestant identity.[25]

What emerges from this recent work is that identities are constructed from many sources: they are not static, and they can be adopted—chosen—as well as inherited. Identities also have very local connotations, denoting difference within larger groups. The English in New England saw themselves as all-English when arrayed against Native Americans in King Philip's War, for example, yet in times of peace made much finer distinctions among themselves, based on status, religion, or place of origin. Thus members of British communities in Massachusetts were not simply defining themselves against the dominant population—such as Scots against English, dissenters against Puritans, or laborers against landowners—but were also creating identities as colonists, as inhabitants of Massachusetts, with a place within this society.

By necessity, the discussions of British identity and its intellectual construction in the colonial world focus on the educated elites. These men and women wrote sermons, pamphlets, and books for public consumption, and letters and journals for more private correspondence. Without such sources, it is much more difficult to understand how common people saw themselves and their world. Yet, though less literate, common people also constructed identities and formed communities and social networks that reinforced those identities. This study attempts to understand some of the conceptions held by lower-status settlers in Massachusetts by looking at the social organizations that they formed, the communities that they associated with, and the kinship networks that rooted them in the colony. Without documents written by them, we can only rely on such associations to see how these residents saw themselves at certain times. Nevertheless, what we find is that non-English settlers did not become "English," although they accepted, for the most part, the strictures of English and Puritan society in Massachusetts.

As early as the 1640s and 1650s, then, communities of laborers and agricultural workers began to exhibit British characteristics—groups of people of various national backgrounds, religious beliefs, and cultural traditions working together and forming families and social networks. These communities generally existed on the outskirts of larger villages and towns, and consisted of residents who do not fit into the traditional conception of New England settlers as English Puritan landowners. Yet these common people—yeomen, artisans, servants, tenant farmers, and laborers—created mixed communities of English, Scottish, Irish, and Jersey Islanders similar to those in the better-known mercantile communities at the end of the century. These residents exchanged work, shared tools, married within the group, and kept their ethnic or national identities intact while becoming settled and respectable members of their towns and the colony—in short, becoming Massachusetts men and women, as well as colonials. Similar networks developed among merchants in the port towns of Salem and Boston, yet these networks were much more expansive, stretching across the Atlantic world.

The existence of such alternative communities also explains how people who were not Puritan, nor even necessarily English, thrived in early Massachusetts. Distinct cohorts of Scots, Irish, or Welsh residents were too small to influence the political and economic development of the colony, as they could in Pennsylvania or New York. Yet collectively, non-English settlers supported members of their groups, provided outlets for national identity, and allowed some colonists to maintain cultural traditions. Massachusetts society had elements of diversity long before the eighteenth century. People from all strata of society had learned to live together, and they understood that national differences did not necessarily overshadow commonalities, in the same way that similar religions did not sublimate national identities. Modern elements thus crept into Massachusetts in ways that the colony's founders could not have foreseen, and the groundwork for the development of a British provincial identity had been laid well before the Acts of Union in 1707.[26]

The argument presented here does not presume that non-Puritan residents had only one, or even one, overriding identity or community affiliation. We will meet many individuals in different contexts—people who identified themselves as Scots, for example, while espousing loyalty to an English colony, becoming Congregational church members, and trading primarily with Dutch and French merchants. Multiple associations constituted the core of colonial identity. The colonies were places where peoples from many areas and with different religious and cultural traditions met. Yet this does not imply assimilation or the outdated concept of the "melting pot," out of which, through some alchemy, "Americans" emerged. In the seventeenth century, the social, economic, and political relationships between colonies and home countries were still being defined, and therefore colonial identities were also under development.

At the same time, the Bay Colony did not develop through consensus. Conflict among the many elements of Massachusetts society did occur. That this conflict did not result in violence, such as Bacon's Rebellion in Virginia, until 1689 can be attributed to the "social web" that developed, the many ties that settlers had within and among their communities. The "social cohesion" discovered by T. H. Breen and Stephen Foster was not simply the result of homogeneity, but came from the extensive communities and multiple identities that tied colonists together across social and economic boundaries.[27] Servants were church members, middling farmers who were church members participated in government, Irish captives became landowners, and Scottish merchants became wealthy and influential within an English colony before 1707. Limits, however, did exist. Religious dissidents were persecuted, Scottish and French merchants did not break into the upper ranks of Massachusetts society until the eighteenth century, and many settlers who started as servants and laborers remained poor. Massachusetts was not a land of unlimited opportunity and certainly cannot be described as "the best poor man's country." But bonds among colonists did develop across social boundaries, in part because of overlapping networks and multiple identities grounded in the communities that non-Puritans developed over the course of the seventeenth century.

LABORERS IN EARLY MASSACHUSETTS:
IRONWORKERS AT SAUGUS

A key component of the formation of British communities in early Massachusetts was the need for labor. As the Bay Colony grew and its economy diversified over the course of the seventeenth century, a need for labor developed that could not be provided primarily by families and godly servants.[1] In particular, certain desirable industries, such as iron manufacturing, required a highly skilled labor force that could not be found in Massachusetts. Colony leaders quickly discovered that economic growth meant that they needed to accommodate laborers who did not necessarily meet their standards of conduct and religious beliefs. Puritans hoped to control these potentially unruly elements in their society, but as the population of non-Puritan laborers grew, these settlers began to form their own communities, composed of peoples from England, Scotland, Ireland, the Channel Islands, and France. To understand the development of British communities in early Massachusetts, we must first examine the origins of the land-based non-Puritan labor force in Essex County and the work performed by these families.[2]

Labor constituted the crucial aspect for development in all of England's North American colonies, and was as important in Massachusetts as in Virginia. In the Chesapeake, the labor problem was resolved by the development of indentured servitude and slavery. New England depended heavily on family labor, since most early immigrants arrived in family groups, and on servants brought as part of a family. Some large landowners and wealthy investors in the Massachusetts Bay Company, such as Matthew Craddock, the first governor of the company in England, sent over servants to work their land, whereas others in the colony recruited young men and women for service on speculation.[3] Historian David Cressy estimates that servants composed 25 percent of New England's population and were "hired more for their labour than their religion," although many servants among the early settlers were from godly families and became church members.[4] Even though New England leaders wanted to encourage the migration of godly servants—or at least those "of good conversation," who were sympathetic to Puritan social and religious ideals—the colony also received servants who had been charges on the poor rolls in English towns. Many of these servants signed indentures for four or five years, and usually worked at a variety of tasks for their masters. Yet, whereas Virginians continued to attract workers throughout much of the century despite poor demographics and the diminishing availability of land, New Englanders had a much more difficult time recruiting laborers. The desire of Puritan leaders for a godly workforce, and the "competency" available in New England, which could not compete with the potential for riches in the Chesapeake and West Indies, made Massachusetts a far less attractive destination, especially for skilled workers, even though the region had a much higher life expectancy.[5]

Massachusetts leaders faced the shortage of workers soon after settlement began. In 1633, John Winthrop recorded in his journal that "the scarcity of workmen had caused them to raise their wages to an excessive rate . . . so as it grew to a general complaint." A carpenter, Winthrop complained, "would have 3s. the day, a laborer 2s. 6d." Usurious rates, however, were not just a problem with craftsmen. Winthrop also noted that some merchants charged almost double what they had paid for commodities in England. The General Court responded to inflation by setting wage and price controls, restricting skilled laborers to wages of two shillings per day and general laborers to eighteen pence. Merchants, in turn, could not sell goods "above 4d. in the shilling more than it cost for ready money in England," with perishable commodities, such as "oyle, wine &c. & Cheese," exempt from this order. The money to sustain the economy came from the prices charged to new arrivals: "Corne at 6s. the bushel, a Cowe at £20, yea, some at £24, some £26, a mare at £35, an ewe goat at £3 or £4." Settlers arriving in the colony with cash to set up farms kept the economy afloat during the first decade.[6]

By the early 1640s, however, the economic situation in the colony changed. Immigration to Massachusetts virtually ended as political tensions in England and Scotland rose. The economy, which had been sustained by the money brought by new settlers, declined as well. The lack of ready cash caused prices to drop precipitously. Winthrop noted in December 1640 that "corn (Indian) was sold ordinarily at three shillings the bushel, a good cow at seven or eight pounds, and some at £5."[7] Many settlers decided to try their fortunes elsewhere—either returning to England to participate in the "thorough reformation" that many Puritans saw coming, or moving south. Viscount Saye and Sele, Lord Brook, and the Earl of Warwick, who were all involved with the settlements in New England, had invested in a colony on Providence Island, near the Central American coast. They urged New England residents to join the new settlement there, much to the dismay and anger of Massachusetts leaders. Small Puritan enclaves had also developed in Virginia and Maryland—residents repeatedly contacted Massachusetts about sending ministers—and a few New England settlers contemplated a removal to the Chesapeake.[8]

Fearing that their colony would be stripped of settlers as well as of vital economic assets, Massachusetts leaders attempted to stimulate the economy. One of their first actions was to repeal wage and price controls in February 1640/1. The regulations had never been effective, since laborers could easily move to get the wages they wanted, they could be paid more by private arrangement with an employer, or they could take up other occupations, such as farming. Each tactic undercut the law, and so magistrates decided to leave wage controls to the towns, hoping that community pressure would keep wages reasonable. "But," Winthrop noted, "it held not long."[9] Labor costs continued to rise, and the continuing shortage of workers forced the Court to find new solutions. By April 1641, the Court of Assistants had started levying fines, ranging from ten shillings to five pounds, to keep masters from freeing their bound servants, and in 1646 the General Court ordered that "artificers or handicrafts men" could be forced to work for their neighbors during the harvest at the prevailing daily wage for agricultural labor.[10] In 1645, Winthrop repeated his 1633 complaint that wages had risen to "unreasonable" heights due to the wars in England, Scotland, and Ireland; the general lack of servants; and the scarcity of specie.[11]

The servants who did come to Massachusetts in the first decade of settlement were overwhelmingly English, and many hailed from Puritan families. Most migrated to New England voluntarily, negotiating their indentures with prospective employers or being recruited by the friends and family members of colonists who had remained in England. Many were also young males, although New England saw a greater proportion of older female servants than did the southern colonies because of the emphasis on family migration and the greater variety of work that needed to be performed.[12] The indenture agreement of Jeremy Boutman in 1651 was typical for young servants. Originally from Suffolk in England, he agreed to work for Matthew Nixon in Salem for seven years. Nixon was to teach Boutman the fishing trade and "the same service at sea in which he was engaged." Boutman promised "not to frequent houses of common entertainment" and "to behave himself as an apprentice ought." For these services, he received £7.4, part of which was paid at the beginning of the term and the remainder at the end.[13]

Older servants also came to New England under contracts. Richard Crane, for example, left a wife and children in England to serve a five-year indenture in Newbury. He may have chosen this course because of the money—a letter from his wife, Dorothy, in 1639 reveals that he received thirty-five pounds for five years' service—or as a trial run to see if he wanted to move his family to the colony. Dorothy noted in her letter that she did not have the money to bring the family to Massachusetts and that she was "not as yet minded to com thither."[14] Catherine Lemon came to New England in 1649 as an unmarried older woman and signed an indenture with John Winthrop, Jr., for four years. She agreed to "abide in all Needfull servis to her best abillitie," for which she received food, lodging, and "such like necessaries," along with forty shillings per year wages.[15]

The most prized servants, however, were like the unnamed maid sent by Margaret Winthrop, wife of the Massachusetts governor, to Lucy Downing, John Winthrop's sister, in 1640/1. She had strong character references from trusted family members: Lucy Downing's "Cosen Nab" traveled with her from England and "gives her the report of a very good carigd," and Abigail and John Goad, sister and brother-in-law of Downing's husband, Emanuel, lived near the servant's family in England and "repute them to be people of a very godly conversation." Downing wrote that "many times hereditary blessings are perpetuated and virtue followes them"; thus these reports gave her "good hopes" for this young woman.[16]

Yet servants with such good references were hard to come by, and the behavior of many servants caused great consternation to Massachusetts colonists. Young and unattached, servants were seen as potentially disruptive to the good order of society, even those from Puritan families and with godly masters who took responsibility for their moral and physical care. Although the governors of the Massachusetts Bay Company had carefully chosen the settlers in the Winthrop fleet, colonists faced problems with servants from the beginning of settlement, even on board the *Arbella*, John Winthrop's flagship, in 1630. During the Atlantic crossing, Winthrop noted two male servants who fought on the ship and were placed "in bolts till night, with their hands bound behind them," and a female who, feeling ill, drank too much and almost killed herself from alcohol poisoning. Winthrop mourned, "We observed it a common fault in our young people, that they give themselves to drink hot waters very immoderately."[17]

Once in New England, behavioral problems multiplied. Discontented servants at times ran away to the Indians, which not only harmed their masters but put the entire community at risk by undermining Puritan belief in the superiority of their society. Others raised "foule scandalous invectives" against the churches and society. Such transgressions were punished by the courts, but could also bring divine retribution, as with two young men who drowned shortly after one of them declared, "If hell were ten times hotter, he had rather be there than serve his master."[18] More common complaints, however, were that servants were disrespectful, disobedient, and insolent.[19]

Such problems, along with the lack of servants in general, caused many residents of Massachusetts to look to Indians and Africans to solve their labor needs. Emanuel Downing, John Winthrop's brother-in-law, wrote to Winthrop in 1645 about the possibility of a "just war" against the Narragansetts, which would bring captives that the colony could exchange in the West Indies for black slaves. Downing believed that slaves were necessary for the success of the colony, "for our Childrens Children will hardly see this great Continent filled with people, soe that our servants will still desire freedom to plant for them selves, and not stay but for verie great wages."[20] Slavery was not unknown in the colony: William Wood, in *New England's Prospect*, noted the presence of a "black-more" in Massachusetts as early as 1633, and the colony had sold captive Pequots to the West Indies in 1637 in exchange for African slaves. John Josselyn also noted the presence of African slaves at Samuel Maverick's house on Noddles Island in 1639.[21] In addition to African slaves, in 1646 the General Court relaxed its restrictions on the presence of Indian servants in English towns.[22]

Another response to the economic downturn of the 1640s was to encourage the development of industries. The Massachusetts Bay Company had looked toward economic self-sufficiency from the earliest days of settlement. In 1631/2, Richard Saltonstall wrote Emanuel Downing about the possibilities of Massachusetts, "I doubt not but wee shall rayse good profit not only by our fishing trade . . . but by Hempe, flaxe, pitch, tarr, pottashes, sope ashes, masts, pipe staves, clapboards (and Iron as wee hope) for wee find here are minerals, but for want of skill and Lime cannot yet Certainly satisfie either our selves or you, of what kinds they are."[23] Shipbuilding, textiles, and salt making also received special encouragement from the General Court in the form of bounties, monopolies, and reduced taxation. Winthrop noted the beginning of a shipbuilding industry in early 1641, undertaken by subscription from the citizens of Boston and Salem.[24] In addition, the General Court encouraged merchants to find new markets for Massachusetts's agricultural products and awarded monopolies to investors to develop manufacturing and other industries.

In terms of economic development, three of the most important industries encouraged by the General Court were iron manufacturing, shipping, and shipbuilding. The need for skilled laborers in these industries led to the migration, voluntary and coerced, of hundreds of non-Puritan laborers to coastal Massachusetts. The iron industry in Essex County employed English and Welsh ironworkers in the 1640s and stimulated the importation of hundreds of Scots in the 1650s, whereas shipping and shipbuilding attracted mariners and marine carpenters from the island of Jersey and other regions throughout the Atlantic world. The general laborers who arrived in the 1640s and the 1650s became the core of British communities and other labor networks in the region, and Puritan officials had to be willing to overlook some transgressions in behavior if they hoped to keep these skilled workers in the colony.[25]

THE DEVELOPMENT OF THE IRONWORKS AT SAUGUS

The industry most desired by the General Court, and ultimately the one that had the greatest impact on the early non-Puritan population of Massachusetts, was iron production. Iron was an essential commodity in the early modern world, used in household goods as well as farming, shipbuilding, and other important industries. Iron implements also became standard trade items with Native Americans. Although settlers could not trade guns and ammunition, they eagerly bartered away cooking pots, hoes, and hunting knives to the Indians.[26]

The Bay Colony also had the natural resources to support an iron industry, along with the desire of its leaders to start one. Massachusetts contained extensive forests to provide fuel for furnaces, and large deposits of bog ore and fluxing material. Of equal importance were swift-moving streams to supply water power for furnaces and forges. These assets looked even more promising when compared with the state of iron production in Britain and Ireland. The industry in these areas had fallen on hard times by the 1630s. Iron smelting required 265 bushels of charcoal for every ton of iron produced; many people in Britain and Ireland believed that iron manufacturing was depleting wood supplies, which were still needed for everyday household use. Thus opposition existed to increasing iron production in Britain and Ireland. The Irish industry was further affected by the rebellion that broke out in 1641, which forced many ironworkers to leave the country.[27]

Massachusetts lacked the capital, however, to begin iron production. In 1641, the General Court tried to encourage local investment by giving to "such as will adventure for the discovery of mines" the exclusive use of any ores or minerals discovered, along with "a fit portion of Land," for twenty-one years. Moreover, even though Massachusetts in general forbade private land purchases from the Indians, land containing ore could be purchased directly from Indians, as long as such a purchase did not infringe on "any man's property without the owner's leave." Yet the onset of hard economic times in Massachusetts made few residents willing or able to invest in such a project.[28]

Therefore, when John Winthrop, Jr., sailed for England as an agent for Massachusetts in 1641, he also had the consent of the General Court to find English investors for an iron industry. Winthrop, as New England's leading scientist, had the knowledge of metallurgy, the influence in New England, and the connections in England needed to convince investors to gamble on iron production in the wilderness.[29] Although unsettled political conditions in England made investors wary of any large undertaking, men of wealth and prominence gradually began to take an interest. By the spring of 1643, Winthrop had obtained enough support to form the Company of Undertakers of the Ironworks in New England. The twenty-four English investors in this private joint stock company included men with a wide range of interests—from Puritan clergymen to public officials and London merchants—but who also shared many overlapping concerns.[30] The experience of the company's leaders, plus the wealth and connections of the other investors, boded well for the success of the enterprise, especially since the General Court was willing to encourage the Undertakers with liberal grants of land and other concessions.

Winthrop may have enticed these investors with the initial promises made by the General Court in 1641, but once the company was formed, stockholders demanded more concessions from Massachusetts's leaders. From 1643, when Winthrop returned to the colony, to 1646, the Undertakers and the General Court traded a series of petitions and responses. The company wanted to have the flexibility to operate the ironworks at a profit, and therefore hoped to obtain land cheaply and to gain access to any land where useful minerals had been found. They also insisted on receiving tax and military exemptions for the ironworks and their laborers. The Court agreed to these demands but made a few of their own in turn. The Assistants wanted to insure that the colony benefited from iron production by insisting that the Undertakers sell their products in Massachusetts first, and at a price no higher than twenty pounds per ton. The company could sell excess iron anywhere it wished, except "to any person or state in actuall hostility with [the colony]." Massachusetts leaders also expected the company to provide ministers for ironworkers and their families who lived "remote from a church or congregation."[31]

Although bargaining went back and forth for several years, in the end the Court acquiesced to most of the company's demands. Far from dictating the terms of the monopoly, Massachusetts leaders proved their eagerness to encourage the Undertakers and promote economic growth. They retained the condition of selling iron to Massachusetts residents first, but ameliorated the demand not to sell to "Indians or enemies." Most interestingly for the development of British communities, the Court also dropped the demand that the company provide ministers. This may have been a tacit admission that ironworkers would be hard to recruit, especially if forced to live under church discipline, or a recognition that with many ministers returning to England at the outbreak of the civil war, it would be difficult to find men willing to remove to "remote" areas.[32]

While petitioning the General Court for more concessions, the Undertakers began to establish their facilities, first at Braintree, south of Boston, and a few years later at Saugus, in Essex County. John Winthrop, Jr., chose the initial site at Braintree due to the availability of bog iron, building sites, and unskilled labor, and he constructed a furnace and forge in 1644 and 1645. The water supply, however, was inadequate for the extensive facility envisioned by the company, and in 1646 construction began at a new site on the Saugus River. This became the primary production facility, although the company continued to operate the forge at Braintree as well.[33]

Iron production was a well-understood process by the middle of the seventeenth century, and the manufacturing complex at Saugus followed European standards.[34] Although the scale of the enterprise was not unusual for seventeenth-century iron-making facilities, the Saugus ironworks was located in a lightly settled region half a world away from Europe, which caused major problems for the Undertakers. The experience of the principal investors in iron manufacturing in Britain and Ireland led them to envision a highly sophisticated, integrated production facility.[35] The New England complex used an indirect process for smelting ore and producing cast iron, and the Walloon method for turning cast iron into wrought iron. Although both methods of processing iron ore were common in England, they were expensive to set up and operate. The Undertakers had unnecessarily complicated their expectations for the Saugus plant. One result of the decision to build such a technologically sophisticated plant was that the company had to import highly skilled workers who did not necessarily adhere to Puritan values.[36]

From the start of iron production, the Court treated ironworkers like fishermen—giving them some encouragement and leniency in order to keep their labor, yet closely watching their activities. Fishing communities had been among the first European settlements in Massachusetts; the Dorchester Company sent fishermen to Cape Ann in 1623, and members of this group lived at Naumkeag (Salem) when John Endicott and his advance party from the Massachusetts Bay Company arrived in 1628. Northern New England's proximity to the fertile fishing grounds of the North Atlantic had long been known and Puritan leaders understood that fishing would be an important component of their economy. Yet fishermen posed problems for the Bay Colony leaders. Like the later iron-workers, fishermen rarely met the standards of behavior demanded by Puritan ideology, and their frequent and long absences from home kept them from proper religious services and the watchful eyes of their neighbors. Fishing was also a physically dangerous and financially precarious occupation, and therefore fishing communities were insular, violent, and competitive, and composed of peoples from many regions of Britain and the Atlantic world. This rough-and-tumble world of fisher families, then, was important to the colony's economy, yet potentially disruptive to Puritan society, a situation also seen among ironworkers.[37]

Massachusetts leaders clearly placed a high premium on development, knowing that the settlements would fail without a strong economy, and they showed great faith in their ability to curb the excesses of unruly laborers (although this faith may have been slightly overrated). Yet by the middle of the 1640s, this belief also allowed them to accept and encourage the immigration of "strangers," as they had accommodated fishermen, and to give these new settlers room to adjust. In the process, these laborers created alternative communities in Massachusetts society.

EARLY EMPLOYEES AT SAUGUS

Although the company faced many problems developing its ironworks, the most persistent was the shortage of labor. As noted above, workmen in general commanded high wages, and skilled ironworkers were rare in Massachusetts. Available workers were expensive, young, and mobile. These conditions forced the Undertakers to recruit skilled labor in Britain and Ireland and to hire Mass-achusetts men for unskilled jobs and piecework. Thus the labor force at Saugus consisted of a mix of full-time and part-time employees, and skilled and unskilled laborers. In addition, some of the workers were free, whereas others were indentured. Many workers also had long-standing ties to the larger com-munity, which meant that ironworkers would not be isolated from Puritan society. Such conditions resulted in a constantly changing workforce and a continual struggle by managers to hire competent employees and keep labor costs down. The Undertakers searched Britain and Ireland for skilled workers for many years. In June 1643, Dr. Robert Child—an alchemist, friend of John Winthrop, Jr., and important investor in the company—wrote to Winthrop that he was searching for a bloomer for the ironworks; in September, another principle Undertaker, London ironmonger Joshua Foote, informed Winthrop that the search continued but so far had been unsuccessful, and suggested training a blacksmith to take over this important job.[38] In 1648, the Undertakers wrote to Winthrop about the problems of finding and keeping qualified servants: "And want of experience in the Minerals in most of our workmen hath bin loss, and charge to us: And worse qualificacions in some of them have beene a trouble to you: It is our earnest desire, and we have endeavored all wee can to be furnished with better men than some of them are: But notwithstanding all our care we have bin necessitated to send some for whose civilities we cannot undertake, who yet we hope by the good example, and discipline of your Country, with your good assistance may in time be cured of their distempers."[39] Although the company continued to send workers to Massachusetts, few were the highly skilled laborers that Saugus required, and even fewer had the religious ideals prized by leaders of the colony.

Puritan leaders tried to control the behavior of the ironworkers while also recognizing the value of their labor. The need for laborers resulted in accommodation, whereby Puritan authorities asserted their prerogative to punish ironworkers' transgressions, but not so severely that these families would take their labor elsewhere. Eventually, as the population became more diverse and as more important political issues occupied the attention of the courts, the compulsion to control non-Puritan residents diminished.[40]

The ability of the courts to accommodate laborers can be seen through the experiences of the Pinnion family, one of the most incorrigible families at Hammersmith. Nicholas Pinnion and his wife, Esther, came to Saugus before 1647 as bound servants of the Undertakers, where Nicholas worked as a carpenter and skilled ironworker.[41] The catalogue of misbehavior in the family runs long; the Pinnions clearly had no intention of abiding by Puritan standards of conduct. Nicholas first appears in the records in December 1647 for beating his wife and common swearing. In February 1647/8, he was fined for swearing, along with six other ironworkers; Esther was presented for swearing in a separate charge. At the same time, he faced charges for absence from meeting four weeks running, "spending his time drinking, and profanely." His wife was also fined for breaking a previously imposed bond for good behavior. At the same court session, Nicholas Russell, another ironworker, was fined "for remaining in Nicholas Penyon's house after he had ordered him to keep away, being jealous of his wife." Pinnion suspected Russell and Esther of having an affair, a suspicion no doubt heightened by her declaration "that if Nicholas Russell departed the house she would depart also." At the same time, Russell was fined for drinking with Pinnion on a Sunday, spending the better part of the day in this activity, and cursing and swearing. At the next court session, in March 1647/8, Esther accused Pinnion of killing five children; she was presented for fighting with her husband three times "since she was bound to keep the peace." The murder charge was not pursued, although the court did acknowledge that Nicholas had beaten Esther and caused a miscarriage during this time.[42]

After this flurry of presentments, the Pinnions did not appear in court again until September 1649. Nicholas was once again fined for swearing "three oaths" and admonished for "striking Charles Hooke," also an ironworker. At the same time, Pinnion and fellow ironworker Quentin Pray got into a fight, which turned into a regular brawl, involving at least seven other ironworkers. Yet for all the disturbance, Pinnion and Pray were simply hauled into court, fined, and admonished. Harsher punishments, such as confinement to the stocks or whipping, were not imposed. None of the other men received any punishment.[43]

Over the next three years, Pinnion only appeared in court for debt. In November 1652, however, Nicholas and Esther were both fined, along with several other members of ironworks families, for breaking the new sumptuary laws by "wearing silver lace."[44] Nicholas Pinnion appeared as a defendant in the court records again in 1656, when he and Esther were presented for absence from meeting. Neither of the Pinnions bothered to appear, however, and no action was taken against them. Nicholas and his son Robert were presented for slander in late 1659 and early 1660, and in 1663 Esther was charged with hitting the wife of another ironworker.[45]

Although the Pinnions tested the patience of the Massachusetts authorities, they remained in the colony until the early 1660s, when they left voluntarily, recruited by John Winthrop, Jr., for his new iron facility in New Haven, a colony noted for being stricter than Massachusetts. The catalog of presentments against Nicholas and Esther Pinnion did diminish over the course of ten years, and the charges reflected different social concerns. The earliest presentments focused on drinking, fighting, and swearing, whereas the later presentments, in 1652 (breaking sumptuary laws) and 1656 (absence from meeting), although not the result of violent misbehavior, carried serious social implications. The sumptuary law passed in 1651 was an attempt to maintain social order during a time of severe stress. The civil wars had ended in England in 1649, but threats of further fighting remained high among England, Scotland, and Ireland, creating uncertainty in colonists as well as among residents of the home islands. This was also the time when many non-Puritan laborers began to arrive in Massachusetts, most notably several hundred Scottish and Irish prisoners of war. The colony faced new challenges in defining its relationship to the Protectorate of Oliver Cromwell as well, and feared being pulled too closely into the English fold. The first of the Navigation Acts passed by the English government in 1651 made merchants unhappy and raised economic concerns. At the same time, the First Anglo-Dutch War (1652–54) brought forth the specter of fighting with New Netherland and its Indian allies. Thus wars and the Navigation Acts threatened to disrupt the economy, and recently arrived "strangers," with their ancient enmities against the English, posed a challenge to society. Sumptuary laws became one method of imposing order on potential chaos.[46] In addition to these economic and political problems, the 1656 charge of absence from meeting came in the context of debates over the status of adult children of church members who, although baptized as infants, did not become full members of the church. The Pinnions had not been charged with absence from meeting since 1648 and, given their behavior in Massachusetts and New Haven (discussed below), it is difficult to believe that they had attended church regularly in the intervening eight years.[47]

Stephen Innes has recently argued that the decline in court appearances among ironworkers illustrates the power of Puritan discipline over these unruly strangers in the colony.[48] Yet the same pattern can also be read as a form of accommodation that developed over time. Magistrates initially felt the need to exert control over these unknown laborers, as they did with fisher families, but soon realized that these laborers served important functions in the colony and could not realistically be held to the standards set for church members. Although an important aspect of Puritan jurisprudence was to punish sin rather than simply stop crime, unless magistrates wanted to spend much of their time policing the ironworks, the best that they could do was to hold such sin and disruption to a minimum.[49]

At first the magistrates did try to control the ironworkers. The court sat at the ironworks at regular intervals during the 1640s.[50] This practice apparently ended by the 1650s, when charges against ironworkers become interspersed with others throughout the county. The need to assert direct control over the ironworkers diminished, although the presentments against them continued. Offenses that fell within English folk culture (such as drinking and premarital sex between betrothed couples) could be permitted, although not officially condoned, whereas serious transgressions that threatened the health or reputations of others (such as fighting and slander) or the peace of the colony continued to be punished. This accommodation on the part of Massachusetts leaders is supported by the later experiences of the Pinnion family in New Haven.[51]

The Pinnions moved to New Haven between 1663 and 1665. Once there, the family quickly reestablished a pattern of frequent court appearances. In January 1664/5, Esther charged Patrick Moran, clerk of the ironworks, with sexual abuse of her daughter Hannah. The same month, son Robert was charged with "contemptuous speeches in reference to the authority." In August, Robert was charged with stealing alcohol and assorted other goods from Moran, along with profaning the Sabbath, and in December daughter Ruth was charged with several counts of lascivious behavior. Ruth was fined £4.6 and ordered out of New Haven. Through the end of the 1660s, the Pinnion children—Ruth, Robert, Hannah, and Thomas—continued to flout New Haven authorities.[52] The behavior of the Pinnion family clearly had not changed with their residence.

In August 1665, the New Haven town leaders wrote a letter to the operators of the ironworks, complaining "about those disorderly persons that were at the iron-works." Although it did not specifically mention the Pinnions, one can surmise that they were among the culprits, given the number of court appearances the family had in that year alone. Town leaders insisted that the owners of the plant obtain certificates of good behavior for future employees, on pain of a forty-shilling fine for each employee without one. An employee without a recommendation would be dismissed and sent back to his previous residence. Moreover, the overseers of the ironworks had to give bond to the town to obey these rules and certify that employees, even those with certificates, would not be chargeable to the town later.[53] New Haven leaders had clearly had enough of the unruly behavior of ironworkers, and took action to compel their employers to control them, although few were forced out of the colony. In New Haven, the behavior of the ironworkers required strict regulation. Essex County magistrates had struggled with the same issues during the 1640s and early 1650s, yet never felt constrained to make any orders similar to this. For Massachusetts, then, the need for labor outweighed the social disruption caused by the workers.[54]

Many other families at Saugus also tested the limits of Puritan patience, including Richard and Mary Pray and the Turner family. Pray viciously abused his wife, and Mary frequently fought back. They appeared in court on several occasions, not only for assaults on each other, but also for abusing family members and neighbors. In March 1647/8, Richard was presented for beating Mary, cursing, swearing, and showing contempt for the court. He was "fined 10s for swearing, 10s for cursing, 20s for beating his wife, and 40s for contempt of court, or to be whipped."[55] The fines were substantial, and this was not the Prays' first appearance in court. Yet, like the Pinnions, the Prays remained at Saugus for many years, until they moved voluntarily to Providence, Rhode Island, in the early 1660s.[56]

The Turner family—John, his son Lawrence, and daughter-in-law Sarah— also appeared before the Essex County court many times for violent behavior. In December 1647, John Turner was presented for stabbing Sarah, "swearing by the eternal God that he would kill John Gorum" (another ironworker), and for being drunk. He was sentenced to be "severely whipped at Salem" and, after a period of recovery in the Boston jail, to be whipped again at Saugus. Yet for an unstated reason, this sentence was overturned. John moved, on his own volition, to the Taunton ironworks in Plymouth Colony, and Lawrence and Sarah left for New Haven. The behavior of Lawrence and Sarah did not change in their new location, and they were warned out of New Haven Colony in 1651.[57]

The need for labor in Massachusetts meant that these families were not punished in an unduly harsh manner. Their behavior, though troubling and unacceptable, did not seriously threaten the colony. In contrast, in 1661 William Ballantyne, a cooper and merchant in Boston, received a fine of one hundred pounds and was sentenced to stand in the pillory for an hour, to have an ear cut off, and to pay triple damages for "counterfeiting the seal of the packer," or falsely certifying that the contents of barrels had been properly packed. This crime threatened Boston's reputation with merchants in the Atlantic world, bringing severe punishment on Ballantyne. The transgressions of ironworkers, however, did not reach this level, and as early as the late 1640s Puritan authorities could make such distinctions.[58]

Overall, the workers sent to Massachusetts in the 1640s had uneven careers in the region. Many families disappeared from the records when their indentures ended or after the ironworks went bankrupt in 1653. At least six families moved to New Haven to work in the iron manufactory there, including John Hardman, Richard Post, John Vinton, Ralph Russell, Roger Tyler, and Nicholas Pinnion. Patrick Moran, the former servant to Oliver Purchase at Saugus, and William Osborne, the Hammersmith clerk under John Winthrop, Jr., also appeared there. Three other ironworkers—John Turner, James Leonard, and Robert Crossman—moved to the Taunton ironworks in Plymouth. Other families moved further away, to Barbados (Francis Perry) and Rhode Island (Richard Pray). These ironworkers followed a familiar pattern in early America: once they had moved across the Atlantic, they continued moving, searching for better opportunities elsewhere. Because few of the ironworkers had any connection with the Puritan religious ideals prevalent in Massachusetts, they had little incentive to stay when their skills were in high demand elsewhere, even if that meant moving to other Puritan colonies.[59]

Though the fact that many early ironworkers left the colony within a decade of their arrival seems to point to a lack of community among them, such a conclusion cannot be completely sustained. John Winthrop, Jr., specifically recruited the ironworks families that left Massachusetts for New Haven, and they continued to associate with one another. As noted above, the Pinnion and Ralph Russell families appear in the New Haven town records together frequently, and other migrants maintained close ties to former colleagues still in Massachusetts. When John and Elinor Vinton died within a few months of each other in New Haven in 1661, for instance, their teenage children elected to return to Saugus under the care of Oliver Purchase. By the 1670s, John and Blaze Vinton worked for Henry Leonard, a former Saugus employee, at the Rowley ironworks and so were ensconced in a network of ironworkers and former ironworkers that included Oliver Purchase and Thomas Leonard, the son of Henry. Blaze Vinton fought in Thomas Lathrop's company from Lynn during King Philip's War.[60] Miner Richard Post also returned to Saugus around 1670, living among former colleagues such as John Gifford, Joseph Armitage, and Samuel Bennett before his death in 1671.[61] In addition, in 1674 Henry Leonard fled the failing Rowley ironworks, allegedly owing money to the owners, for the Tinton ironworks in New Jersey. Yet by 1679, he was back in Essex County with his family. His son Thomas's service with Captain Thomas Brattle during King Philip's War may have mitigated local anger with the family. Patrick Moran also maintained a correspondence with Oliver Purchase, although he never returned to Essex County. While an argument for a network of ironworkers stretching along the East Coast cannot be made, many families from Hammersmith did maintain ties, attesting to the strength of the original community.[62]

Many other ironworkers, however, did remain in Essex County. Some of these men, such as blacksmith Samuel Harte and sawyer Richard Hoode, married into respectable, prosperous families, although few joined the economic and social elite. Because some of the ironworkers came from within the established community, they differed very little in their behavior, although there is no record of any of these men joining churches. The managers of the works—Richard Leader, John Gifford, and Oliver Purchase—did join the church. These men had been recruited by the Undertakers, however, and so presumably were chosen for their religion as well as their expertise. Few ironworkers held town or colony offices; Samuel Harte served as constable and on several trial juries and juries of inquest, and Oliver Purchase represented Lynn in the House of Deputies.[63]

Several English and Welsh ironworks families sent to Massachusetts by the company settled fairly well into the larger English communities, but maintained their ties to other ironworkers, thus contributing to the development of broad social and labor networks in the region and providing connections among the disparate elements of Massachusetts society in the mid-seventeenth century.

Blacksmith Joseph Jenks arrived at Hammersmith in 1646 and worked for the company as well as on his own, fabricating iron tools for the local market. He eventually operated a forge, a rolling and slitting mill (operations that turned bar iron into smaller rods from which items such as nails and pins were made), and a gristmill. Although he branched out from his original occupation, Jenks remained in ironworks networks, acting as agent for Oliver Purchase in 1658, probating the will of Scottish ironworker James Moore in 1660, and investing in the Concord ironworks in the 1670s. Social connections existed as well; his son Daniel was suspected of fathering the illegitimate child of Abigail Harte, daughter of blacksmith Samuel. Although members of the Jenks family remained active in iron production and blacksmithing for many years, they do not appear in extant records as joining a church or holding public office.[64]

The Leonard family provides the best example of the ties among ironworkers, even after the bankruptcy of the Saugus plant in 1653. Henry Leonard, a Welsh ironworker, arrived in New England in 1642 with his brother, James. The Leonard brothers did not play a major role at Hammersmith but were instrumental in starting and operating other ironworks in the region. In the mid-1650s, James followed former Saugus employee John Turner to the Taunton ironworks in Plymouth Colony, where he quickly established himself and became a highly respected member of the community. His son and grandson, both named James, served as selectmen and sat in the Massachusetts legislature for Taunton in the eighteenth century.[65]

The career of Henry and his family, however, was more colorful than that of his brother. The Leonard family is frequently cited as one of the most incorrigible at the ironworks, and they did appear in court accused of many crimes, including physical abuse, lewd and lascivious behavior, and arson. The family first appears in the records in 1649, when Mary Leonard was fined for "speaking opprobrious words." Over the next thirty years, Henry went before the court for debt numerous times. Other, more serious, confrontations with authorities also occurred. In 1674, Hannah Downing, the Leonards' maid and daughter of Scottish ironworker Macam Downing, accused sons Nathaniel, Samuel, and Thomas Leonard of "lascivious carriages" toward her. Although several young women in the community supported Hannah's story, the depositions in this case quickly degenerated into allegations of improper behavior on all sides. The Leonards accused Hannah of walking "abroad at unseasonable times in the night," and "unbecoming conduct" with other men. A male servant claimed that Mary Leonard "took great care to prevent sin and that she often arose in the night to chide said Hannah for her carriages." In response, local leader John Gould accused Samuel and Nathaniel Leonard of swimming naked in the mill pond and "act[ing] indecently" when Faith Black appeared. Samuel Symonds insinuated that Mary Leonard and a Dr. Taylor committed adultery one afternoon in the woods. The authorities took no action on these accusations, however, and the whole affair ended with the Leonard sons piously suing Hannah for defamation. The next year, Nathaniel Leonard was suspected of burning the Rowley Village forge, managed by his father, as retaliation for the owners' lack of trust and their attempts to fire him. Although most people believed that the fire had been deliberately set, and probably by the Leonards, no one was convicted of the crime. Even with these problems, however, members of the family were consistently given responsible positions at ironworks throughout Essex County, and Henry returned to Massachusetts after several years at ironworks in New Jersey. By the late 1670s, the family contributed to the church at Topsfield. There is no evidence that they belonged to the church, however, nor evidence that any member of this branch of the Leonard family held public office in seventeenth-century Massachusetts.[66]

Henry Leonard's activities at other Essex County ironworks show the extent of ironworks networks long after the close of Hammersmith.[67] At the Rowley Village ironworks, which Leonard operated for a consortium of local owners, he worked with Thomas Looke and Thomas Tower, formerly of Saugus, as well as Ambrose Mackfashion and John Ramsdell, part-time employees at Hammersmith.[68] The forge also connects the Leonards to other alternative communities in northern Essex County. Daniel Black, a general laborer associated with agricultural communities near Ipswich, cut wood and coaled for Leonard. Leonard also leased land from Irishman Anthony Carrell of Ipswich, who in turn worked for Mackfashion and Ramsdell. Leonard had agreements to supply iron to blacksmith Edmund Bridges, who was also connected, through the marriage of his daughter Faith to Daniel Black, to these agricultural communities.[69] In addition, the employment of Hannah Downing illustrates his continuing connections to Scottish ironworks families. The Leonards therefore provide an excellent example of horizontal relationships among ironworkers in Essex County. Movement among various iron-making facilities strengthened contacts among Massachusetts residents and with the Atlantic world. These networks provided avenues for communication and trade to develop, tying the region together.[70]

The ironworkers of the 1640s and early 1650s provide one of the first opportunities to study non-Puritan residents in seventeenth-century Massachusetts. Few of these families had any religious motive for emigrating to New England, yet many settled into the region without controversy. Massachusetts authorities monitored their behavior, as they did with all residents, but rarely punished their transgressions severely. Although they did submit to Puritan leadership, ironworkers did not necessarily accept Puritan values. There is little evidence of church membership among ironworkers, and, aside from Oliver Purchase, none ever held the town or colony offices that would have required such an affiliation.[71] From an early period, then, Massachusetts leaders were willing to make concessions to non-Puritan residents who brought needed skills to the colony. This trend became even more evident in the 1650s with the much larger influx of Scottish prisoners of war to Massachusetts.

LATER IRONWORKERS AT SAUGUS

The lack of skilled ironworkers willing to move to Massachusetts hindered the Undertakers' efforts to generate a profit from Saugus. The company, desperate for inexpensive labor, turned to men captured in the wars between England and Scotland in the early 1650s. The Scottish army suffered heavy losses in two important battles, at Dunbar and Worcester, in 1650 and 1651. More than four hundred Scottish captives from these battles were sent to New England and many hundreds more were deported to the West Indies and the Chesapeake. These Scots provided much-needed labor for the ironworks and for Massachusetts.

Fighting between Scotland and England began with the Bishops' Wars in 1639 when Scottish troops invaded England after Charles I attempted to impose an Anglican-style Book of Common Prayer on the Presbyterian Scottish Kirk. The wars with the Scots set the stage for the English civil wars of the 1640s, since Charles I was forced to call a Parliament for money to muster troops against the Scots. This Parliament, however, because of its struggles with the king throughout the late 1620s over royal prerogative, taxes, religious issues, and the eleven years of Charles's sole rule, was not inclined to do his bidding. War broke out between the king and Parliament, raged across England, and spread to Ireland and Scotland. In 1649, Parliament's New Model Army beheaded Charles I. The next year, the new Commonwealth government in England began to fear another invasion from Scotland, this time led by Charles II, who had secured Scottish support and the throne in exchange for signing the National Covenant and the Solemn League and Covenant.[72]

In a pre-emptive strike in July 1650, Oliver Cromwell led the New Model Army in an invasion of Scotland. On 3 September, the two armies clashed at Dunbar, east of Edinburgh, and the English defeated the Scots easily. Almost four thousand Scots died in the field and ten thousand were captured. Wounded prisoners were freed and allowed to return home, but five thousand healthy men marched south to Newcastle. In the summer campaign of 1651, the

Scottish army decided to move south, forcing the war onto English soil. The English and Scottish armies met in late August near Worcester, in south-central England, and again, on 3 September, the English army routed the Scots. The Scots estimated their losses at two thousand dead and another ten thousand captured.[73]

After the Battle of Dunbar, Cromwell and the Council of State had to decide how to dispose of the prisoners at Newcastle. Captured soldiers traditionally would be ransomed or exchanged, but military leaders feared that healthy men would return to the Scottish army to fight again. The English also did not want to deport Scots to Europe or Ireland, for fear that they would join the armies of the Commonwealth's enemies. The Council finally decided to send most prisoners to English colonies in the Americas—in particular, Barbados, Virginia, and Massachusetts. In early November 1650, the Council ordered Sir Arthur Haselrig, the governor at Newcastle, to deliver 150 prisoners from Dunbar to the agents of John Becx and Joshua Foote, two of the principal investors in the Company of Undertakers, bound for the Saugus ironworks in Massachusetts Bay. These men sailed to London, where they boarded the *Unity* under master Augustine Walker of Charlestown. The ship departed from Gravesend on 11 November 1650.[74]

The *Unity* arrived in Boston in mid-December, a remarkably quick voyage for that time of year. The number of Scots who survived the voyage is unknown, as are most of their names. Of the 150 men who left London, however, the Company of Undertakers kept sixty-two for ironworks operations. Thirty-six prisoners went to Saugus, and seventeen worked for manager William Aubrey in the company's Boston warehouse. The remaining nine intended for the ironworks were sent to the Braintree forge or sold to local farmers and artisans soon after their arrival. Fifteen *Unity* prisoners went to the sawmills in Maine under the management of Richard Leader, the former manager of the Saugus ironworks, and his brother George. Fifteen more went to other mills in Maine and New Hampshire. The remaining men were sold to farmers and merchants in New England. Thus of the 150 Scots sent to Massachusetts in 1650, only the thirty-six sent directly to Saugus can be positively identified as part of the *Unity* contingent. Many others can be tentatively associated with this group, however, based on the dates that they begin to appear in court records.[75]

After the Battle of Worcester in 1651, the Council immediately ordered Scottish prisoners to London for deportation to the colonies. John Becx received permission to send approximately three hundred men to New England. The prisoners sailed on the *John and Sarah* under master John Greene in November 1651, and were consigned by Becx to Charlestown merchant Thomas Kemble. Two hundred seventy-two men arrived in Boston on this ship in late January or early February 1651/2. Because Kemble had sawmills in Maine and New Hampshire as well as Massachusetts, most of this group of prisoners probably went to the northern regions.[76]

Because Congregationalists and Presbyterians shared many religious affinities, Scottish prisoners had an advantage over other non-Puritan migrants in their reception by the Puritan community. Although the two groups differed in their church governance, both based their religious beliefs on Calvinist principles. New England leaders had even tried to recruit Presbyterian settlers in the 1630s. Scottish minister John Livingstone, leader of a Presbyterian congregation in northern Ireland, for example, wrote to John Winthrop, Jr., in 1634 to inquire about settling in New England. Livingstone was a well-known evangelical preacher in Scotland who fled to Ulster because he refused to conform to the Episcopalian establishment imposed on Scotland in the late 1620s. He was highly respected by Massachusetts leaders, illustrating the connections among Reformed denominations. In 1635, Livingstone and his group of Irish Protestants actually embarked for New England, but were turned back by a hurricane.[77]

Moreover, whereas earlier ironworkers had been sent by the Undertakers with apologies and trepidation, John Becx never showed the slightest hesitation about sending the Scots. His letters convey anxiety that the men would be treated well but not lavishly, joy at the prospect of bound servants replacing expensive contract labor, and delight at the profit to be made from selling excess servants to others. In short, Becx believed that he was performing a service to the colony rather than burdening it with undesirable inhabitants, as had been the fear of Joshua Foote in the 1640s.[78]

Even Puritan leaders in Massachusetts wanted to ensure the well-being of the prisoners. John Cotton carefully reassured Oliver Cromwell that the Scots had received fair treatment in New England, writing, "We have been desirous (as we could) to make their yoke easy. Such as were sick of the scurvy or other diseases have not wanted physick and chyrurgery. They have not been sold for slaves to perpetual servitude, but for 6 or 7 or 8 yeares, as we do our own."[79] This last phrase acknowledged that although the Scots deserved special care as fellow Calvinists, they were different from English residents of Massachusetts. As prisoners of war and strangers, the men were not "our own," although they received terms equal to those of English servants. Many of these men married between 1656 and 1659, indicating that they served terms of five to seven years, which was common throughout the English colonies. Scottish servants were even obligated to serve in the militia. Thus Cotton and other Massachusetts leaders believed that the prisoners would settle into life in New England and become stable members of society during and after their terms of service.[80]

At Saugus, the Scots worked with and for free employees. John Becx clearly hoped that the Scots would reduce labor costs at the ironworks, but they could not take over all the jobs of free employees. Becx expected to employ eighteen Scots as woodcutters, calculating that these men could cut four cords of wood per week, resulting in at least 3,600 cords per year. This arrangement would "make a good round stock for supply with the help of other cutters: but methinks you should have no less than 24 scotts men to constantly cut wood." Woodcutting was one of the Scots' primary occupations; an inventory of stock and tools taken 21 September 1653 listed sixty axes for thirty-seven Scottish laborers, not all of whom were employed in woodcutting. By 1652, the accounts credit Scots with cutting and cording over four thousand cords of wood, at a savings to the company of almost five hundred pounds. Yet partial accounts for 1653 also record payments to five local residents for cutting almost two hundred cords of wood.[81]

Furthermore, the Undertakers hoped that free employees could train one Scot as a hammer man, saving five shillings in every ton of bar iron, and two Scots as carpenters in order to cut back on outside carpenters, except for extraordinary works. They also wanted six Scots to work as colliers to save all coaling expenses except for the supervision of a master collier. Free employees did teach their trades to several Scottish servants. For example, Samuel Harte trained John Clarke as a blacksmith, earning four pounds for doing so. Transferring this work to a bound servant saved the company forty-four pounds per year. Undated partial accounts also indicate that James Mackall, John Mackshane, and Thomas Tower learned different aspects of forging and founding, which saved the company seven shillings for every ton of iron. Scots frequently lived with the free employees with whom they worked. Collier William Tingle, for instance, housed James Danielson and George Thomson while he taught them to make charcoal, and carpenter Francis Perry boarded and trained Robert Meeny.[82]

Aside from their work at Hammersmith, Scots "kept Gifford's and the people's cattle, fifty or sixty head, two summers, for which they were to pay 5s. p cow to the keeper."[83] In other words, they did odd jobs for residents of Saugus and Lynn, work that paid wages, allowing these men to accumulate small estates during and after their terms of service. One example of this is Arzbell Anderson, a Scottish captive working at Saugus who died in 1661, leaving an estate worth thirty-eight pounds to his relative Allester Grime, also a servant at the ironworks. James Moore, a collier, had gathered a small estate as well, leaving his wife and daughter fifty-six pounds at his death in 1659. Although these are small sums of money, the Scots had only been released from their indentures a few years before. Thus they were clearly doing work for hire before the end of their terms.[84]

Several of the Scots known to have been at Hammersmith disappear from the records in the mid-1650s. Some of them moved to New Hampshire and Maine, where a fairly large community of former captives developed around the sawmills. Maine, of course, was part of Massachusetts at this time, but the low population of the northern territories allowed many of these Scots to settle near one another in an area of York called "Scotland" by 1668. The lives of these men differed little from those of their counterparts in Essex County. A few held minor town offices, such as in 1678 when Alexander Maxwell and James Grant served as surveyors of highways for Scotland. Like their southern counterparts, several owned land but many remained tenants, and they all worked with and for their English neighbors.[85] Some Hammersmith Scots moved to ironworks in other colonies. Patrick Moran, as noted above, had been a servant of Oliver Purchase, manager at Saugus after 1658, and later became the clerk of the New Haven ironworks.[86] A few went to Boston, where there were more work opportunities for general laborers. Others may simply have died before leaving any record of themselves behind.

For the Scots who remained in Essex County, those who received training in a craft generally continued to work in these trades after their indentures ended, attesting, in part, to the need that such laborers filled. John Clarke, trained as a blacksmith by Samuel Harte, purchased land near the ironworks and continued to ply his trade until his death in 1685. Thomas Tower, a collier, worked in several of the ironworks that opened up after the Saugus facility went bankrupt in 1653. In the 1660s he made coal for, and may have been a manager of, the Concord ironworks. By the 1670s he was making coal for John Gifford, a former manager at Saugus who had opened a new bloomery in North Saugus, and for Henry Leonard and his sons at Rowley Village.[87]

Most of the later ironworkers, however, continued to work as laborers in Essex County. Arzbell Anderson chopped wood and grazed livestock as a tenant on ironworks land.[88] Anderson's kinsman and heir, Allester Grime, tried to establish himself in Salem but never managed to prosper. He worked for Edmund Batter, a Salem merchant with ties to the ironworks; then tried farming, probably on rented land; and later worked for blacksmith Daniel Rumball in Salem.[89] Macam Downing and Macam Macallum also continued to work as woodcutters and carters for colliers associated with various ironworks in Essex County, and Alexander Bravand performed agricultural labor near Wenham.[90] Many of the Scots who stayed in Essex County thus continued to work and socialize within ironworks networks. Few of the ironworks Scots held public office or joined a church, as far as the extant records show. John Clarke served as a marshal's deputy in 1662, Allester Grime served as a hog reeve in Salem in

1663, and Allester Mackmallen sat on a jury of inquest in 1668. Alexander Bravand, who attended the Wenham church, left a bequest of five shillings to minister Joseph Gerrish, and Martha Macallum, daughter of Macam, joined the Lynn church and transferred her membership to Salem in 1686. John Mackmallen, son of Allester, joined the Salem church in 1693.[91] Many of the Scottish iron-workers remained poor. The selectmen of Salem paid three families to care for Allester Grime in 1690–91, the final year of his life. Alexander Bravand was cared for by Charles Gott of Wenham for ten weeks before his death and left an estate of five pounds in 1678; Allester Mackmallen left an estate worth forty-eight pounds at his death in 1679.[92] For the most part, however, they were able to support their families until old age reduced their ability to work. That they could support families as general laborers, again, illustrates Massachusetts' need for labor throughout the seventeenth century.

A few of these former servants did obtain land, however, exemplified by John Upton and George Darling. Upton first purchased forty acres of upland near Salem Village in 1658 and continued to acquire land throughout his life. In the 1670s he moved to a large farm near Reading, in Middlesex County, but held on to much of his Essex County land, bequeathing it to his sons upon his death in 1699. Upton was unusual among the Hammersmith servants in accumulating so much acreage; out of an estate worth £984, his landholdings totaled £813 in at least sixteen parcels. For all his wealth, however, Upton apparently never joined a church or held public office. He was, in fact, sued in 1675 for refusing to pay the Salem Village meetinghouse rate. Most Scottish ironworkers acquired sig-nificantly smaller parcels, if they had any land at all.[93] George Darling eventually acquired at least twenty acres, purchasing a tract on the Salem-Marblehead town line in 1672. Like many of his fellow former servants, before buying land Darling had worked as a laborer and tenant farmer around Lynn. Once settled, he opened an inn, obtaining his license to sell beer and wine in 1676.[94] In com-parison, Allester Mackmallen purchased twenty rods of land (about one-third of an acre) in Salem for thirty shillings in 1667, and Allester Dugglas obtained a two-acre grant from Lynn in 1688.[95]

THE BRITISH COMMUNITY AT SAUGUS

The British community near Lynn developed out of living arrangements and marriage patterns at the ironworks. Although John Gifford, the manager of the ironworks, had built a dormitory for the Scottish prisoners in 1650, not all the men stayed there. The Company of Undertakers lodged and boarded many indentured servants with free workers who lived in ironworks housing; at least eight workers' houses were on the property, along with the manager's house and a "longhouse with 4 tenements."[96] Company records show that between September 1652 and September 1653, at least eight free workers boarded eleven Scots for varying lengths of time.[97] As noted above, many of the Scots also worked closely with free employees. Samuel Harte trained Scot John Clarke as a blacksmith, and James Moore, James Danielson, George Thomson, and Thomas Tower were taught to be colliers. In addition, Gifford hired out several of the Scots to other employees of the plant, who agreed to provide the men with food and clothing in addition to the fee given to the company for their hire. Collier William Tingle, for example, had four Scots for three years, and Thomas Looke, Thomas Wiggens, and Richard Hoode hired one Scot apiece for three years. John Adams and John Stewart, while on the books as working for the ironworks, lived with Gifford and looked after his personal business. Scots also kept cattle owned by the ironworks and by residents of Lynn, thereby building ties within the ironworks community as well as with local inhabitants.[98]

At times these work and living arrangements developed into more formal unions. John Clarke lodged with Francis and Jane Perry during his term of service. Perry worked as a carpenter and general handyman at Hammersmith, but he and his wife actually arrived in Massachusetts in 1631 as servants. The Perrys became landowners and church members in Salem, but they never quite conformed to Puritan ideals. They appeared frequently before the court for fighting, drinking, and "ill-speeches," and eventually moved to Barbados. John Clarke, however, married Perry's daughter after his indenture, and in 1658 purchased six acres of land next to ironworks property. He established an independent blacksmith shop and continued to do piecework for Hammersmith. He lived in Lynn until his death in 1685, and remained associated with other ironworkers, serving as administrator for the estates of two fellow Scots, Arzbell Anderson and James Moore.[99]

Moore, trained as a collier, also married into the ironworks community. In 1657, he wed Ruth Pinnion, the daughter of Nicholas. As noted above, the Pinnions were one of the most troublesome families for local authorities, but remained in Lynn until the early 1660s, when they moved to New Haven. As a collier, Moore was a highly skilled worker, and at his death in 1659, he left an estate worth fifty-six pounds, including some livestock and his working tools, but no land. The Moores lived on ironworks land, either as tenants or in exchange for work, a pattern followed by several other former servants. His will was witnessed by Joseph Jenks, a blacksmith formerly at Saugus, and Moore appointed John Clarke and Oliver Purchase administrators of his estate, thus continuing to rely on ironworks connections to protect his family.[100]

Arzbell Anderson also died while still enmeshed in ironworks networks. After his indenture, he continued to chop wood and graze livestock on ironworks land. The estate inventory noted his ownership of "a small mare & 2 Colts, 18 li.; A Small Cow, 4 li.; 2 steers." Like many unprotected estates, Anderson's suffered from the depredations of unscrupulous neighbors. Corporal John Andrews claimed that he had hired Anderson's two steers and "fetched them away," killing one and selling the other, before the administrators resolved the issue. Anderson's kinsman Allester Grime was his heir, the administrators of his estate were Oliver Purchase and John Clarke, and the estate inventory was performed by Edward Baker, John Divan, and Oliver Purchase, all of whom were connected to the Saugus ironworks. Anderson thus followed a pattern familiar to him from home: he was a tenant farmer who grazed livestock on common lands and owned little else. He also remained connected to a wider Scottish community in Essex County and in Massachusetts. He owed money to William Gibson, a Scottish shoemaker in Boston, and to Rowland Mackfashion and Macam Downing, both associated with Hammersmith. He also owed a tavern debt to John Hathorne, whose establishment was the gathering place for Saugus ironworkers.[101]

Through marriage the community that formed in the 1650s around the ironworks began to incorporate people with few connections to the plant, and so spread kinship ties throughout southern Essex County. Macam Downing and Allester Dugglas married women with no known links to ironworkers, but who most likely worked as servants near Lynn. In 1653 Downing wed Margaret Sullivan, and in 1659 Dugglas married Hannah Meadows. No information about Margaret or Hannah has been found except for their marriages and the births of their children. Downing continued his association with ironworkers from Saugus, working as a laborer on the ironworks property and putting his daughter Hannah to service with Henry Leonard in the 1670s. Hannah later married and moved to Chebacco Parish in Ipswich; her sister Priscilla married Nathaniel Carrell, of Irish descent and connected to a British community near Ipswich, and lived in Salem Farms (now Danvers). The second-generation Downings thus expanded their contacts within British networks throughout Essex County.[102]

Downing and Dugglas also lived near Teague Brann on the outskirts of Lynn, considered "in the woods" according to Brann's probate inventory. The land that these families occupied was far enough from town that Elisha Fuller was paid five shillings "to fetch the goods" after Brann's death. The Brann, Dugglas, and Downing families were quite close; in fact, Dugglas and Downing split the bulk of Brann's estate after he died in 1677 during the Battle of Black Point in King Philip's War. The three families shared labor and equipment, according to the estate inventory, which was also a pattern common in rural Scotland. Another beneficiary of the estate was Oliver Purchase, who had remained close to many former ironworkers, even though he later served as a deputy from Lynn to the General Court. Thus the community centered around ironworkers began, in the 1660s, to expand and incorporate other non-Puritan residents in the region, while also maintaining ties to local leaders in the Puritan community.[103]

Other marriages and liaisons connected this community. In 1662, Scottish ironworker James Adams married Priscilla Ramsdell, the daughter of John Ramsdell, a part-time employee of Saugus and a man later connected to Henry Leonard and the Rowley Village ironworks. In 1684, Sarah Paul, the daughter of Scottish ironworker John, was presented for fornication with John Darling, son of George; Priscilla Downing and Nathaniel Carrell were also charged with the same offense. Macam Macallum's daughter Anne married Peter Twist, a servant in Lynn who was associated with the ironworkers, although the plant did not employ him.[104]

Non-Puritan residents also maintained connections with one another even after leaving their initial geographical community. George Darling, for instance, an unskilled Scottish laborer at Hammersmith, married Irishwoman Katherine Lary in 1657. Lary had been a servant in the household and tavern of John Hathorne near the ironworks, which served as a gathering place for local laborers. In the 1670s, the Darlings opened a tavern of their own on the Salem-Marblehead town line, a location that straddled the mixed-nationality fishing community in Marblehead and the equally diverse population along the Salem waterfront. The centrality of the tavern made Darling's house a meeting point for locals, as well as the starting point for the yearly perambulation of the Salem and Marblehead town lines. The Darlings also had a young servant, Ingram Moody, who was probably the son of another Scottish captive from Saugus. Thus, although the Darlings left the ironworks community near Lynn, they moved to a marginal area, as did so many other non-Puritan residents, and continued their association with these communities. Philip and Hannah Welsh, who were closely enmeshed in the agricultural communities discussed in the next chapter, were neighbors of the Darlings for several years, as was John Blaney, a former part-time employee at Saugus.[105]

Thus the need for labor in the early decades of settlement in Massachusetts brought unanticipated consequences to the Puritan commonwealth. In order for the colony to survive—in light of the political situation on England in the 1640s and the establishment of other Puritan-sponsored colonies—Massachusetts's leaders had to diversify their economic base. The solution to these problems, however, made immigration more difficult to control and even encouraged the migration of people with little sympathy with Puritan ideals. Yet because these families did not openly challenge Massachusetts authorities, an accommodation could be reached. Laborers were less threatening to the intellectual basis for the colony than were prominent religious and social dissenters, such as Roger Williams, Anne Hutchinson, John Underhill, and Robert Child.[106] Yet these laborers were not willing to be completely enfolded into Massachusetts society and subsumed in Puritan culture. They formed localized communities and wide-ranging social networks, particularly in marginal areas of Essex County, that were neither static nor completely separated from the larger Puritan community. Some ironworkers left these communities, but many more remained in Essex County or returned after living elsewhere. Members of these alternative communities also had ties to the larger society of Massachusetts; just as the colony could not remain isolated from the larger Atlantic world, no particular group of colonists could remain isolated from society.

Three

BRITISH COMMUNITIES:
AGRICULTURAL LABORERS AND TENANT
FARMERS IN ESSEX COUNTY

In early Massachusetts, non-Puritan residents constructed social relationships based on physical proximity (in neighborhoods, for example), but also on nationality, shared experiences as captives or servants, and marriage and kinship. These mixed communities and social networks consisted of non-Puritan English—most of whom migrated for economic reasons—Scots, Irish, Channel Islanders, and Welsh settlers, in differing degrees. Some communities were largely Scottish, others Irish, and some had fairly even mixes of non-Puritans of several nationalities. What they all had in common, however, was both a lack of affiliation with Puritan religious ideology and lower-to-middling social and economic status.[1] Yet these communities flourished within and alongside more traditional kinds of communities. Non-Puritan residents, as with all colonists, belonged to many communities and held several identities simultaneously. Although this chapter emphasizes several less-noticed forms of community in Essex County, non-Puritan agricultural workers did not separate themselves from larger social cohorts. This lack of sharp divisions between communities meant that all residents joined in the construction of society.

Mixed-nationality communities of tenant farmers, servants, and laborers began to develop in Essex County in the late 1650s and early 1660s as a result of demographic pressure. The Scottish prisoners sent to New England in 1651 and 1652 were all male, as were many of the Irish who had been spirited to the colonies. Scottish and Irish men, therefore, married Irish- and lower-status Englishwomen, precluding widespread endogamous marriages even if these men had wanted to marry within their national group. Although historians generally interpret exogamous marriage as a dilution of ethnic identity, such marriages were common among groups with extensive international ties. Scots, for instance, with their long history of emigration, did not see exogamous marriage as extraordinary. In Massachusetts, out-group marriage allowed the Scots and Irish to begin families and to carve places for themselves within coastal communities. Far from being set apart by endogamous marriage, the Scots and Irish became part of networks of non-Puritan residents, living under English law and Puritan religious strictures without necessarily assimilating into Puritan society.[2]

Filling in the geographical and economic interstices of Massachusetts society, laborers and tenant farmers developed extensive networks that substituted for kinship ties left behind in England, Scotland, and Ireland. These communities consisted of people who shared similar places in society, who had common experiences of servitude, and who supported each other in lieu of long-standing family ties. The presence of such networks contributed to the colony's development by providing stability for the "lower sorts," believed by contemporaries to be the most volatile and untrustworthy segment of the population. Members of these communities also constituted a fairly settled labor pool, which allowed the local economy to develop and expand.[3]

British communities can be seen most easily in northern Essex County, near Ipswich.[4] In Essex, unlike Suffolk County, official records survived remarkably well, and the diversified economy supported occupations unrelated to farming. Inland counties were more dependant on subsistence farming for a longer period, although in a few places, such as Springfield, similar communities appear to have developed as well. Springfield, of course, was a fur trade center as well as an agricultural community, and traded extensively with other Connecticut River towns.

In Springfield, Stephen Innes notes the presence of a small group of Scottish men, most of whom arrived as captives from the war between England and Scotland in the early 1650s. He estimates that the numbers of Scots "never exceeded a dozen men," although "their impact on the community was considerable," and argues that the Scots "were suffered to remain in the community because of their contributions to the local economy," but that they "tested the limits of social tolerance" as well. As described by Innes, the Scots in Springfield were more contentious than those in the coastal counties; appearances before the magistrates included the usual presentments for drinking, fighting, and slander, but also card playing, an offense not found in the Essex County records. The less restrictive atmosphere in Springfield, being further from the center of authority in Boston, and the almost complete dependence on one employer,

John Pynchon, may have made these non-Puritan residents more of a challenge for local magistrates.[5]

Geographically, British communities in Essex County were centered around three areas—Lynn and Saugus, Salem, and Ipswich—but the ties among members of these communities stretched across such governmental boundaries. Near Lynn, the British community focused around ironworkers at Saugus, including the early ironworkers from England and Wales, Scottish workers from the 1650s, and other English laborers who did piecework for the plant or worked in peripheral crafts, such as potters and carpenters. The communities near Salem and Ipswich were more diverse. At Salem, French-speaking servants from Jersey joined the Scottish and English in mixed communities composed of farmers, fishermen, craftsmen, and general laborers, a diverse workforce that reflected the occupational needs of a flourishing port town. Around Ipswich, British communities contained a larger proportion of Irish inhabitants, along with Scots and non-Puritan English. The primary occupation in this region was farming.

The towns where British communities concentrated were also very different. Salem was a large town with a busy port, and contained approximately 2,000 residents by 1690. Ipswich, a prosperous agricultural center involved with the supply of sailing ships, supported a population of around 875 in 1690, and Lynn was smaller and less wealthy, with a population of 600 in 1690. Topsfield, which contained a subset of the Ipswich British community, was completely agricultural and comprised 279 residents in 1687. Marblehead, a subset of the Lynn community, was a much larger town, with approximately 1,030 residents in 1690, but, because a large population of transient fisher families, was very poor. In the typology of towns developed by Edward Cook, Salem falls into his first category, an urban center. Ipswich meets the criteria for the second grouping, a major county town, and Lynn and Marblehead fall into the third category, secondary centers. Topsfield, Wenham, and Saugus fall into the fourth type of town, small, self-contained villages. Non-Puritan communities were not centered in one kind of town in Essex County. Social, economic, and national ties connected these non-Puritan residents, and many moved easily and frequently among communities.[6]

British communities in coastal Massachusetts thus comprised a mix of Scots, Irish, English, Jersey, and Welsh colonists. Some members of these communities owned their own land, some were tenant farmers, and others remained servants and laborers. Although non-Puritan residents had wide connections to prosperous, churchgoing Puritan families in the region, the settlers discussed here frequently appear in the court records in close association with one another. They clearly knew one another's business very well, they shared labor and tools, their children frequently married into other non-Puritan families, and they looked to one another for support. The bonds were tighter than simply those of neighbors and acquaintances.

Complaints brought by members of mixed communities against one another were rare, even suits for debt, which are ubiquitous in the seventeenth-century court records. Scottish and Irish settlers in particular rarely appeared in court in opposition to each other. (Jerseyans, particularly merchants, behaved differently, as discussed in the next chapter.) Members of these newly formed British communities appear as either defendants or plaintiffs in ninety-nine cases in the published records of the Essex County Quarterly Court. Two of these cases were between Scottish and Irish men, and both cases involve William Paterson and Anthony Carrell. Only ten of the ninety-nine cases were between members of mixed communities of any nationality, and five of these were suits for debt. In no instance did a Scot bring another Scot to court, and the same holds true for the Irish. In other words, when members of mixed communities came before the court, they had been charged by the magistrates (for offenses such as excessive drinking, fornication, or fighting) or another colonist (generally for debt) who was not part of their usual social network. These numbers are striking, given the general litigiousness of New England society in the seventeenth century, and they attest to the strength of these communities and the abilities of members to mediate problems among themselves.[7]

This preference for settling local disputes out of court stands in contrast to relationships that members of British communities had with the larger society. Non-Puritan residents did use the courts to resolve problems with settlers who were not part of their communities; a few even appealed local decisions to the Court of Assistants in Boston.[8] They therefore understood the laws and how the legal system functioned; moreover, because court costs could be expensive, these residents had the resources to file lawsuits. In general, non-Puritan residents trusted the courts to settle disputes between them and members of the larger community equitably, and served on petty juries and as constables themselves. The lack of formal legal actions within British communities was, therefore, a matter of choice rather than necessity. David Thomas Konig has argued for the integrative function of the courts in early Massachusetts, which may account in part for this difference. Non-Puritans needed to establish their place within the town or county community and used the legal system to do this. Within their own communities, however, they depended on mediation and social pressure to settle disputes.[9]

Their trust in the legal system was not misplaced. There is little evidence that the courts were heavily skewed in favor of Puritan residents. Juries, composed mostly of common settlers who may or may not have been church members, at times appeared more sympathetic to the viewpoints of non-Puritans, people of similar socioeconomic status to most jurors, than those of Puritan magistrates. For instance, in a case against Scot John Upton, discussed in chapter 5, the jury was not willing to censure Upton for aiding a servant who ran away from his master in Boston. The magistrates did not agree with this verdict, but no punishment for Upton was recorded. Similarly, in a case brought by magistrate Samuel Symonds of Ipswich against his Irish servants Philip Welsh and William Downing, also discussed below, the jury decided that the two men should serve longer terms only *if* the indenture contract between Symonds and ship captain George Dell was valid. In short, the jury was willing to consider the Irishmen's argument. The magistrates, however, ruled for their colleague Symonds.[10] Social status was more important than church membership or nationality in influencing these court cases: magistrates supported the positions of other elites, and juries were more attuned to the needs of lower-status residents.

AGRICULTURAL WORKERS IN NORTHERN ESSEX COUNTY

As shown in the previous chapter, immigration to Massachusetts declined in the early 1640s, leaving colony leaders searching for new sources of labor. Scottish captives from the Cromwellian wars of the early 1650s proved to be one such source, the majority of whom were sent to New England under the auspices of John Becx to benefit the Company of Undertakers of the Ironworks in New England. Those servants not needed at the ironworks were sold to local landowners and craftsmen, primarily in northern Essex County. Therefore, most of the Scots in Massachusetts before 1680 arrived as indentured servants in the early 1650s. The English government, however, also sent many young Irishmen and -women to the colonies after the conquest of Ireland by Oliver Cromwell in the late 1640s. And so, as Scottish captives arrived, Massachusetts's leaders also began to allow the importation of Irish workers of unknown backgrounds.

Aside from the long-standing prejudice that the English felt against the Irish, Massachusetts's leaders had practical concerns about settlers from Ireland. As long as potential immigrants were Protestants from Scottish-dominated Ulster, or from Anglo-Irish families (particularly the New English), they were welcome, as evidenced by John Winthrop, Jr.'s correspondence with John Livingstone in

1634/5.[11] But native, or "wild," Irish were suspect. Not only were these people likely to be Catholic, but they were also believed to be barbaric and uncivilized, and thus a physical, as well as religious, danger to English Protestants. The events of the 1640s heightened such fears in England and Massachusetts.[12]

In 1633, Charles I appointed Thomas Wentworth as lord deputy of Ireland. Wentworth aggressively protected the interests of the king in Ireland, which had been badly mismanaged by the previous royal favorite, George Villiers, the Duke of Buckingham. Through his diligent attention to Charles's affairs, as well as his own interests, Wentworth managed to alienate all factions in Irish society. When Wentworth became a pawn in the disputes between the English Parliament and Charles (and lost his head after being convicted of treason in 1641), many Irish saw an opportunity to gain more control over domestic affairs, if not outright independence, and therefore rebelled. Catholics and Protestants alike committed atrocities against the other, but in England, Protestant victims of Irish Catholics received great sympathy. Their tales of horror were given wide publicity, which hardened English Protestant anger against, and fear of, Catholics. Charles was unable to stem the rebellion because of the developing civil war in England, and thus after 1642 Irish lords ruled Ireland, virtually independent of the English.[13]

The Parliamentary victory in England in 1649 and the beheading of Charles I opened a new chapter in Anglo-Irish fighting. Parliament decided to use Catholic actions during the 1641–42 rebellion as an excuse to reward its supporters with land, and began a wholesale confiscation of Irish property. Oliver Cromwell and the New Model Army invaded Ireland in the summer of 1649, attacking soldiers and civilians alike and committing atrocities unheard of in earlier conflicts. The English were faced with controlling an angry and newly dispossessed population, and so began to deport young men and women to the colonies, using Elizabethan statutes against "rogues and vagabonds."[14]

Most of the Irish spirited out of their country during this time were sent to the West Indies and the Chesapeake. Indentured laborers brought higher prices in these areas, where the cultivation of staple crops and the high mortality rate created a constant need for servants. New Englanders needed laborers but did not have the steady demand found in southern regions of North America.

Massachusetts's policy toward Irish settlers was inconsistent. Ship owners and captains may have avoided the colony, in part because they never quite knew what reception to expect. In October 1652, for instance, David Selleck, a Boston merchant, appeared before the Court of Assistants, charged with (and fined for) "bringing some of the Irish men on shoare." The Court eventually remitted the fine and gave Selleck permission to provide medical care for another man, "provided he [Selleck] give bond to send him out of this jurisdiction when he is well." A week later, Martha Brenton of Boston asked permission to acquire two Irish children as servants, which the Court granted as long as both were "borne of English parents." Both cases indicate a concern over immigration and a desire to keep Gaelic Irish, or those of unknown backgrounds, out of Massachusetts.[15] Yet eighteen months later, after Selleck had obtained a license from the English government to bring four hundred Irish children to the colonies, his ship, the *Goodfellow*, discharged in Essex County at least part of its complement of servants, including fourteen-year-old Philip Welsh and sixteen-year-old William Downing.[16] Selleck had investments in New England and Virginia, and so most of the children went to the Chesapeake, but close inspection of the Essex County records indicates that many Irish servants arrived in Massachusetts around this time. These forced immigrants faced a slightly different reception from that received by their Scottish counterparts. They were more likely to be presented to the court for minor infractions, to be warned out of town, and to be suspected of criminal activity because of their "Irish bloud."[17] And so, although Scottish, Irish, and non-Puritan English joined in mixed communities, they did not all face the same conditions in Massachusetts.

Little information about the Irish deported to Massachusetts has survived. There is no record of their arrival, no ship passenger lists, and, aside from the men who appear in the Symonds-Welsh case discussed below, no indication of why or when these servants were allowed to settle in the colony. Although the Massachusetts government had discouraged the settlement of Irish in the colony in general, it did not officially prohibit them, and thus left no record why, in the mid-1650s, clusters of Irish servants and laborers begin to appear in the records in Boston and Essex County.

Non-Puritan servants also arrived in Massachusetts in the 1650s under individual contracts. Alexander Gordon, for example, petitioned the Middlesex County court in 1653 to stop the sale of his labor by his master, John Cloise. Gordon had been captured during the Battle of Worcester in 1652 and sent to Tothill Field, near London, to await deportation. While there, he agreed to go to Massachusetts with Cloise "with out any agreement for time or wages, only his promise to be as a father in all Love and kindness." Gordon paid for his passage by working on the ship and then worked for Cloise for a year without pay, receiving only room and board. Cloise later sold him for seventeen pounds, prompting Gordon's complaint. In addition, in 1655, "severall Scotsmen" petitioned the Court of Assistants for their freedom, which was denied. Although it is possible that these men were part of the ironworks contingent, it is more probable that they, like Gordon, had entered into informal work contracts that brought them to Massachusetts, and which they interpreted differently from their employers.[18]

In contrast to the workers at Hammersmith, the servants who had been sold to landowners and craftsmen in northern Essex County became tenant farmers or agricultural laborers at the end of their terms. This difference was due in part to the skills developed by ironworkers that allowed them to support themselves by practicing a craft, and to the fact that northern Essex County had good agricultural land that could support commercial farming. Much of this land was held in large parcels, rather than as smaller family farms, and could be let to tenant farmers. Northeastern Massachusetts, where these agricultural laborers lived, had been divided into large land grants in the 1630s and given to colony leaders as compensation for public service. John Winthrop, Jr., John Endicott, Emanuel Downing, Samuel Symonds, Richard Dummer, and others received farms of several hundred acres each in the 1630s and early 1640s.[19] Those who chose to improve the land needed servants to work it. Because godly servants and laborers were difficult to obtain, involuntary indentured servants, such as Scottish or Irish captives, became the next-best, and cheapest, choice. John Endicott, for example, purchased five men for his farm from the Dunbar prisoners sent by John Becx, and Samuel Symonds employed at least three young Irish men—John King, Philip Welsh, and William Downing—and probably several more.[20]

Tenant farming was common in England, Scotland, and Ireland. In New England, however, early settlers were given land in new towns, making this a region of family-run freehold farms. Tenancy, then, was far less common in Massachusetts, and New England as a whole, than in Britain, Ireland, and the southern colonies in North America. Yet, according to Daniel Vickers, tenant farming "flourished in those parts of Essex County where adequate land that was close to the sea made commercial agriculture possible." He estimates that Ipswich, Newbury, and Rowley, which together accounted for 35 percent of the population of Essex County, held about 68 percent of the county's tenant farmers. In addition, agricultural districts near Salem and Marblehead held large numbers of tenant farmers. Vickers also notes that most of the tenant farmers in these areas arrived after 1640, when land in the coastal regions had already been apportioned to the towns.[21] As remaining land continued to be divided among town proprietors, usually limited to early residents, tenancy among new arrivals increased. Many Scottish and Irish tenants neatly fit the description offered by Vickers. By the mid-1660s, they were concentrated in Ipswich, Topsfield, and Wenham, although many non-Puritan tenant farmers also lived near Salem and Marblehead. All arrived after the Great Migration and with few resources to acquire their own land. Tenancy filled a need to put land under cultivation at the least cost to the property holder, and was a step to land ownership for some non-Puritan residents.

Tenancy in the commercial agricultural areas near the coast differed from tenant farming in inland communities. In Springfield, Stephen Innes found tenancy to be "a swift route to economic hardship," due in large part to the control that the Pynchon family had over the economy of the region. Tenants of John Pynchon frequently paid high rates for their land and were usually required to help develop the tract by clearing ground or constructing houses or outbuildings. Lessees were not given allowances for these improvements, unlike typical lease arrangements in coastal areas. The 1660 agreement between Richard Dummer and Irishman Daniel Grasier in Ipswich, for instance, gave Grasier credit for building a house and putting the land under cultivation. As in Britain and Ireland, tenants in Springfield found that their condition was lifelong and entailed dependence on a powerful landowner. In Essex County, the greater extent of landownership and competition for laborers meant that tenants had wider choice of landlords and therefore more advantageous terms, although here, too, lease holding was frequently a permanent status.[22]

Although few Scottish and Irish servants and laborers moved into the ranks of landowners, farming good tracts of land may have been an improvement on their prospects at home. Scottish and Irish captives generally came from backgrounds of very small landholdings, tenant farming, or common-land livestock grazing. In both Scotland and Ireland, most of the land was held by large landowners who rented it out at their pleasure. Scottish landlords had almost unfettered authority over their lands. In Scotland, according to Ned Landsman, "leases were rare and, where they existed, quite short, often lasting only a single year," leaving landless farmers at the mercy of great landowners. In Gaelic regions of Ireland, land was frequently controlled by groups of kin and could be redistributed often, depending on local custom. In Anglo-Norman areas, tenancy was common, as was subletting smaller tracts of land to subtenants. The seventeenth century was also a period of enclosure in Britain and Ireland, which meant even fewer prospects for tenants or landless men. Thus even a middling- or lower-status laborer or tenant farmer in Massachusetts had opportunities not available in his home country.[23]

Non-Puritan leaseholders in Massachusetts became tenants on short-term leases, with few requirements outside of yearly rents, and settled near their original places of residence. Alexander Thomson, for example, had been sold to a "Master" Starkweather of Ipswich in 1652, and rented land in 1663 from Matthew Whipple of Ipswich.[24] Daniel Davison rented from Daniel Ringe of

Ipswich in 1661, living on land adjoining Thomson. William Danford also rented land in this same area, which was close to his former master, Sergeant Jacobs.[25] The terms of these leases are not known, but may have been similar to the agreement between Daniel Grasier and Richard Dummer. This agreement required more than a simple lease payment, which probably reflected Grasier's poverty and the fact that he rented undeveloped land. Grasier agreed to "build a house, break up land and hold it ten years," but was to be allowed "to hold the ground four years for the fencing and breaking up." Grasier also rented a cow and calf at a lower rate in exchange for his labor on the house. When the term of the lease ended, the livestock and house were to be appraised, and if they were worth more than Grasier's payment, Dummer would pay him the difference. If they were worth less, Grasier would have to pay the difference. He forfeited this agreement and was ordered by the court to pay Dummer for his loss. As noted above, however, the terms of this lease were more generous than the Pynchon leases in Springfield.[26] Other men obtained their landholdings directly from their former masters. Edward Nealand purchased seven acres of land in Ipswich from Joseph Medcalfe for half a mare and an agreement to work for Medcalfe for four pence less than the rate that laborers usually commanded. Nealand later acquired from Philip Fowler an additional two acres of meadow nearby.[27]

Some laborers in Essex County combined agricultural work on small tracts of land while working for others, piecing together a living for themselves and their families. Daniel Black, a non-Puritan laborer closely associated with iron-workers and other members of the British communities, chopped wood for Henry Leonard at the Rowley ironworks, working with colliers Thomas Tower and Thomas Looke, and worked in an unstated capacity with Ambrose Mackfashion, also a collier. All these men had worked at the Saugus ironworks. In addition, Black did agricultural work, on his own or on leased land, and kept at least one cow and some pigs.[28] Philip Welsh also supported his family through day labor. Welsh, however, moved his family frequently in search of work. Although he had been a tenant of selectman Moses Maverick in Marblehead, when he returned to Ipswich he worked for many landholders, including Edmund Potter of Ipswich and John Gould of Topsfield.[29]

By 1660, non-Puritan laborers had been accepted as part of the social fabric in Massachusetts. After the brief flurry of concern over the ironworkers and Scottish and Irish captives in the 1640s and early 1650s, non-Puritan laborers received little comment from town or colony leaders.[30] Non-Puritan English, Scots, and Irish arrived throughout the century and were absorbed into these mixed-nationality communities of laborers. Few of these immigrants were presented for swearing, fighting, and lack of respect for religion, unlike the ironworkers of the 1640s. Only

William Danford and Philip Welsh faced presentments for these offenses, although drinking continued to be a problem, with Downing, Welsh, Edward Nealand, and John Morrill, among others, being presented for this offense.[31]

Even with the recent wars in England, Scotland, and Ireland, and the long history of violence among these peoples, most laborers settled into life in Puritan-dominated Massachusetts with few overt problems. Tensions between these non-Puritan residents and their Puritan neighbors did exist, attested to by the ethnic slurs discussed below, but violence or mistreatment of non-Puritan servants and laborers was rare.[32] That such laborers became settled residents of the Bay Colony, however, does not mean that they assimilated into the Puritan population. The tightly knit communities formed by non-Puritan agricultural workers and laborers allowed these residents to maintain old identities and develop new ones as colonists.

BRITISH COMMUNITIES IN NORTHERN ESSEX COUNTY

As tenant farmers and agricultural laborers, members of these communities tended to be more stable, not moving quite as often as ironworkers, and many remained near their former masters, either renting land from them or from neighboring landholders. The area around the Topsfield-Ipswich town line near Wenham held one such community, focused around several families, including Alexander Thomson and Daniel Davison. Other non-Puritan settlers, such as Philip and Hannah Welsh, moved in and out of the region frequently. Thomson and Davison arrived in Massachusetts in 1652, as prisoners from the Battle of Worcester, and were indentured to landowners in Ipswich. They were released from their indentures around 1658 and began leasing land, Thomson from Matthew Whipple, and Davison from Daniel Ringe. Thomson married Deliverance Hagget of Wenham in 1662, and Davison married Margaret Low of Ipswich in 1657.[33] Deliverance was the daughter of Henry and Ann Hagget, a poor family that arrived in Massachusetts before 1644; her sister Hannah married Philip Welsh. The Low family had long been settled in Chebacco Parish, near Ipswich. Mary Thomson, the daughter of Alexander and Deliverance, married another member of this family, Jonathan Low, in 1693/4. Although Thomson may have acquired a few acres of land, he remained a tenant farmer most of his life. Daniel Davison, however, owned at least eighty-eight acres of upland and meadowland at his death in 1693. He therefore was one of the few Scottish residents to move from tenancy to ownership, although his property was still within the same Ipswich neighborhood where he had served his indenture and rented land.[34]

This circle of families had wide connections throughout northern Essex County. For instance, Thomson, Davison, and William Danford all lived near one another and subleased meadowlands from John Warner. Danford, an Irishman who had arrived in Essex County before 1660, had more brushes with the law than did his neighbors Thomson and Davison. He was presented several times for drinking and fighting, and, more seriously, for stealing and killing a steer. Yet, for all these problems, he served in the Newbury militia during King Philip's War. Danford was also closely connected to several other Irish families in the area. He was one of four Irishmen to petition for the estate of Robert Dorton, along with Thomson's brother-in-law Philip Welsh, Edward Deere, and John Ring. No record of Dorton exists before this petition. He left Essex County in 1672, giving twenty-five pounds in specie to John Ring with the instructions "that if he came not here within the space of three years, then he willed the said sum with the use thereof to four of his countrymen," the men who filed the petition. The court approved the distribution of money, allotting ten pounds to Edward Deere and five pounds to the other three men.[35]

Deere lived in Ipswich, near his countrymen, but also enjoyed ties to the larger community, serving as bondsman for Holick Country in 1667, on two juries of inquest in 1669 and 1676, and testifying in other court cases involving his neighbors. Deere also had ties to Daniel Black, who, in 1660, used his house to woo Faith Bridges of Topsfield, daughter of Edmund Bridges, a prosperous but cantankerous blacksmith, against her father's wishes. William Danford helped Black lure Faith to the house.[36]

John Ring became a farmer in Ipswich, where he worked closely with other Irish residents in the area. He hired Richard (no last name given), also from Ireland, who ran away when presented for fornication with Mary Greeley, a servant of Nathaniel Wells. He also allowed William Downing, who arrived on the *Goodfellow* with Philip Welsh, to keep a sow in his barn. Ring lived on the geographical outskirts of the larger British community around Topsfield and Ipswich, but became part of a smaller grouping of non-Puritan settlers. This neighborhood was near the establishment of innkeeper John Fuller, whose Irish servant Katherine Brummigen later married Luke Wakelin, another newcomer with no known relatives in Essex County, and settled in the area.[37] This small grouping of families resembles the clachans of rural Ireland, wherein small groups of families lived near one another and farmed in common. As with most communal enterprises, whether undertaken by families or unrelated people, members of these communities bore responsibilities to one another. Although the extent of shared responsibilities in the Topsfield neighborhood is not clear, many non-Puritan communities in coastal Massachusetts exhibited similar characteristics. Also reminiscent of the farmtouns of rural Scotland, such communities may indicate a preference among Irish and Scottish residents for smaller, more intimate groupings of people than was common in traditional English-style villages established in Massachusetts.[38] Ring and Deere apparently lived quiet lives, as they appear in the court records infrequently. Both men married, had children, and acquired modest competencies (since neither appeared in court for debt), yet they also left no recorded wills or estate inventories.

Edward Nealand also lived in the area, embedded in both the mixed-ethnicity communities of former servants and captives as well as his neighborhood community. He arrived in Ipswich in the 1650s and was indentured to Joseph Medcalfe, from whom he purchased land in the early 1660s. This purchase brought him into a number of land disputes over the years with his neighbors John Kimball and Philip Fowler. The men sued and countersued one another several times between 1668 and 1682 over property boundaries, which was not an unusual occurrence in early Massachusetts, but Nealand frequently initiated the suits, indicating that he was familiar with the court system and believed that he would get a fair hearing. He won many of his suits, justifying his faith in the courts.[39] Nealand was associated with the leading men and church members of the town—such as John Gould, John Warner, and John Whipple—and appeared as a witness in several cases involving other neighbors' disputes. He also served in the trainband and in the militia during King Philip's War, and in 1684 was appointed a marshal's deputy.[40]

Yet, as shown above, Nealand was also part of the mixed-ethnicity communities around Ipswich. He kept in close contact with other Irish residents as well as his Scottish and English non-Puritan neighbors; for example, he was deposed along with Alexander Thomson about cattle earmarks in 1674, and was apparently not associated with the Congregational churches. In fact, Nealand purchased a house and land from his countryman Anthony Carrell that sat atop the Topsfield-Ipswich town line. According to local legend, he avoided paying the Topsfield minister's rate by being "in Ipswich" when the constable came to collect it.[41]

Like Nealand, most non-Puritan residents were closely involved in the larger communities, working for Puritan landholders in addition to farming their land. Alexander Thomson worked with Irishmen John Morrill and Daniel Grasier at Edward Colburne's farm, along with Englishman John Clarke. Grasier rented land from Colburne after defaulting on his lease with Richard Dummer, and Morrill owned land in Ipswich. Both Grasier and Morrill had been warned out of Ipswich in 1661, when Grasier was a tenant of Dummer, but neither had been forced to leave the town. In 1667, Grasier entered into a dispute with Colburne. He was unhappy with his landlord for taking away a cow and other unstated offenses. When Colburne's Indian corn was destroyed, suspicion fell on Grasier, since he and his wife had not suffered in silence but had threatened to "do Colburne some scurvy trick to pay him for what he had done about the lease." Deponents in the case included John Morrill, Alexander Thomson, Ann Hagget, Deliverance Thomson, and Daniel Black, who was working for John Morrill. These families were clearly part of a neighborhood, consisting of Scottish, Irish, and English colonists. They were connected on several levels: through proximity, kinship, nationality, and shared experiences of captivity. Yet members of this community had ties to wider networks as well.[42]

Alexander Thomson stayed in touch with his countrymen in Essex County, receiving a bequest of a pair of stockings from Alexander Bravand, who had arrived in Massachusetts in 1651 and worked at Saugus. Bravand died in poverty at Wenham in 1678. Other Scots receiving bequests from him included Robert Mackclaffin, Alexander Maxey, and John Ross. Bravand also left five shillings to Joseph Gerrish, the pastor of the Wenham church, which he attended, and a doublet to John Fiske, the son of the previous minister. Although it is not clear how closely tied Thomson was to these Wenham Scots—they only appear together in this one instance—Bravand's will illustrates not only the existence of communities based on nationality in Essex County, but also that small groups of non-English residents lived throughout the county and, probably, the colony.[43]

Little is known about the other Scots mentioned in Bravand's will. Robert Mackclafflin's arrival in Massachusetts went unrecorded, although he married Joanna Warner in Wenham in 1664, and he and his wife joined the Wenham church before 1674. Mackclaffin also served in the militia in the late 1680s.[44] Alexander Maxey probably arrived in 1652, since a Sander Mackey is listed on the 1652 manifest of Scottish prisoners from Worcester, and was indentured to merchant William Browne of Salem. He lived in Wenham by 1660, where his wife, Mary, and his children became church members, although Alexander apparently did not join. Upon his death in 1684, he left a house and sixteen acres of land. His total estate was worth approximately £130.[45] Three John Rosses appear on the 1652 manifest, but it was a fairly common name, appearing in the Sudbury, Charlestown, Malden, Ipswich, and Kittery (Maine) records. Most likely this John Ross was the Ipswich man, but it is not possible to identify him further.[46] These men rarely appeared in the court records and were never identified by nationality when they did appear, which raises the question of how many other non-English residents lived in the same manner. For historians, those who remained tenant farmers or laborers and had few appearances in court most likely will never be identified, and so we cannot get an accurate picture of diversity in seventeenth-century Massachusetts.[47] Yet, as Bravand's bequests show, non-English residents did recognize bonds based on place of origin. Their small numbers in Massachusetts, as well as their distance from home, gave meaning to nationality, however broadly constructed, although it was not the only, or sometimes even the primary, bond.

Non-Puritan residents also maintained ties to their Puritan neighbors. Like the ironworkers, non-Puritans participated in the larger community in many ways, primarily by holding minor town offices and serving on juries and in militias. Daniel Davison, Edward Deere, and Allester Mackmallen each served on several juries of inquest, and Edward Nealand and John Clarke of Lynn acted as marshal's deputies. Allester Grime was appointed hog reeve for Salem Village, and Philip English and Nathaniel and Samuel Beadle, among other Jersey Islanders, served as constables in Salem. Davison, Thomson, Mackmallen, and others also performed smaller services, such as appraising damage to livestock or crops in disputes or caring for the indigent at the town's expense. As minor as such service was, it was the glue that held local communities together. Constable was an onerous position that few men assumed gladly, yet without it, the most basic legal functions could not take place. Fence viewers and hog reeves kept potential problems between neighbors from becoming large issues. Mediators—men who appraised damages according to commonly accepted standards—maintained equity within the community.[48] Non-Puritans were part of the structure of their towns and villages. Participation in community affairs signals a commitment to that community, and these duties were shared among all residents, not just church members.

Although non-Puritan agricultural laborers generally lived in fairly stable neighborhoods, some families moved throughout Essex County, usually remaining within the orbit of more settled British communities. These extra-local ties can be outlined through the wanderings of Philip and Hannah (Hagget) Welsh. Welsh arrived in Massachusetts in May 1654, at the age of fourteen, and his indenture was sold to Samuel Symonds, a wealthy landowner, magistrate, and assistant from Ipswich. In a suit brought by Symonds against Welsh and his fellow Irish servant William Downing in 1661, Welsh claimed that he, along with many others from his village in Ireland, had been taken by force, placed aboard David Selleck's ship, the *Goodfellow*, and brought to New England. The voyage of the *Goodfellow* corresponds to an English Order in Council (May 1653) authorizing the punishment of idle or lazy people. One such punishment, of course, was to send indolent persons to the colonies, thereby ridding Ireland of unproductive (and probably Catholic) residents while also providing the colonies with labor.[49]

The disputes between Welsh and Symonds also illustrate the need for labor in Massachusetts. In 1660, Symonds had lodged a complaint with the court about Welsh's "stubbornness." When Welsh was sentenced to spend time in jail, Symonds requested that the punishment be held in abeyance "until he has cause again to complain of him." Symonds retained Welsh's labor while retaining a cudgel to hold over him to regulate his behavior. The new cause for complaint came the next year, in 1661, when Welsh and Downing refused to serve Symonds any longer because they had already worked for him for seven years. They appealed to the fairness of the court, arguing that seven years was the common length of service in England and was "3 yeeres more then ye used to sell them for at Barbadoes, when they are stollen in England." Symonds pled hardship; he needed the continued work of the men to stave off "destitution" for his family. Not surprisingly, Symonds won the case, retaining their labor for another two years, but the Irishmen were willing to argue for their rights. They also received support from the jury, which was willing to consider their position, although the magistrates decided in favor of Symonds.[50]

Philip Welsh served Samuel Symonds until 1663 and three years later married Hannah Hagget. Philip and Hannah oscillated among Ipswich, Wenham, and Topsfield for the rest of the 1660s and the early 1670s, working for Puritan landowners such as John Gould, but never straying far from the British community containing Hannah's parents, sister, and brother-in-law, as well as other Irish residents. In 1675, Welsh was drafted into service in Captain Joseph Gardiner's company, which attacked the Narragansett Indians during King Philip's War.[51] Shortly after his service, the Welshes moved to Marblehead, where they became tenants of Moses Maverick, a Marblehead selectman and prosperous landowner. Though warned out of Marblehead in 1676 because of poverty, the family continued to live there for the next several years. They became incorporated into a community composed of former Saugus ironworkers, living near and working with John Blaney, who had done piecework at Saugus through the 1650s and 1660s, and George Darling, a captive from Dunbar at the ironworks, who owned a tavern near the Salem-Marblehead town line. By 1680, the family had moved back to Ipswich, where they were once again warned out of town, yet continued to reside in the area, living near the Thomsons and Davisons. Through marriage, work, and nationality, the Welshes remained tied to British communities in different parts of the county.[52]

Like Philip Welsh, Daniel Black also had extensive ties to non-Puritan residents in Essex County, casting a wide net in his associations and jobs, which helps illuminate the networks among Puritan and non-Puritan Essex County residents. Black came to Massachusetts as a servant in the mid-to-late 1650s.[53] He first appears in the Essex County records in 1659, in a suit for debt against Alexander Thomson. As noted above, he was a poor laborer who cut wood and did piecework for the Rowley ironworks in the 1670s, working with colliers

Thomas Looke and Thomas Tower, former employees of Saugus; in addition, he cut wood for Henry Leonard. Ambrose Mackfashion, who was also associated with Hammersmith, owed him money. Black therefore worked with many former employees of Saugus who were plying their trades in the smaller ironworks that opened after the Undertakers' Saugus monopoly ended in the early 1660s, connecting him to ironworker networks throughout the county.[54] Yet he had close ties to non-Puritan agricultural laborers. Along with Thomson, Morrill, and other non-Puritan residents, he testified in the case against Daniel Grasier for threats against Edward Colburne. In 1674, his wife, Faith Bridges, gave a deposition against Thomas and Nathaniel Leonard, the sons of Henry Leonard, in the suit for lewd and lascivious behavior brought against them by Hannah Downing. These ties again place Black within wide-ranging networks of non-Puritan ironworkers, laborers, and agricultural workers.[55] Although more settled in the Topsfield-Ipswich area than Philip and Hannah Welsh, Black had wide connections among non-Puritan residents and provides a connecting link among many members of these Essex County British networks.

Yet Black also had ties to Puritan communities as well. In 1660, he was charged with courting his wife, Faith, against her father's will. As noted above, Black used William Danford as a go-between to bring Bridges secretly to Edward Deere's house, where they spent half an hour alone together. Daniel Black and Faith Bridges later married, again without her father's permission, but did not live easily together. In 1664, they were both sentenced to sit in the stocks, he for abusing her and she for "gad[ding] abroad."[56] This court case illustrates the mixed nature of non-Puritan communities and their connections to Puritan society.

The witnesses and deponents in the case between Daniel and Faith Black outline a mixed neighborhood of families in Topsfield, which included respectable church families and town leaders, such as the Hows, the Goulds, and the Perkins; the rather more contentious and numerous Bridges clan; and apparent newcomers, such as Luke and Katherine (Brummigen) Wakelin. The depositions in the case do not break down along church or ethnic lines: the Bridges men (not church members) defended Faith, as did the Wakelins (not church members) and John How (a church member). Lining up in defense of Daniel Black were church members William Smith, Zacheus Curtis, and Thomas Dorman, as well as non–church members John Danfed (perhaps an incorrect recording of William Danford?) and Thomas Hobbes.[57]

Faith Black's behavior was the core issue of the case, stemming from disobedience first to her father and then to her husband, rather than any deeper rift in the community. Yet the image that emerges is of a poor man, not a church member, with close ties to non-Puritan laborers and mixed-nationality communities, yet who is defended by the respectable and churchgoing residents of Topsfield. Thus, while providing support and stability for the lower stratum of society, these mixed British communities did not exist apart from the larger Puritan-dominated society.

Through such networks we see the layers of associations among Massachusetts residents. Settlers of European descent identified themselves within the larger context of "Christian" and "European," as seen by the service of non-Puritans in King Philip's War. These men saw their homes and families endangered by Native American attacks, just as were those of Puritan families.[58] Non-Puritans also identified with "countrymen," whether English, Irish, or Scottish. This was a more broadly based identity than in Britain and Ireland, where regional or confessional loyalties predominated, although it is unlikely that Irish Catholics identified closely with Protestant Irish or Ulster Scots, even in the colonies.[59] In addition, bonds of kinship and proximity gave many non-Puritans roots in Massachusetts. Alexander Thomson and Philip Welsh would have had little in common had they not married sisters. They did, however, and the peripatetic Philip and Hannah continually returned to the community surrounding the more settled Alexander and Deliverance. Through their participation in town affairs—and the colony's wars—non-Puritans also made a statement about their loyalties. They built homes and lives for themselves in their towns, further identifying themselves with the Massachusetts colony. These layers of identity intersected and clashed with other identities, allowing a British colonial identity to develop after the turn of the century.

As a part of larger communities, as well as their own communities of interest, non-Puritan residents came into conflict with their Puritan neighbors, which many times exposed ethnic rancor. The lack of overt violence among peoples of different British and European nationalities did not mean that complete harmony existed in the towns where non-Puritan settlers lived, although it does help explain the traditional interpretation that non-Puritan residents assimilated easily into Puritan society. There were problems between Puritan and non-Puritan settlers, although these issues did not always divide communities clearly along national lines.

In one case in 1669, for instance, Irishman Daniel Musselway was accused of "abusing Henry Short's maid and daughter." The depositions in the case refer only to Musselway's threats against John Ewen, the father of Henry Short's maid. Sarah Short, Henry's wife, testified that she warned the Ewens of Musselway's anger, because "his being of the Irish bloud made me fearfull of some mischeivous intent." Musselway was sentenced "to be whipped, pay a fine, to be imprisoned until he pay it and satisfy his master forty days' work after his time was out." Although it is not known what Musselway did to the young women to deserve such a stiff sentence, his threats against Ewen and his "Irish bloud" apparently exacerbated the offenses. Yet his Irishness did not preclude his service in King Philip's War.[60]

In a similar vein, Alexander and Deliverance Thomson were sued by John Clarke of Wenham for slander in 1667. According to the depositions, Deliverance had accused Clarke of assaulting her while her husband was out reaping grain. Clarke had been helping Thomson, but came inside to smoke and "tried to kiss her." Hannah (Hagget) Welsh, Henry Hagget, and Daniel Davison gave depositions in support of Thomson, and Robert Colburne (son of Edward, mentioned above in the dispute with Daniel Grasier) testified that Clarke wondered why Thomson would "raise such false reports of him." Three days later, Hannah Welsh made a similar complaint about Clarke. Clarke was not a man of high status and most of the depositions supported Deliverance's version of the story, yet Clarke won the case. Although the initial issue of assault never made it to the courts, the words of Deliverance Thomson did. Clarke believed that his reputation was compromised and took steps to resolve it. Given Clarke's lack of social status, we must wonder whether his suit had its basis in the poverty of the Hagget family and the Thomsons' connections with British communities.[61]

Words as well as deeds were at issue between Samuel Lummas of Ipswich and his neighbors. Lummas was a bad-tempered man, frequently before the court for verbal and physical abuse of people and animals. His land bordered the farm of Daniel Davison, with whom he was often at odds. In 1680, Lummas was accused of assaulting his neighbor Nathaniel Browne, and in the course of depositions it became clear that he had threatened many others in the neighborhood as well. In particular, he called Daniel Davison "a Scotch rogue," and Alexander Thomson testified that he heard Lummas call Davison "a limb of the devil, saying that all the Scotchmen were hypocrites and devils." He also threatened Davison's wife, Margaret, with an axe and said, "If she went to heaven, he wished he might never go there."[62] Although Lummas only used ethnic slurs against the Scots, he was equally abusive toward his other neighbors, threatening them and their livestock. In 1686, the community had suffered enough, and publicly humiliated Lummas by holding a charivari. A group of men—including local landowner Edmund Potter; Daniel Davison and his two sons; tanner Thomas Clarke and his brother John; trumpeter Thomas Manning; and several others—met early one cold morning in February and "in a riotous way several hours before day mischievously tore in pieces and threw down a house of Lummas' and carried it away the same day." Manning sounded his trumpet to alert the neighbors to witness the deed. Potter claimed that he had purchased the house and land from Lummas and was simply taking his own property. The intent of the action, however, was clear to the community. Neighborhood farmers, Scottish and English, punished another landowner who had at one time or another harmed each of them, their families, their crops, or their livestock. This incident was not about divisions between English and non-English residents, yet there is an element of ethnic tension present, at least on Lummas's part.[63]

In other instances, Englishmen did try to throw the blame for their crimes on their non-English partners. William Longfellow, for example, when arrested for killing a bullock of Joseph Plummer, made a properly pitiful submission to the court, asking forgiveness from the magistrates, God, and his neighbors. Although acknowledging his crime, he also claimed that he "was for a Considerable time frequently & earnestly solicited to join in doeing what I did; & after the fact prevailed with by the same ill meanes not to disclose it," implicitly blaming Irishman William Danford, at whose house the butchering of the bullock occurred. Danford left Ipswich and did not defend himself, but Longfellow was allotted six pounds of Danford's forfeited bond to pay part of his share of the damages to Joseph Plummer.[64]

Within any group of people disputes will arise. Even relatively homogeneous agricultural villages such as Dedham, which was formed explicitly around the concepts of harmony and Christian love, experienced difficulties maintaining that ideal.[65] It should not be surprising that in less idealistic towns, such as Salem (founded initially by the Dorchester Company in 1624 to house fishing families) and Ipswich (settled in 1633 to guard against French incursions from the north), dissention occurred frequently.[66] Among the English, Scots, and Irish, however, few incidents exposing ethnic anxiety came before the court. The structure of British communities mitigated these potential problems. Non-English residents built bonds—communities—among themselves and with non-Puritan English settlers for support, while also participating in more traditional town communities with their Puritan neighbors.

At the same time that these communities and social networks were develop-ing, life in coastal Massachusetts was changing rapidly. As with many utopian experiments, the idealism of the early years bumped against the realities of eco-nomics and politics. After the Restoration in 1660, Massachusetts saw increasing numbers of royal commissioners, officials, and laws, although the Stuarts were not able to impose their will on the colony until the 1680s. These years also saw an increase in trade and shipbuilding, as well as larger markets for fish and grain, all important elements of the coastal economy.[67] Non-Puritan farmers and agricultural laborers finished their indentures and started families in a period of expansion, which also helped ease potential tensions between them and their Puritan neighbors. Although the Scots and Irish did not become "Englishmen," they contributed to the growth and general prosperity of the colony, which gave them a place in Massachusetts society.

MASSACHUSETTS MERCHANTS:
FROM BRITISH TO ATLANTIC NETWORKS

At the same time that British communities developed among tenant farmers, servants, and laborers in agricultural districts of coastal Massachusetts, merchants in the major ports formed commercial communities based on economic interests. Initially, many of these merchants traded primarily with their countrymen in other ports and formed partnerships with countrymen in Massachusetts, even while they settled into life in the colony, marrying colonial women and participating in town affairs. By the end of the century, however, commercial communities incorporated colonial merchants regardless of nationality or Protestant confessional affiliations. After 1700, these families became part of an interlocking group, pulled together through trade and kinship, with connections throughout the Atlantic world. Unlike non-Puritan farmers and laborers in Essex County, merchants looked outward. They saw themselves as participants in an Atlantic commercial community and became active players in the English, then British, Atlantic world.

As with other aspects of life in early Massachusetts, commerce was dominated by the English: it was governed by English laws, as far as these could be enforced, and the most prominent merchants were English, or New Englanders of English descent, who enjoyed close connections to London merchants.[1] At mid-century, the most influential mercantile families, such as the Hutchinsons, Gibbons, and Stoddards, had all been involved with New England from the earliest years of settlement. Yet because the Navigation Acts (the laws regulating overseas trade) defined colonial ships and crews as those built and owned by settled residents of the colonies, after 1660 Scottish, Jersey, and French merchants began to arrive in ever-increasing numbers, trading on equal terms with merchants of English descent.[2] Scots gained access to colonial trade under the ruling established in Calvin's Case in 1608, which declared mutual naturalization for Scots and English born after 1603 in regions ruled by James VI and I.[3] Jerseyans received special privileges due to their status as subjects of the monarch (see below), and many Huguenot merchants sought denization or naturalization in England before immigrating to the colonies. Non-English merchants became part of the wave of non-Puritan commercial immigrants after the Restoration, and took an active role in the North American coastal trade, gathering fish in Piscataqua, flour in Pennsylvania, and tobacco in Virginia. They also developed close trade connections with merchants in other Atlantic ports, such as Barbados, Jamaica, and Surinam in the Caribbean; Rotterdam, La Rochelle, and Cadiz in Continental Europe; Ulster, Glasgow, and Edinburgh in Ireland and Scotland; and Bristol and London in England.

This movement into the Atlantic world, however, did not occur only after 1660. As discussed earlier, New England merchants entered into overseas trade in the 1640s and 1650s as part of the colony's attempts to stabilize the economy during the wars of the three kingdoms in Britain and Ireland. The fish trade helped merchants establish connections to Spain and southern Europe and, through these ties, develop an exchange in barrel staves and other wooden products essential to the wine trade in the Canary Islands and Madeira. Early merchants also developed commercial ties to the West Indies in these decades, first exchanging food and lumber for tobacco and cotton, then adding horses as the islands switched to sugar production. New England ships also became the prime carriers of sugar out of the islands. Among the merchants who helped define these trade connections were those who disagreed with Puritan political and religious leaders in New England. Samuel Maverick, for example, had lived near Massachusetts Bay before the arrival of the Winthrop fleet in 1630 and never reconciled himself to Puritan control of the region. Thomas Breedon and Richard Wharton, who arrived in the 1650s, also immigrated for the economic opportunities that New England represented, and not out of religious affinity with Puritanism. Thus Massachusetts had trade connections in the Atlantic world, and with non-Puritan resident merchants, before the 1660s.[4]

As the expansion of trade brought more English, Scottish, Channel Island, and Continental European merchants and mariners to Massachusetts ports, the balance of power in the region shifted. Merchants were instrumental in bringing Massachusetts into the developing British Empire, since their economic and social self-interest frequently coincided with the political and economic goals of the English government after 1660.[5] As merchants gained wealth and their trade became more important to the regional economy, they wanted to share the political power and social prestige that rested with Puritan leaders and old families in the colony. In some instances mercantile interests matched those of the Puritan leadership, as in their common opposition to closer regulation of trade by the English government. Merchants involved with smuggling goods from French and Dutch colonies resented threats of more powerful admiralty courts. Puritan political leaders and ministers saw the same enhancement of royal authority as a breach of the colony's charter that would surely lead to their loss of power and influence. In general, however, merchants supported attempts by the English government to curb local autonomy. The activities of the Carr Commission of 1664—which polarized the merchant community throughout New England— the opening of the Newfoundland trade, and the growing importance of the naval stores trade made many merchants recognize the benefits of closer coop- eration with the English government.[6]

Most studies of New England's seventeenth-century commerce have focused on English colonial merchants, since they were the largest, most prominent group and were actively involved in colonial politics. Yet although these men pulled Massachusetts into England's political and economic orbit, Scottish, Jersey, and French merchants helped align the colony within wider Atlantic commercial circles. Scottish merchants, for example, had long-standing ties with Dutch merchants. Even though the Navigation Acts cut the Dutch out of England's carrying trade in the 1650s, these connections in the Netherlands brought great advantages to New England. Jersey Islanders, too, enjoyed extensive commercial connections, particularly with France, due to their favored position in English law. Yet these were not simply two-party trade connections. Merchants may have had stronger ties to certain areas based on long-standing national affinities, but they traded wherever they could find reliable partners and vendible goods. Thus by the turn of the eighteenth century we see not just local British communities, such as those in Essex County, or early hints of a provincial British society in Boston and Salem, but the development of an Atlantic society as well.

COMMERCE IN EARLY MASSACHUSETTS

Although early leaders of Massachusetts wanted to keep merchants under tight control, they understood that trade with England and other colonies was neces- sary to their well-being. As Perry Miller acknowledged, "These Puritans never intended that their holy experiment should eventuate in a conflict, let alone a contradiction, between the religious program and civil employments."[7] Men were expected to follow their callings diligently, in glorification of God, and to participate in the world as part of the struggle against sin. Some callings, however, exposed men to more temptation than others, and therefore required careful attention by practitioners and greater oversight from the authorities. Commerce was among the most dangerous of occupations, since merchants regulated the flow of goods and cash. Most items necessary to society and the economy moved through merchants' hands, thereby giving them control over individuals as well as the community. Many Puritans advocated the concept of the "just price," an ideal that allowed merchants reasonable profits on their goods while keeping costs for buyers within acceptable limits. The "just price" fluctuated, based on the availability of merchandise, but in theory it was always a figure on which reasonable, knowledgeable men could agree.[8]

Massachusetts leaders tried to provide the necessary oversight of merchants in the 1630s, as seen in their prosecution of Robert Keayne, a member of Boston's First Church and one of the wealthiest merchants in the first two decades of settlement. In 1639, Keayne was accused of inflating prices and, although he denied the charges, was fined eighty pounds by the court and censured by the church.[9] The magistrates also tried to control wages and prices in the economically troubled 1640s. As the colony grew, however, and trade became more important to the regional economy, these attempts foundered. By mid-century, Massachusetts's commerce was firmly entrenched in Atlantic trading networks that were, in many ways, immune to local control.

Although local authorities were unable to establish firm control over their economy and prices, the English government attempted to regulate the overseas trade of the colonies. In 1651, the Commonwealth government passed the first of the Navigation Acts, attempting to drive the Dutch out of the English carrying trade, thereby funneling colonial trade through English ports. The 1651 acts restricted trade between England and its colonies to ships owned by English or colonials with crews that were primarily English and colonial. After the Restoration in 1660, Charles II needed to control the flow of goods to and from England and Scotland in order to provide more revenue to the royal treasury. He also wanted to place further restrictions on the Dutch, and to control smuggling with the French and the Spanish. He chose to strengthen and enforce the Navigation Acts, closing loopholes in earlier legislation by enumerating certain colonial products, such as sugar and tobacco, that had to be shipped to England or a colonial port before being reexported to the Continent. Non-enumerated items could still be carried directly to Europe, and cargoes from these ports could be brought directly to the colonies as long as they were carried in English or colonial ships and without any intermediate stops. The Staple Act of 1663 closed this loophole in colonial trade by forcing all imports to the colonies to arrive via England or Wales. Scotland, Ireland, and the Channel Islands were also cut out of colonial markets, since only servants, horses, and provisions could be directly shipped from these areas.[10]

Thus a British mercantile community in Massachusetts, which included merchants and mariners from many parts of the Atlantic world, coalesced after 1660 in part around the need to find creative responses to the Navigation Acts. For instance, as commercial networks grew after the Restoration, the restrictions on direct trade between Scotland, Ulster, Jersey, and England's North American and West Indian colonies forced merchants to conduct business through factors in London or the English outports. This increased the attractiveness of sending resident merchants to the colonies, since settled residents could trade on an equal footing with English merchants. The result was an increase in non-Puritan participation in intercolonial trade, as well as in trade with Britain and Europe. With resident traders, many of the restrictions on non-English trade were legally circumvented, and because enforcement of the laws was less stringent in the colonies, illegal methods of avoiding the Navigation Acts were more easily undertaken.[11] The Scots had a long history of providing extra sets of passes and of renaming ships to avoid privateers or the English navy during times of war. Although no clear evidence of smuggling has been found before the 1680s, on two occasions (in 1686 and 1688) Boston merchant John Borland wrote to his partner Andrew Russell in Rotterdam about their cargoes being scrutinized by customs agents in Amsterdam for "not touching in England." In 1696, Daniel Campbell of Glasgow gave instructions to his supercargo, James Robison, that told him how to avoid a stop in England to pay duties on a cargo during a voyage from Virginia to Glasgow.[12] It is not improbable that merchants followed similar practices in earlier decades. Slowly, then, throughout the 1650s and 1660s, a mixed commercial community developed, with merchants at first trading largely through their countrymen in other colonies and with their home countries, then joining in wider, more diverse networks. By the 1680s, these men had become full-fledged participants in Massachusetts and Atlantic mercantile communities.

NON-ENGLISH MERCHANTS BEFORE 1680

Merchants from Scotland, the Channel Islands, and France joined their English counterparts in the Bay Colony during the 1650s, at the same time that non-Puritan laborers and agricultural workers arrived. The economic opportunities that made laborers necessary for landowners and craftsmen also attracted merchants. Massachusetts leaders were eager to expand the shipping and shipbuilding industries and encouraged merchants to search for new markets, which they found in the West Indies. In the 1650s, the islands were making the transition to sugar, and therefore becoming more dependant on imports of food. For the Scots, the West Indies was an obvious market, since the Dutch, their close trading partners, introduced both sugar production and slaves. A further move to Boston and Salem, to enter the fish and provisions trade, would have been a natural outgrowth of their activities in the islands. Merchants and ship captains from the Channel Islands, particularly Jersey, also saw New England markets as an extension of their existing fish trade in Newfoundland, Nova Scotia, and Europe. French Protestants, too, sought to open commerce with their fellow Calvinists in Massachusetts.

Scots were among the earliest non-English merchants in Massachusetts, arriving in Boston in the 1650s to take advantage of the growing provision trade as England's island colonies became more focused on sugar production. Many of these merchants came from Glasgow or other west coast ports. Glasgow's rise to commercial prominence in Scotland began in the seventeenth century, when the west coast ports first challenged the dominance of Edinburgh and the port of Leith. The development of Scottish settlements in Ulster stimulated trade in western Scotland and the growth of commerce in general, and so the move into transatlantic trade was a logical course, given the favorable location of these ports compared to Edinburgh and Leith, which continued to dominate trade to the Baltics and northern Europe.[13] In addition, the wars of the 1640s and the occupation of Scotland by Cromwell's army in the 1650s slowed trade, and some merchants may have taken the opportunity to relocate to North America. The divisions within the Scottish Kirk that began to emerge in the late 1640s and deepened in the early 1650s soon spread throughout Scottish society. After Cromwell's conquest of Scotland in 1652, his government saw both sides as potential threats, a distrust shared by the Scots, who saw Cromwell's attempts to enforce toleration as undermining religious and civil society. These disruptions may also have pushed merchants on the west coast, where support for hard-line Presbyterian principles was strongest, to North America. There, they began to construct the commercial networks that flourished after 1660.[14]

After the Restoration, the Scottish government attempted to encourage manufacturing in order to reduce imports and relieve pressure on the country's money supply. Certain industries, such as sugar refining, soap boiling, and textile production, received exemptions from duties on imports of raw materials. Sugar refining and rum distilling became the most successful of these industries, and they, in turn, further stimulated trade with the West Indies. Voyages from Glasgow to the West Indies increased after 1666, and by the 1680s three major sugar houses had been established in Scotland.[15]

Scottish merchants in the Americas were trading with each other before the sugar houses opened, however, and these new merchants and manufacturers in Scotland tapped into preexisting colonial networks, following trade patterns that Scots had developed in Europe. Ned Landsman describes Scottish traders in Europe as "develop[ing] informal trading networks of their countrymen overseas, often on the peripheries, where competition was limited." He also notes that "Scottish merchants aggressively carved out distinctive niches for themselves" in these peripheral areas.[16] In the 1650s, as Scottish merchants began arriving in Boston, primarily from Barbados, a similar pattern appears. These men traded among themselves, within fairly extensive networks given the low number of Scots in the Americas at the time, but they also had close commercial ties to countrymen in Ulster and western Scotland.

Letters written by merchant Thomas Dewer to Robert Scott outline the trade established between Boston and Barbados in the 1660s, and probably earlier. They also demonstrate that Scottish merchants and mariners traveled easily and frequently among the ports of the Atlantic world and had commercial contacts in many of them. Dewer moved to Boston from Barbados in 1650; by the 1660s, he had become extremely active in trade to that island and was associated with Scottish merchants throughout the Atlantic.[17] Dewer's correspondence indicates that he often traveled to the West Indies and had a wide range of contacts, singling out more than fifteen Scots in Barbados alone for personal greetings.

One exchange between Dewer and his Barbadian partners depicts several aspects of this trade in the middle of the seventeenth century. Dewer, Robert Scott, and several unnamed partners owned a ship, the Katherine, which had been severely damaged in a hurricane in 1666. Repairs and lost voyages cost the owners dearly, and Dewer desperately sought to sell his share. In September or October 1667, he wrote to Scott about the arrival of Alexander Reid and a Mr. Duncan in Boston. The men were on a voyage from Barbados to Virginia and Londonderry when their ship had been damaged by another hurricane, forcing an unexpected layover in Boston for repairs. Reid inquired about purchasing the Katherine, and Dewer urged Scott to complete the transaction. The sale did not occur, but these merchants—Dewer, Scott, Reid, and Duncan—clearly participated in a commercial community that flowed through Barbados to the North American colonies, and then to Britain and Ireland. Their networks made it possible for merchants to connect with countrymen even in unfamiliar ports.[18]

In addition to trade connections described in the letters, the frequency of communication testifies to the strength of commercial networks. Dewer wrote at least five letters to Scott within nine months, three of which were sent in September and October. Although some letters repeated news sent earlier, they were not duplicates. Dewer urged various actions on his Barbados partners and expected them to react quickly to his suggestions. For Reid and Duncan, Boston was not a scheduled stop, yet they easily connected with a fellow Scot— and, more important, one with access to a replacement ship. Thus Scottish mercantile networks in North America and the Caribbean were well developed by the late 1660s, and travel and communication among colonial ports was frequent, regular, and quick by contemporary standards.[19]

Dewer was a merchant in the early modern sense of the word: a man trading in commodities to overseas markets. He and his partners sent provisions, lumber, and sugar throughout the Atlantic world, with no evidence that Dewer retailed any of the goods that passed through his hands. Many merchants in Boston, however, were concerned with Atlantic markets and local retailing. William Ballantyne is one example. He arrived in Boston before 1652, but when and why he came to Massachusetts is not known.[20] Ballantyne died in December 1669, leaving an estate valued at £677, mostly in merchandise. His estate inventory is quite detailed, providing a glimpse of the kinds of goods that a large merchant and retailer in Boston carried.[21]

The inventory indicates that Ballantyne had many connections to the Atlantic trading system. "In the shopp" were many different kinds of fabrics, of varying colors and qualities, most of which had been imported from England and Scotland. The shop also contained several dozens of horn books, knitting needles, knives, paper, thread, ribbon, lace, wooden boxes, turned boxes, stockings, gloves, mirrors, combs, beads, Jews' harps, scissors, tobacco tongs, tobacco boxes, gimlets, and buttons. The merchandise spilled over into the dwelling house as well. In "the little Room next the hall," Ballantyne stored thirty pounds of whalebone, one hundred pounds of cheese, and fifty pounds of hard soap. The "great chamber" contained, along with beds and other furniture, a dozen diaper napkins, one and a half dozen other napkins, and twenty-four gross of "tobacco pyes [pipes]." The "little chamber" held six dozen brooms, thirty pounds of starch, and another sixteen gross of "tobacco pyes," and the "little garret" held three dozen glass bottles, nails, pepper, handkerchiefs, children's whistles, oatmeal, rice, figs, and currents. The warehouse contained five kentals of fish, thirteen barrels of mackerel, cooper's tools, hoops, timbers, and "cask made in the house." Ballantyne therefore participated in the fish trade, most of which he shipped overseas, and he carried many varieties of imported goods for sale. The warehouse and wharfage rights also indicate that he was not simply a shopkeeper, but had direct connections with overseas merchants in many locations in the Atlantic basin.[22]

Scots were not the only non-English merchants in Boston in the 1650s and 1660s. French merchants also established themselves in Massachusetts by the 1660s, although their trade in the region did not become substantial until the 1680s. However few these early French residents were, by the 1660s increasing restrictions placed on Protestant religious practices in France drove some Huguenots to seek new homes in Massachusetts. In August 1661, for example, Jacques Pepin, a merchant from La Rochelle, petitioned the General Court to allow him to settle in Massachusetts with a group of Huguenots. In addition to bringing several Protestant refugees, Pepin brought "an estate," which he hoped to unload and sell. He also wanted permission to negotiate with Boston merchants to send his ship back to La Rochelle with a full cargo. The Court granted Pepin and his group permission to live in Massachusetts, but refused to allow him to trade, "contrary to the Act of Parliament bearing date 25th April 1661." The Court seemed unwilling to challenge English law so soon after the Restoration. Pepin settled in Salem and by the 1670s was once again involved in trade.[23]

French merchants continued to see potential in the New England market throughout the 1660s, despite disruptions in France and the English government's attempts to tighten control over colonial commerce. Stephen Bellocque, a merchant from Bayenne, petitioned the General Court in 1665 for permission to sell his goods in Massachusetts in spite of the Navigation Acts. Bellocque stated that French merchants believed that "a free trade was by law established in this country with all Christian nations," and with this understanding he had sailed for New England from western France with a shipload of goods "proper for this place." To his dismay, upon his arrival he discovered that "there is lately a decision made by his Majesty of Great Britain that no stranger shall Trade into these parts." He asked permission to trade anyway, "since the law both of god & nations hath always bin to acquaint men with their Comands & Ordinances before any punishment can be rightly inflicted for the breach of them." The General Court's reaction to this petition was not recorded, but given the Court's response to Pepin and the fact that the Carr Commission was then investigating breaches of the Navigation Acts in New England, it is likely that they refused Bellocque's request. Nevertheless, although various forms of the Navigation Acts had been imposed on the colonies since the 1650s, Bellocque and other French merchants still hoped to establish direct trade. Thus Boston and western French ports had a history of commercial activity before the larger Huguenot immigration of the mid-1680s.[24]

Merchants from the Channel Islands, particularly Jersey, also became part of Atlantic trading communities in Massachusetts in the 1660s. The Channel Islands lie in the English Channel, geographically much closer to France than to England, and came under the rule of the English Crown in 1066. The two main islands, Jersey and Guernsey, had active maritime cultures that revolved around fishing, trading, and privateering. Culturally French but ruled by England, the Channel Islands played an important intermediary role between the two nations throughout much of the seventeenth and eighteenth centuries.[25]

The islands occupied a unique place in English law, largely governing themselves. Residents were subjects of the English monarch, not of Parliament, and had received special privileges from successive rulers. Perhaps the most important privilege was neutrality, granted by agreement between the English and French kings in 1480 and confirmed by each new monarch thereafter. The islands were thus safe from attack, reducing the need for military protection from England, and merchants continued to trade with both countries in wartime. In addition, neutrality meant that privateers could not legally operate in the waters surrounding the islands. The islands' trade therefore could be exploited for political gain in times of war by both France and England.[26]

The islands were also exempt from English customs duties, which encouraged trade, especially after 1689. Imports such as food, salt, wool, and other goods came into the islands under licenses and official quotas from specific ports along the southern coast of England. Although the English government carefully controlled the distribution of licenses, the system remained open to abuse, especially in the reexport trade. Privy Council received numerous complaints over the years from the islands' governors that leather and wool came into the islands without duty from England and then went on by night to St. Malo or other French ports. In addition, in the early seventeenth century, goods produced in the islands could be exported to England without paying duties. This prompted complaints that French goods were being smuggled into the islands and then sent duty-free to England as products of the Channel Islands.[27]

By the middle of the seventeenth century, these commercial privileges, combined with the Channel Islanders' participation in the North Atlantic cod fisheries, opened an active trade between the islands and New England. Jersey ships entered Boston and Salem harbors with increasing frequency to load fish and other commodities, and the commerce between Massachusetts and Jersey became important enough for both sides to ignore the Navigation Acts until

well into the 1670s. Established commercial networks can be seen in the contract between John Brown, Nicholas Balhach, and John Balhach, merchants in
Jersey, and William Stevens, a shipbuilder in Gloucester. In 1661, the Jerseyans
contracted with Stevens to construct a ship in Gloucester. Payment for the ship
was to be £50 in goods from either Walter Price, William Browne, or George
Corwin, merchants in Salem; 150 pounds of Muscovado sugar, worth two pence
per pound in Barbados; and £100 in New England money. Thus Jerseyans had
established commercial ties to at least three Salem merchants and had access to
West Indian sugar, indicating that an extensive mercantile relationship had
developed among Barbados, Jersey, and Massachusetts by 1661. John Brown
himself moved to Salem shortly after this contract; in accounts dated 1666 he
was owed money in gilders and stivers as well as in Virginia tobacco, indicating
the continued expansion of trading ties.[28]

During the 1660s, contacts between Massachusetts and Jersey began to
increase. In 1663, William Hollingsworth, a Salem merchant, contracted with a
Boston-based sea captain to pick up tobacco in Maryland, sail to Plymouth,
England, then to Jersey and the Netherlands. Hollingsworth's contacts with
Jersey merchants continued, and became stronger through kinship ties. Philip
English (né Philippe L'Anglois) of Jersey arrived in Salem in 1666, probably with
established connections to Hollingsworth. English became the most prominent
Jerseyan in Salem, if not in all of Massachusetts. His success was facilitated by an
advantageous marriage to Mary, the only daughter of William Hollingsworth,
in 1675. English combined Hollingsworth's extensive commercial connections
in the North American colonies and Europe with his own knowledge of Jersey
trade routes to build his highly profitable commercial empire in Salem, with
trade connections reaching to the West Indies, England, France, Spain, Portugal,
Sweden, and Jersey.[29]

Philip English was active in local community affairs in Salem and with the
Atlantic community of merchants. In Massachusetts, he served on a jury of
inquest in 1675, on trial juries in 1682, 1684, and 1685, and was elected a constable
of Salem in 1683, and as selectman in 1692. He had many business connections
with English, Scottish, and French merchants in Boston and Salem, including
Richard Wharton and William Browne, Sr., and sponsored and employed Jersey
residents of Essex County, bringing many of his countrymen and -women over
as indentured servants. Female servants worked in town, frequently for other
merchants or artisans, and males generally went to sea. English himself was
said to have kept fifteen Jersey servants in his household, many of them
mariners working the fishing grounds or the trade routes. English also hired
out his servants to other shipmasters, spreading his influence throughout the

Salem fishing industry.[30]

His visibility in all these communities in Salem contributed to perhaps the most harrowing moment in his life, when in 1692 he and his wife, Mary, were accused of witchcraft. Historians have posited several reasons for these accusations. English had recently been elected as a selectman for Salem and was politically connected to the Porter family. He had frequently held other town offices, such as constable, in which office he had shielded Jersey fishermen from paying town taxes. English also made no secret of his Anglicanism, frequently rowing to Boston to attend services at King's Chapel. In addition, he was clearly the leader of the French-speaking community in Salem, bringing many of his countrymen there. Jerseyans, as discussed in the next chapter, tended to separate themselves from the larger community and had many conflicts with Puritan authorities in town. In the context of King William's War (1688–99), fought against the French and their Abenaki allies, French-speaking residents were viewed with suspicion. All these sources of irritation were enhanced by the fact that English was quite wealthy and had married into an old, influential Salem mercantile family. He thus became a prime target for the resentment, hostility, and fears of Salem Villagers. Mary herself was also a target; her mother, Elinor, had been accused of witchcraft (though not prosecuted) in the early 1680s and Mary had inherited her father's estate after Elinor's death. She therefore met several criteria common in witchcraft accusations. After being arrested and sent to Boston, the Englishes escaped from jail with the help of friends and fled to New York, where they lived until the hysteria had passed. The Englishes later returned to Salem, where they rebuilt their business and reputations. Philip, in fact, served in the Massachusetts House of Representatives in 1700.[31]

The many modern studies of witchcraft have shown that no one factor was the root cause of witchcraft accusations. Historians have examined social, psychological, economic, gender, and political issues related to witchcraft, some focusing specifically on the 1692 Salem outbreak and others more broadly based, but a fear of witches was deeply ingrained in early modern societies. One generalization that can be made is that many of the people involved in witchcraft outbreaks, as accusers and accused, were marginal in some way. For example, women who had inherited property that would traditionally have gone to men, or who were poor and therefore drained a community's charity and patience, were more likely to be accused than others. Witchcraft accusations have also been linked to people associated with Quakers, whose extraregional ties and religious dissent had long made them suspect in Massachusetts. The stresses of frontier wars precipitated many witchcraft accusations as well. In the case of Salem in 1692, renewed fighting with the French and their Native American allies in Maine brought waves of refugees into town, thereby straining supplies and increasing fears of attacks in Massachusetts. Widows and orphans further depleted local charity, and the loss of men in the war increased the insecurity that many young women felt for their own futures. These fears fed on one another and resulted in accusations of witchcraft in Salem in 1692, which tore apart not only the community but the entire colony.[32]

Yet none of the Scottish or Irish inhabitants of the region were directly involved in the witchcraft trials, as accusers, accused, or witnesses, and the Englishes were the only prominent members of the Jersey community to be accused.[33] Even in previous witchcraft accusations in New England, very few non-English people were involved, and many of these were women who had married into non-English families, giving them an ambiguous status in the community.[34] Witchcraft outbreaks reflected internal social tensions that cannot be connected directly to outsiders, although such a status could exacerbate other problems. Considering the number of non-English residents in Essex County, especially French-speaking settlers, and the number of people with extra-regional ties, the wonder is that so few of these residents were involved. Most non-English settlers in Essex County had become integrated enough into the community that they were not seen as threats; their loyalties in times of war were known to be with Massachusetts. The service rendered by non-Puritans in King Philip's War probably contributed to this perception. At the same time, they were not so assimilated into the Puritan community as to take part in the accusations or trials.[35]

These early non-English merchants established themselves in the Boston and Salem communities as well as in the commercial world. Thomas Dewer was not just a member of Atlantic mercantile communities, but was also involved in the affairs of Boston. He held minor town offices, being named surveyor of highways in 1657/8, clerk of the market in 1659/60, and constable in 1663/4. He was called as a juror several times in the 1660s and 1670s, and collected money from First Church members who had pledged but not paid their subscriptions to Harvard. He also helped establish other Scots in town, including tailor James Fowle in 1681, Robert Nevin in 1684, and David Kincaid in 1684/5, giving bond for their good behavior, and witnessing wills and estate inventories.[36] Philip English, as discussed above, married a Massachusetts woman of English descent and served in many offices in Salem and in the colonial legislature.[37] William Gibson, a shoemaker and merchant, and his wife, Hannah Hazen, the daughter of an old Massachusetts family, joined Boston's First Church in 1676; his first wife, Sarah Purchase, had joined in 1662/3. Gibson served as constable in 1676, tithing man in 1690, and as a sealer of leather and clerk of the market several times from the 1660s through the 1680s. Gibson also gave bonds for the good behavior of several non-English residents of Boston, owned land with Thomas Dewer, and maintained ties to Scots in Essex County. Gibson may have been one of the prisoners sent to the colony by John Becx for the Saugus ironworks in 1651. Although he does not appear in the ironworks records and lived in Boston by 1662, his first wife was the daughter of Oliver Purchase, the clerk at the ironworks and a man who later became active in local and colony politics. Gibson, then, provides a link between laborers in Essex County and the Boston commercial community, as well as with long-settled families. Thus, while these men had close and lasting connections to their own countrymen and -women in Massachusetts, they also established themselves, through marriage, church membership, and town offices, with the wider community in Boston and coastal Massachusetts.[38]

Although largely staying out of colony politics, at times non-English merchants joined with their English colleagues to petition the General Court about issues affecting commerce and government in the middle decades of the century. In 1662, for instance, twenty-six merchants in Boston, including Thomas Dewer, asked the General Court to halt grain shipments out of the colony, owing to a perceived lack of food for local consumption. Because Dewer supplied provisions for fishermen in return for fish, such a scarcity would have constrained his business as well as threatened Boston's poor. Several non-English inhabitants of Boston, including Scots Thomas Shearer, Alexander Bogle, and John Anderson, along with many prominent Englishmen in the city, also signed a petition in 1664 supporting the actions of the Massachusetts government in thwarting the instructions of the Carr Commission.[39] In general, however, non-English merchants stayed out of issues between the Massachusetts and English governments, perhaps being unwilling to draw attention to themselves or believing that disagreements with the English government could best be handled by Englishmen or colonists of English descent.

Other Scottish, Jersey, and French merchants came to Boston and Salem throughout the 1650s and 1660s, but not until after the disruption of King Philip's War did these merchants move strongly into the Atlantic world. The war greatly retarded overseas trade. In a letter to John Pollock of Glasgow in 1675, supercargo George Hutchinson wrote that the market in Boston had been flooded with goods from London and other places in England, with two more heavily loaded ships expected in port soon. Hutchinson looked for other outlets for his goods but thought that it might take a year before he could find advantageous markets. He also noted that there was no money in the "country touns," and he was forced to trade in "wheit malt and fush [fish]."[40] The devastation of the war, which killed several thousand colonists and Native Americans alike and pushed European settlement back almost to the seacoast, also set the stage for the growth of the Massachusetts economy.

The end of the war in 1676 not only reinvigorated trade, but also opened up new fronts in the long-running, if intermittent, struggle between Massachusetts and England. Royal commissioner Edward Randolph's reports to London on trade and government in Massachusetts gave Crown officials the leverage that they needed to assert royal influence in the colony more forcefully. By 1684, the English government was ready to take action, and finally voided the colony's charter. Massachusetts was placed under the governance of a council headed by Joseph Dudley, the politically ambitious son of Puritan leader Thomas Dudley, and merchant Richard Wharton, who came to Boston in the 1650s. In 1686, after the accession of James II, Massachusetts was incorporated into the Dominion of New England, subject to an appointed governor and council, and under much closer supervision from the home government. Many old settlers vehemently opposed this arrangement, whereas non-Puritan merchants initially supported the new regime, which promised them influence and participation in government commensurate with their wealth and social status. The Dominion government under governor Edmund Andros, however, proved no more sympathetic to the needs of merchants than the charter government had been. In 1689 many merchants who had formerly supported the change in government, including William Browne and Bartholomew Gedney of Salem, and Samuel Shrimpton and Peter Sergeant of Boston, joined with the charter party to overthrow Andros in the wake of England's Glorious Revolution.[41]

However disruptive the war and political upheavals of the late 1670s and 1680s had been, at the end of the period non-Puritan merchants had the power and influence in Massachusetts that they felt they deserved. The new charter of 1691, promulgated by William and Mary, brought an influx of royal officials from England and Scotland, and instituted property ownership or personal wealth as the basis for political citizenship in place of church membership. These political changes, and the related loss of religious homogeneity that had unified the colony through most of the century, reduced the hold of old Puritan families on government and opened the way for merchants from many parts of the Atlantic world to further expand the trade networks emanating from Boston. Between 1680 and 1700, the commercial community in coastal Massachusetts became an interlocking group of families—English, Scottish, French, and Jersey, and of several religious backgrounds—who began to see themselves as provincial Britons.[42]

Social, political, and economic transitions in Massachusetts combined with events in other parts of the Atlantic world to bring more non-English merchants to New England after 1680. London commercial houses, intent on entering and dominating colonial trade, sent resident factors to Boston to oversee trade from the primary marketplace in North America. Other merchants, attracted by the assertion of royal authority, sought to make or increase their fortunes through political patronage, hoping to gain land or monopolies on colonial products. Wealthy, well-connected English merchants altered Boston society and politics in ways that troubled Puritan residents. In 1686, Samuel Sewall complained about prominent merchants Samuel Shrimpton and Peter Lidgett coming into Boston from Roxbury drunk and stopping again in town, where they "drink Healths, curse, swear, talk profanely and baudily to the great disturbance of the Town and the grief of good people. Such high-handed wickedness has hardly been heard of before in Boston." Politically, merchants allied with Joseph Dudley and Richard Wharton controlled the council set up by James II to govern the region before the formalization of the Dominion of New England, and they used this power to further enhance their wealth.[43]

As important as the influx of English non-Puritan merchants was for Massachusetts, the opportunities that attracted them brought more non-English merchants as well. These men too were influenced by events in the colonies, in England, and in their home countries. By the last quarter of the seventeenth century, for instance, Scottish overseas trade had developed, and merchants in Scotland regularly conducted business through resident factors, who handled accounts and consignments from many merchants. Andrew Russell in Rotterdam was one of the most important of these "free" factors in Europe, and by the 1680s he also handled many European consignments shipped by Scottish merchants in Boston. Russell became an important node in this segment of New England's trade, connecting Scots in the colonies, Europe, Scotland, and Ireland.

Scotland had also experienced a period of economic expansion in the 1670s, which ended in the early 1680s. In response, James, duke of York, and the Committee of Trade for the Scottish Privy Council embarked on an ambitious plan to redevelop the economy. A major part of the plan was predicated on establishing overseas colonies, such as those in South Carolina and East

Jersey, and in general encouraging the expansion of trade to the Americas. With established contacts in Europe and the blessing of Scottish political leaders, merchants, particularly from Glasgow and other west coast ports, began pushing more actively into North America.[44]

French and Jersey merchants as well found opportunities in Massachusetts that were denied them at home. The most obvious problems for Huguenot merchants were the restrictions on their rights under Louis XIV and the increasing brutality of French soldiers against Protestants after 1675, which culminated in the revocation of the Edict of Nantes in 1685. Huguenots tended to concentrate in the merchant and artisan classes in western France, whence came most of those who fled to England and its North American colonies in the wake of the revocation.[45] The Channel Islands faced a general economic downturn after the civil wars and Restoration, adding to the initial impetus to settle in New England. After 1680, however, the most important reason for the immigration of Jerseyans was the increasing wealth of men like Philip English and their importation of indentured servants. The growth of the fish trade in the last two decades of the century and the wealth and influence of established merchants also contributed to the increase in Jersey participation in Massachusetts' overseas trade.[46]

The Scots constituted the largest group of non-English merchants in Boston. As the sugar houses in Scotland grew, merchants demanded more sugar and expanded their contacts with Scots in New England. As noted above, the Scottish pattern for trade in Europe consisted of setting up mercantile houses in smaller ports, where competition was not as strong, and trading through networks of countrymen. Northeastern Massachusetts had the infrastructure for these Scottish patterns to develop. The initial community of several hundred Scottish captives in Massachusetts had grown as these men married and had children, as well as through the arrival of merchants such as Thomas Dewer and William Ballantyne and their families before 1680. Many of these merchants had already established connections to the West Indies, and had contacts in the fish, lumber, and provisions trade from New Hampshire and Maine. In addition, the Scots' Charitable Society (SCS), a fraternal organization founded in 1657/8, had maintained bonds within this expanding Scottish colonial community throughout coastal Massachusetts. After 1684 the society had been transformed to provide commercial connections among far-flung merchants in Atlantic commerce.[47]

Along with the core group of merchants in New England, craftsmen and artisans provided goods and services necessary for the West Indies trade. Many new members of the SCS after 1684 were craftsmen: shoemakers and tailors, such as William Gibson and James Fowle, providing work shoes, pants, and shirts for sailors and West Indian slaves; and coopers, such as William Ballantyne, supplying the barrels and casks to transport both dry and wet goods. Boston even hosted a Scottish innkeeper, Andrew Neale, whose well-appointed house was near the center of the commercial district. By establishing themselves in Boston, newly arrived merchants could tap into a wide range of local goods and services provided by other Scots.

New Scottish residents of Boston easily moved into this already defined community of Scots. Alexander Clemy, for example, was a mariner who arrived in Boston in the late 1680s. He married Elizabeth English, the daughter of Scot James English and Joanna Farnum, after 1690. James English, a merchant, had been in Massachusetts since the 1650s, became a founding member of the scs, and joined Boston's Second Church in 1688. Clemy joined the scs in 1688 and quickly established trade connections throughout the colonies and Britain through this network of Scottish merchants. When his estate was settled in 1693 and 1694, he had more than two hundred pounds in "goods from England," as well as flour and tobacco from Pennsylvania and tobacco from Virginia. The men who appraised these goods for the estate were all Scots in Boston: John Borland, Thomas Hill, John Campbell, and John Maxwell. Clemy owed debts to several Boston Scots, such as David Dewer, grandson of Thomas, and John Maxwell, as well as to George Jaffrey of Piscataqua, one of the leading Scottish factors in the New Hampshire fish trade. He also owed debts to other merchants, such as Elias Heath, Edmund Mountford, and Samuel Holland, all members of established commercial families in Boston. Thus although Clemy established himself through Scottish networks, he did not limit himself to these networks. He developed ties with non-Scottish families: his wife was part English, one of a growing number of Massachusetts-born children of "mixed" marriages.[48]

Aside from appraising Clemy's estate, Thomas Hill acted as attorney for several merchants in Britain, such as Alexander Long in London and William Arbuckle in Glasgow, and for Scots in other colonies. Hill also represented Robert Clemy, brother of Alexander, at the probate hearings, indicating that Clemy retained close ties to his family in Scotland. A sign of the growing connections between Scotland and England's colonies, merchants and mariners in the last quarter of the century frequently left bequests to their families in Scotland, unlike the earlier group of laborers and farmers in Essex County. Merchants, of course, were in a better position to keep overseas ties strong, and they generally had greater resources to leave to family members in Britain and Europe. Nevertheless, the increasing ease and frequency of overseas communication also played a role.[49]

Another example of overseas ties can be found in the will of Alexander Cole, a sea captain who lived in Salem in the 1680s. At his death in 1687, he divided his estate between his son and wife, but stipulated that if his son died before he reached twenty one years of age, his share would go to "my two sisters and his Aunts namely Anna & Jannett Coale of Dumbarton in the kingdom of Scotland." As Atlantic commerce grew, non-English residents of Massachusetts seaports clearly had greater opportunities to maintain ties to the home country while settling down, marrying, and raising families in the colonies.[50]

John Borland also tapped into the Scottish network in Boston, cementing mercantile connections with Barbados, Surinam, New York, Amsterdam, Rotterdam, and Glasgow, while also becoming a prominent citizen of the town. Borland moved to Boston in 1682 after two previous trips to New England for his master, Glasgow merchant John Peadie. These trips established Borland in the Boston mercantile community and within Scottish commercial networks. Six months after moving to Boston, Borland left on a yearlong voyage to Surinam and the Netherlands. In October 1683, one month after his return, he married Sarah Neale, the eldest daughter of innkeeper Andrew Neale. In January 1683/4, he again sailed for Surinam and the Netherlands, becoming an active participant in the Dutch West Indies trade and making frequent trading voyages over the next two decades.[51]

Borland established himself quickly in Atlantic trade networks and cultivated extensive contacts. His primary partner in the Netherlands was Andrew Russell, the prominent factor in Rotterdam whose business connections extended throughout Europe and Britain. Borland and Russell cultivated a close personal relationship as well, since Borland was one of the few men for whom Russell continued to act as factor after his partial retirement in 1686. This relationship was based on religious affinities along with commercial ties. Russell was well-known for his opposition to episcopacy in Scotland, and Borland came from a strongly Presbyterian family that had moved between Scotland and Ulster from the 1620s through the 1650s in response to changing religious climates. Borland was also closely associated with the Moy family of Amsterdam, Dutch merchants with commercial networks throughout the Atlantic world. He frequently joined trading ventures with these Scottish and Dutch merchants in Surinam, and participated in commercial circles throughout the western Caribbean. In fact, in 1685 he used his connections to get his brother Francis a position preaching to the European community in Surinam. By 1690, Borland had an interest in so many ships plying the Caribbean that Francis easily managed to find free passage from Surinam to Boston.[52]

Borland became a central figure in Boston's Atlantic commerce in the 1680s and 1690s, tying together merchants in western Scotland, Ulster, the Netherlands, the West Indies, and New England. He did not, however, pioneer any of these networks. He apprenticed in Glasgow, whose residents had many personal and commercial ties with Ulster (and where Borland also had kin). Glasgow merchants had long-established trade with the Netherlands and, through Dutch merchants, its colonies. Boston was simply one more node in this Glasgow-based trade network. The existence of an established Scottish community in Boston made the town an attractive starting point for expansion into North America. When Robert Livingston left the Netherlands in 1672, after a brief stay in Scotland, he sailed for Boston, where merchant and mint master John Hull helped him get started in the fur trade and begin his impressive career in New York. Livingston had other connections as well. The son of Reverend John Livingstone, who had flirted with immigrating to Massachusetts in the 1630s, he was also related to Andrew Russell of Rotterdam. Even within "national" networks, then, kinship and confessional affinity were important.[53]

Records of ships licensed to leave Boston between 1698 and 1700 describe a few of Borland's investments in merchant vessels, indicating the extent of his commercial partnerships. In March 1698, he gave an oath that he was an owner of the ketch *Return*, along with Joseph Bridgham, an English merchant, and David Dewer, the grandson of Thomas Dewer. The next month, he appeared as partial owner of the brigantine *Friendship* with Joseph Bridgham, and in May as the owner of the ship *John and Ann* with several prominent partners, including Boston merchants Andrew Belcher and Henry Gibbs. In June, he acknowledged partial ownership of the brigantine *Susannah and Sarah* with Bridgham and Thomas Steel, another member of the Scots' Charitable Society, and the ship *Hannah and Elizabeth* with seven other owners, including the well-connected merchants Giles Dyer, Andrew Belcher, and Daniel Oliver. In December 1698, he claimed ownership of the sloop *Ann,* along with Bridgham and John Maxwell, another scs member. In 1699, he was listed as partial owner of the ketch *Dove* with John Metcalfe, a merchant in London, and John Campbell, a Scot in Boston. The same year, Borland also owned part of the ship *Amity*, again with Bridgham and Steel.[54]

Borland was thus associated with a diverse community of merchants and town leaders. Joseph Bridgham was a resident of Boston and a deacon of the First Church (which Borland joined in 1702), and had extensive ties within the mercantile community, appearing as a witness to several wills and investing in many ships with English and non-English, and Puritan and non-Puritan merchants. Borland's partners included Andrew Belcher, Samuel Lillie, Daniel Oliver, Henry Gibbs, and Peter Butler, all from well-established Boston merchant families. In addition, Borland had a friendly relationship with Samuel Sewall. Borland and Sewall both belonged to the New England Company and supported the Darien Company, Scotland's failed attempt to establish a colony in Panama in

1698. The men served together as pallbearers at several funerals as well. In his diary, Sewall notes his distress at Borland's legal problems in 1706, when Borland was jailed for treason for trading with the French in Canada during Queen Anne's War. Also implicated in this affair were Scottish sea captain Samuel Lillie and Massachusetts governor Joseph Dudley. Borland and Lillie negotiated the ransom of captives taken during the war with the French. Disappointment over the small number of people redeemed, dismay over the length of time the negotiations took, and general suspicion about merchants' trade combined with political machinations against Dudley to produce these charges. Dudley was not brought to trial, whereas the other defendants were eventually acquitted and their fines remitted. The incident illustrates that the post-Restoration merchant community was not segregated by nationality, and was not necessarily at odds with the old-guard Puritan families. A multi-national, multi-confessional mercantile community had taken shape by the turn of the century.[55]

Borland and Clemy were but two of an extensive network of Scottish merchants in Boston. Most were members of the Scots' Charitable Society, which connected them to a wide community of Scottish merchants throughout the Atlantic world. The SCS counted members in New York, Virginia, the West Indies, and Scotland, including some of the primary merchants with investments in the Glasgow sugar houses. One of the most prominent Scottish members of the SCS was Daniel Campbell of Shawfield near Glasgow (joined 1694), whose cousin Duncan Campbell became a well-known Bostonian, settling in the city around 1684. Another cousin was John Campbell, the proprietor of the first newspaper in Massachusetts, the *Boston News-Letter*.[56]

The Campbell family connects Boston and Glasgow through commerce and kinship, and also provides insight into the political and social aspirations of overseas Scots at the turn of the eighteenth century. Duncan Campbell first appears in the Boston records in 1687, although he joined the Scots' Charitable Society in 1684. He called himself a bookseller, but quickly expanded his activities, becoming a general merchant, postmaster of Boston, and factor for merchants throughout the North American colonies. Like many merchants who came to Boston after the Restoration, Campbell embraced imperial authority. He sought the favor of men with influence in government and used these connections to obtain official positions for himself. He, like many of his mercantile colleagues, apparently saw the imperial system as a way to improve his prospects.[57]

To this end, Campbell cultivated contacts with some of the most influential people in England's American colonies. In 1693, he received an appointment as postmaster of Massachusetts from Andrew Hamilton, a former governor of East Jersey who had instituted the first postal service throughout the colonies.

In addition, before 1693 Campbell established a correspondence with Fitz-John Winthrop, the former governor of Connecticut and son of John Winthrop, Jr. The correspondence began as bookseller to customer, but soon took the form of a manuscript newsletter wherein Campbell informed Winthrop of the latest news and rumors that came into Boston. Campbell's letters to Winthrop reveal other important connections. He at times traveled with Richard Coote, earl of Bellomont, the governor of New York and Massachusetts (1697–1701), and kept Winthrop apprised of the governor's movements. He had connections to Gurdon Saltonstall, governor of Connecticut after 1707; merchant Robert Livingston of New York; Francis Nicholson, governor of Virginia and formerly lieutenant governor of New York; and William Penn of Pennsylvania. As outlined in these letters, Campbell traveled from Massachusetts to New York and Virginia fairly regularly. He also solicited an appointment as sheriff of Suffolk County in 1700, receiving the recommendation of Bellomont for the position. When Massachusetts lieutenant governor William Stoughton was slow to confirm the appointment, Campbell pointedly reminded him that King William had recently proclaimed that "a Native of Scotland is Qualified for any place of Publick Trust in any of his Majesties Plantations." He repeatedly invoked Bellomont's name in this letter and stated his conviction that Stoughton was not trying to disobey the governor. Campbell clearly knew how to use his connections to important people in order to further his career.[58]

Thus a young Duncan Campbell saw opportunities in the colonies and, like so many other Britons, left home. He probably chose to migrate to Boston because of the strong Scottish community there, and for the chance to establish himself in a peripheral market, much like Scottish merchants in Europe did. Once in New England, Campbell realized that participation in the English colonial system could help him increase his fortunes. Like many of his countrymen after 1680, Campbell recognized the colonies as vehicles for advancement. In many ways, he personifies the attitude of many residents of Massachusetts at the turn of the century.

John Campbell continued the pattern set by his cousin Duncan.[59] He joined the SCS in 1684 while living in Glasgow, but moved to Boston before 1695, when he began to appear in the town records. After Duncan's death in 1702, John continued his manuscript newsletter correspondence with Fitz-John Winthrop and became postmaster of Massachusetts. Campbell began publishing the *Boston News-Letter* in 1704, the first regular newspaper in the colonies, taking advantage of his correspondence networks and his privileges as postmaster. Through all these activities, John Campbell became closely tied to the Atlantic mercantile world. His daughter Sarah married James Bowdoin, a Huguenot refugee and merchant in Boston, and his daughter Elizabeth wed William Foy, the son of Captain John Foy, a well-known Boston mariner originally from the Channel Islands. Although he held no offices and did not join a church, by the early 1700s John Campbell had attained a position of influence within Massachusetts and throughout the North American colonies, and his family became firmly entrenched in the upper ranks of Boston society.[60]

Far from being simply booksellers and merchants, the Campbells came to Boston with extensive mercantile connections and soon cultivated influential political patrons. Through these contacts, they managed to gain footholds in visible and potentially lucrative positions of public trust. In this, they were much like the other merchants who arrived in New England after the Restoration. The opportunities available in the rapidly growing New England colonies attracted ambitious men. Merchants' support for royal government increased their influence in England, and their resistance to restrictions on colonial trade gave them status in the Bay colony. Thus the activities of merchants of all nationalities facilitated the incorporation of Massachusetts into the English colonial system.

French and Jersey merchants saw the same opportunities in Massachusetts in the 1680s that Scottish and English merchants did. Huguenot refugees brought important skills and contacts into the economy of New England, which, along with religious affinities, gave them a generous official welcome to the colony.[61] In 1682, for instance, the Massachusetts General Court requested that elders of Congregational churches take up collections for Huguenots after the evening service on a fast day. Thus even before the 1685 revocation of the Edict of Nantes, Massachusetts residents eagerly helped French refugees. By 1686, relief committees existed throughout the New England colonies. For example, John Saffin and Elisha Hutchinson, merchants in Boston, were members of the Narragansett Committee, dedicated to helping a group of refugees settle Frenchtown in Rhode Island. They wrote a letter to Thomas Hinckly, governor of Plymouth Colony, in December 1686 requesting that he ask Plymouth towns to send their relief contributions quickly, so that Daniel Smith of Rehoboth could help sixteen Huguenots in that town recover from a maritime disaster.[62] Although Huguenot families settled throughout the colonies, most notably in New York and South Carolina, many of those in New England built agricultural communities on the western frontier. The two largest towns, Frenchtown in Rhode Island and Oxford in Massachusetts, settled in 1686 and 1687, respectively, were composed of Huguenot settlers who had extensive ties to French merchants in Boston and Connecticut. These communities were dispersed in the wars between France and Britain (and their respective Indian allies) from

1690 to 1715, and the survivors scattered to other French communities in North America.[63] Yet several prominent merchant families came to Boston in the last two decades of the seventeenth century, leaving long-term legacies to the city.

The Bowdoin family exhibits many characteristics common to French émigrés in Massachusetts: extensive trade connections throughout the Atlantic world and kinship ties with prominent Boston families. Pierre Bowdoin fled France in 1685 for Dublin, Ireland, and then came to New England. He first settled in Casco (Portland), Maine, in 1687 and arrived in Boston before 1689. Although known as a physician in France, he quickly established himself as a merchant in the colonies. Bowdoin never held office in Boston or the colony, but sought to enhance his influence by giving five pounds for the construction of King's Chapel in 1689. Like many merchants who saw royal government as a way to prefer-ment, he hoped to curry favor with powerful Anglicans in town. Nevertheless, he was an elder in the French-liturgy church that had been established in Boston in 1685.[64] Bowdoin's mercantile connections stretched to the West Indies, as well as to the north. In 1695, he gave bond for his countryman Abraham Samuel to appear in the Court of Common Pleas in Boston in order to answer to the charges of John Papine of St. Kitts that Samuel had taken Papine's slave from St. Thomas and sold him in Canada. The bond given by Bowdoin was witnessed by Duncan and Mary Mackfarland, indicating his ties with Scottish merchants and illustrating the connections between the Boston mercantile community and the French colonies in the West Indies. Despite attempts by European governments to control trade in the Americas, in the seventeenth century commerce and smuggling was relatively open to merchants regardless of nationality or religion.[65]

As noted above, Bowdoin's son James married Sarah Campbell, and his daughter Mary married Stephen Boutineau, a Huguenot merchant in Boston, thereby remaining within Boston's developing commercial community. Another son, John, moved to Virginia and carried on a prosperous trade with his father and brother in Boston. Thus Pierre Bowdoin's familial and commercial connec-tions spanned the Massachusetts merchant community, and ranged from Canada to the West Indies. Bowdoin died in 1706, leaving one of the largest fortunes in Boston.[66] These networks also illustrate how people, goods, and information moved through the Atlantic world in the early modern period. A multiplicity of contacts among merchants residing in the colonies of many nations and confes-sional loyalties ensured that this flow continued.

The Faneuil brothers—Andrew, Benjamin, and John—likewise extended their social and commercial networks throughout this lightly regulated colo-nial world and became leading members of the Boston merchant community. The three brothers arrived in Boston in 1688 and remained until the end of the century. By 1693, Benjamin Faneuil had cultivated at least an acquaintanceship with Massachusetts governor William Phips, and the brothers had already become well-established in the Boston merchant community. Andrew died in Boston in 1737, a wealthy and highly respected member of the community; his nephew and heir, Peter, donated Faneuil Hall to the city in 1742. Benjamin moved to New York in 1699, and John returned to La Rochelle after 1702. These moves were undertaken at least in part to further extend the family's mercantile connections, which encompassed much of the colonial world. Andrew, for example, in 1695 acted as factor in Boston for Captain John Dobree and Company of Guernsey in a voyage from Boston to Virginia, and then to England (to enter the cargo of tobacco according to the Navigation Acts), and finally to Guernsey.[67]

By 1698, Andrew owned part of several ships with merchants from many segments of Boston's commercial circles. For instance, on 11 April 1698 the brigantine *Neptune* received a license to sail from Boston, the owners being Florence Maccarty, Philip Barger, James LeBlond, Faneuil, and Ruth Huddock. Nothing is known about Barger and Huddock. Maccarty, however, was probably a Scot and had lived in Boston at least since 1688. LeBlond was a Huguenot refugee who became a merchant in Boston in the 1690s and was a member of Boston's Second Church. Later that same year, Faneuil was listed as part owner of the *Peter,* a ship that had been captured from the French at Newfoundland in 1697 and was purchased by nine men, including John Usher, John Hobby, Andrew Belcher, Daniel Oliver, and James LeBlond. Thus, like other non-English merchants in Boston, the Faneuil family moved quickly to develop mercantile connections within New England and overseas.[68]

In the 1680s, Jersey's trade with Massachusetts also had increased to the point where several leading mercantile families of that island sent representatives to settle in Boston and Salem. Daniel Janverin, one of the most active of these immigrants, belonged to a prominent family of merchants who began their overseas trade with Newfoundland. The family concentrated on the fish trade but also imported tobacco from Virginia, and Janverin settled in Massachusetts around 1681 to look after the New England part of the business. Also a ship captain, Janverin made at least two voyages from Boston in the mid-1680s, carrying cargoes of fish, French and English goods, Spanish iron, and sweet oil. Because Atlantic trade was usually quite complicated, voyages frequently ended in the courts rather than with the unloading of the ship in port. Overseas merchants relied heavily on their local factors or family members to represent them in these complex cases.[69]

One voyage that illustrates the nature of Massachusetts's Atlantic commerce at the end of the century occurred from 1681 to 1684. Daniel Janverin owned seven-eighths of the ship *Daniel and Elizabeth*, with the remaining one-eighth belonging to Thomas Mudgett, the shipwright in Salisbury, Massachusetts, who built the ship. Mudgett had given his one-eighth part of the ship to his son-in-law Abraham Murrell, who sailed as the ship's carpenter. While the ship was at Jersey, Murrell sold this part to merchants John Durrell and Edward Demeret. Murrell shipped the goods that he received as payment in John Brown's ship *Maidenhead*, which was in Jersey but bound for New England in April 1682.[70] In addition, William Hollingsworth, the brother-in-law of Philip English, had "freighted one-eighth part of Tho. Mudgett," or in other words had a one-eighth share in the voyage. He lived in Virginia when the ship sailed, but had moved to Bilbao by the time that Janverin arrived there. Thus the *Daniel and Elizabeth* had several partial owners during its maiden voyage and stopped at ports throughout North America and western Europe, including Salem, Jersey, Bilbao, and Lisbon, none of which was out of the ordinary. Bilbao, in fact, was such an important stop that Lawrence Hayne acted as "interpreter of the English nation in the town." Between September and November 1684, Janverin, Mudgett, and Murrell sued and countersued each other over various aspects of voyage. Janverin even tried to get one-eighth of the provisions and wages from Hollingsworth in Bilbao, registering his actions with Spanish officials, thereby giving this Essex County court case an international component.[71]

None of this was uncommon: the stops, the changes of ownership, the changes of residence, or the combination of investors of Jerseyan and other nationalities. The crew as well exemplified the multinational component of trade in the late seventeenth century. Although most of the sailors' names were French, mariners from different backgrounds also sailed on the ship. Janverin, Murrell, Mazury, Mager, Lefavor, Lacrois, and Defew sailed with Simon, Taskett, Gefford, and Gillum. These men made up a floating world of sailors that drifted from port to port and ship to ship, searching for voyages. In this world, men of many nationalities and confessional loyalties (or none at all) lived and worked together on the land and the sea, further expanding Atlantic communities in Massachusetts.[72]

John Foy provides another example of the many layers of community and identity developed by merchants at the end of the seventeenth century. Foy, a sea captain, first appears in Boston records in 1672, and by 1680 regularly sailed the Boston-to-London route, transporting goods, passengers, and letters. In 1686, he contributed £1.10 to the construction of King's Chapel, and in the early 1700s he, along with fellow French-speaking residents James Bowdoin, Andrew Faneuil, and James LeBlond, was elected constable in Boston. Although constable was a minor town office, especially for Atlantic merchants, these men may have seen it as a step into Boston affairs or as demonstrating loyalty to the colony at a time of war between France and England. From the community's perspective, electing trusted, French-speaking merchants to this office was one way to keep track of a potentially subversive segment of the population. At Foy's death in 1715, pallbearers included four prominent men in Boston: Waitstill Winthrop, Samuel Sewall, Anthony Stoddard, and John Campbell. His children also married into several principal families in Boston. His son William married Elizabeth, daughter of John Campbell, and later became treasurer of Massachusetts. Elizabeth Campbell's sister Sarah married James Bowdoin, thereby connecting these French and Channel Island families. Foy's daughter Mary married the Reverend William Cooper, a Congregational minister whose first wife was Judith Sewall, daughter of Samuel, and his son John married Sarah Belcher, daughter of Andrew, the prominent Boston merchant.[73]

Men such as John Borland, Pierre Bowdoin, and John Foy were not simply sojourners in Massachusetts, men who lived in the colony and intended to return home later, but became settled members of the community, much like earlier non-Puritan laborers and merchants. They were all active in the affairs of Boston and Massachusetts, yet maintained ties with their countrymen. Many Scots joined the Scots' Charitable Society, Huguenot refugees supported the French-liturgy church in Boston, and Jersey immigrants kept a close community based on language and culture. Although many of these merchants initially traded predominantly through their countrymen, as had earlier English merchants, by the 1690s Boston's commercial community had become closely entwined. Although kin and country networks remained important when establishing new overseas contacts, within the town these national affiliations became less noticeable. Men of many nationalities and confessional backgrounds in Boston joined in shifting partnerships to take advantage of overseas trade opportunities. These families began to marry as well as trade together. Yet, like earlier laborers and agricultural workers, the non-English members of this merchant community did not become "English." The identities that developed incorporated various aspects of national identities as well as colonial, professional, and confessional loyalties.

Over the last half of the seventeenth century, the European population of Massachusetts became more diverse, much like the composition of England's other colonies. Massachusetts, and New England as a whole, was more homogeneous than the mid-Atlantic and southern regions, but, nevertheless, differences among the colonies at the end of the century were those of scale. Massachusetts was at one end of the spectrum, and New York and Pennsylvania were at the other. Aside from the Huguenot town of Oxford, entire villages of non-English residents did not exist, as in the German towns of Pennsylvania, or even the small communities of Scots in New Jersey. But to assume that non-English settlers in Massachusetts became "good Englishmen"—giving up their identity and traditions, and blending into English-dominated society—oversimplifies the development of the colony. As illustrated in the past three chapters, Scots, Irish, Jersey, and French settlers formed communities within the larger society, offering support for one another as countrymen, while also creating close ties with their neighbors, whether English or another nationality, whether Puritan or not. Because the identities that developed among them were not "English," but combinations of national, colonial, kinship, confessional, and professional identities, these residents adapted well to the changing political climate after the Union of 1707. Thus the overlapping identities that these settlers formed facilitated the development of a provincial British identity in the colonies during the eighteenth century.

Five

COMMUNITY AND IDENTITY IN EARLY MASSACHUSETTS

The formation of British and Atlantic communities in seventeenth-century Massachusetts indicates that these settlers did not simply submerge their identities into the dominant Puritan culture. Through their community networks, they provided support for countrymen and other non-Puritan residents. Traces of cultural patterns brought from the old countries can also be found within these communities, such as Scots who lived in small groups of families in marginal areas, or who moved from town to town following jobs but always stayed within in the orbit of other non-Puritan residents. Many Jersey Islanders continued to speak French among themselves and to litigate mercantile disputes aggressively. Many non-English residents went beyond such cultural traits, however, to join voluntary associations based on nationality: Scots formed the Scots' Charitable Society (scs) in 1657/8 and Huguenots founded a French-liturgy church in 1685.[1] Yet these associations created different meanings of nationality for people in the colonies. When the Scots' Charitable Society was reorganized in 1684, for example, the new constitution defined members as "Scottsmen and the sons of Scotts-men inhabitants of Boston and in the Colony thairof with several strangers of our Countriemen." The list of men pledging to join the society was divided into "Residenters in Towne and Countrie" and "Strangers," most of whom lived in western Scotland. Strangers, countrymen, and Scotsmen could have different meanings depending on context.[2]

Identity is a complex issue to unravel from a distance of almost four hundred years even under the best of circumstances. In this case, the lack of personal documents from non-Puritan residents of Massachusetts makes it difficult to trace the intellectual development of identity as so many scholars of colonial North America have done for more literate colonists. This chapter discusses identity in its most obvious form—how non-Puritan residents saw themselves based on their associations, as well as how Puritan colonists saw them. For most residents, regardless of nationality or religious affiliation, loyalty to the old country and to Massachusetts coexisted. They kept up associations with their countrymen and served their town or the colony. Non-English settlers did not become "Englishmen." At the same time, they did not remain purely Scottish, Irish, or French, either. The process of migration, whether forced or voluntary, created new networks and new identities. As historian Kerby Miller writes, "Ethnic identity is the result of the dynamic conjunctions of social structures, class conflicts and cultural patterns in the old country and the new. Ethnicity evolves from a complex dialectic that exists between an immigrant group and a host society but also among the immigrants themselves and among members of the host society."[3] Along with their Puritan neighbors, non-Puritan settlers began to see themselves as provincial British as the eighteenth century drew on; they accepted that the provinces had much to offer the new British state after 1707, and that they themselves played an important role within these areas.[4]

Colonists from Britain and Ireland had many common sources to draw on when constructing a British identity. They had a long history of interaction and shared a belief, based on the Bible, that all peoples had a common origin in the descendants of Noah. For centuries, Britons had constructed stories that tried to define the relationships among the inhabitants of the British islands. In particular, scholars had looked to the ancient inhabitants of the islands—Celts, Picts, Angles, Gaels, and Welsh—associating them with the various branches of Biblical genealogy, thereby linking the Celtic and Germanic groups together in a common ancestry. The different interpretations of this genealogy gave English, Scottish, and Irish peoples choices when constructing their own identities. By the early modern period, according to Colin Kidd, "The idea of a common descent persisting in spite of waves of superficially different ethnic settlement strengthened the notion of immemorial continuity." Commonalities were even easier to find in the colonies, given the distance from homelands and the presence of mixed-nationality marriages and families.[5]

That Scots, Irish, and English began to build a British identity in colonial Massachusetts should not be surprising. They had common origin myths and shared histories that involved both conflict and cooperation. They had more modern affiliations as well. Doctrinal similarities between Congregational and Presbyterian churches provided a bond among some Scots, Irish, and English. Opposition to the Cromwellian regime in Ireland and Scotland, or loyalty to the Stuart monarchs, also helped to forge links. As discussed in previous chapters, kinship and work also drew Massachusetts residents together. All the common ties among colonists of European descent, however, did not result in a homogeneous identity or the early modern version of the melting pot. The purpose of this chapter is to pull out some of the individual threads in order to see how non-English colonists adapted their cultural traditions to new conditions, thereby creating new national identities alongside colonial and British ones.

Many non-English immigrants did retain aspects of their cultures and identities, even within a predominantly English population. Such traits can be seen most easily among the Scots, Jersey Islanders, and French. The Scots constituted the largest group of non-English immigrants to Massachusetts in the last half of the seventeenth century, whereas Jerseyans remained distinctive through language. Huguenots formed a French-liturgy church in Boston and established separate settlements in central Massachusetts and Rhode Island. Irish cultural traits are more difficult to isolate because these immigrants were a much smaller proportion of the population. Although court records suggest that some of the Irish spoke Gaelic as their first language, no firm evidence of Catholicism has been found. Catholics, of course, would not have been allowed to practice their religion openly and, without priests, probably did not try to maintain it clandestinely. In addition, most of the Irish who have been identified so far as living in Essex and Suffolk counties did not leave wills, or were too poor to do so, and so little can be gleaned from probate records. Nevertheless, the networks formed by non-English residents throughout coastal Massachusetts and the Atlantic world gave many of these inhabitants the opportunity to maintain some cultural traditions.

SCOTTISH AND IRISH COLONIALS IN MASSACHUSETTS

The clearest example of the development of a colonial Scottish identity in Massachusetts lies in the formation of the Scots' Charitable Society by residents of Boston and Essex County in 1657/8. Many founding members were former prisoners from the battles of Dunbar and Worcester who lived in Essex County and had been recently released from their indentures. Other members were merchants and artisans in Boston, some of whom may have been former prisoners as well, whose indentures had been purchased by merchants or craftsmen in the town.[6] The purpose of the society was to provide charity for indigent Scots and their families in New England, which was not only an altruistic motive, but also served to strengthen ties among Scots in the region while drawing Irish and English wives and children into the community.

The founding members envisioned the association as a permanent institution, one formed not simply to alleviate immediate problems but to provide for the future. In organizing the SCS, the original members agreed both to pay quarterly dues and that "there shall nothing be taken out of the box for the first sevin yeers for the releefe of any" in order to build a cash reserve. In addition, members agreed that their sons, many of whom were half Irish or English, would be allowed to enter the society when they reached maturity, with the same rights and privileges as original members. Thus New England, and Massachusetts in particular, was seen as home by these men as early as 1657/8; they saw themselves as laying the foundations for a long-term Scottish presence in the English colony. Yet, even though the founders planned for a permanent society, they had problems perpetuating it. Twenty-seven men attended the initial meeting in January 1657/8, and seven more joined in the following years. By 1661, however, only nine members regularly paid their quarterly fees, and in 1667 the records end. The artisans, laborers, and agricultural workers who constituted most of the membership apparently found it too difficult to pay even the small quarterly dues, and this, along with the malfeasance of some trustees, kept the SCS dormant for almost twenty years.[7]

As the number of Scots in Massachusetts grew, their increasing resources allowed them to revive the organization. In 1684, four of the original members of the SCS joined with recent immigrants to Boston and "stranger" Scots in western Scotland to reorganize the society, which included members throughout the Atlantic world. Men in New England, New York, Virginia, the West Indies, Scotland, and Ulster joined, facilitating trade and commercial connections among merchants. Yet poor laborers living in the North End of Boston were also encouraged to become members, revealing a close affinity with the purposes of the original society. The SCS, in fact, resembled the charity hospitals formed by merchants and craftsmen in Glasgow, described by historian T. C. Smout as "a valued form of social insurance, as it conferred protection on oneself and one's family against the terrors of old age, sickness or the decease of the breadwinner."[8] The association was also modeled on the Royal Scottish Corporation, which developed out of a "box club" that existed by 1613 for the benefit of Scots in London. Box clubs, so named because the charitable donations were kept in locked boxes in the care of trustees, were common in Scotland by the late sixteenth century. Thus the SCS provided an important link to Scottish culture in Boston.[9]

The SCS sustained an active Scottish community, helping immigrants and their American-born children maintain and create identities as Scots. Ned Landsman notes that Scots "maintained a rather complex sense of nationality, and Scotsmen were never simply those who lived in Scotland."[10] The SCS illustrates this idea quite well, embracing long-time residents of New England; temporary residents, such as merchants and mariners passing through on voyages; new arrivals; and the New England–born sons of immigrants. The society also reached out to bring together Scots and their descendants in many parts of the Atlantic world. Yet the experiences of Scots outside Scotland was different from those at home. In seventeenth-century Massachusetts, they had little political power, they could not form separate churches until late in the century, and they had to work within a much more diverse society.[11] The distinction made between members of the SCS in "Towne and Countrie" and "Strangers" indicates that men in Massachusetts felt a closer affinity to one another than with members in Scotland, even though they recognized each other as countrymen and many had established commercial connections.[12]

Members of the first SCS included many of the Scots discussed in chapter 4, such as Thomas Dewer, William Gibson, and William Ballantyne. Members in Essex County included blacksmith John Clarke and laborers Macam Macallum and Allester Dugglas at Lynn; most early members lived near Boston and Salem. Given the dearth of records for the early years, it is difficult to draw conclusions about individuals in the first society, but a collective portrait of the founding members can be compiled. Of the thirty-four men who joined between 1657/8 and 1665, some information has been found for nineteen. For four members, too many men of the same name lived in coastal Massachusetts to distinguish the Scottish resident.[13] The remaining eleven simply could not be found. They may have lived in Maine, Plymouth, or towns farther away from the coast.[14] Of the nineteen men for whom information was found, sixteen lived in Boston and three resided in Lynn. The three Lynn residents—John Clarke, Macam Macallum, and Allester Dugglas—had worked at Hammersmith. Two other members, William Gibson and George Thomson, may have worked there as well and later moved to Boston. Of the fourteen men for whom occupations are known, six worked as laborers or small craftsmen. For example, Thomas Shearer was a tailor and Alexander Simpson a brick burner, whereas John Kneeland, Macam Macallum, and George Thomson were laborers. Two men were mariners, and four members were merchants or shopkeepers. Most members lived in coastal Massachusetts; there is no indication that any of the members came from outside New England.[15] The original members, even those in humble occupations, found the organization important enough to pay the entrance fine and quarterly fees, and many probably knew one another before joining the scs.

Seventeenth-century tax lists from Boston also give some clues about the spatial relationships among early scs members. Of twelve identifiable men who appear in the tax lists, seven lived in the fourth ward, near the commercial center of the town.[16] Other families were scattered throughout other wards. Men who joined the second Scots' Charitable Society after 1684 also tended to cluster in certain wards. The fourth ward still predominated, being home to eleven of twenty-five families, and wards three and six had the next highest totals with five and seven families, respectively. These three wards were all in the central section of Boston.[17]

Some conclusions can be drawn from this information. If the fourth ward was indeed the commercial center of town, then non-English residents were not geographically marginalized from the rest of the community. Unlike the concentration of non-English settlers in upland regions of Essex County, these families lived directly in the center of commerce in an increasingly commercial society, although a similar tendency to cluster together also existed in Boston. In addition, these families had the means to purchase or rent land in what must have been a fairly expensive section of town. There, they had access to the latest news from abroad, receiving it at the same time as other merchants. Thus they were aware of important political and commercial changes and could respond to events quickly. Scottish merchants and craftsmen in the center wards of Boston were well situated to take advantage of expanding commercial opportunities in the late seventeenth century.[18]

The members of the first scs lived in a fairly constricted world. They had few contacts with Scotland or the families that they left behind. Their closest ties were with other Scots in Massachusetts and the British communities they formed there. This characteristic may be related to poverty, although even those men who prospered, such as Alexander Simpson and John Upton, left no evidence that they reconnected with family in Scotland. Nevertheless, as the stories of Alexander and Joseph Simpson illustrate, their identities as Scots remained strong for them and their sons.

Alexander Simpson arrived in Massachusetts in 1652 as a captive from the Battle of Worcester and worked as a brick burner in Boston. He appears in the records infrequently through the years and died in 1707/8. He left his entire estate, worth £188, to his son Joseph, with small bequests to Joseph's children and Mary Kneeland, daughter of John Kneeland, a Scot who had lived in Boston since at least 1658 and was also a founding member of the scs. Simpson lived quietly in Boston, made a competent living, and, like Scots in Essex County, left no evidence that he maintained connections to Scotland. Yet as a founding member of the society in 1657/8, it appears that his heritage was important to him, and he joined the scs again in 1684.[19]

Joseph Simpson, Alexander's son, lived as inconspicuously as his father did. Born in Boston in 1665, he followed his father's craft of brick making and married Hannah Kneeland, also a daughter of John. When Joseph died in 1709, one year after his father's death, he left an estate worth almost seven hundred pounds, which he bequeathed to his wife, Hannah, and after her death to their children. Like his father and many former prisoners of the 1650s, Joseph Simpson left no provisions for family members in Scotland or even acknowledged that family still lived there. In addition, there is no evidence that either Joseph or Alexander had any mercantile interests that would make membership in the scs financially advantageous. Yet, also like his father, Joseph placed enough importance on his heritage to join the Scots' Charitable Society in 1684, and he married into the Scottish community in Boston.[20]

A few of the founding members of the scs did cultivate and prosper from Atlantic connections. Most of these men lived in Boston and attached themselves to the mercantile community there, even if they were not merchants themselves. Such participation in Scottish and Atlantic networks can be seen through the life of Andrew Neale, who joined the first Scots' Charitable Society in 1659. Neale's activities between 1659 and 1676 are not known, but in 1676 he was given a license to sell beer, "provided he make use of John Courcers house & utensells for brewinge." In 1678, the Suffolk County court allowed Neale "to keepe a house for publique entertainment & to retaile beere and cider," and established him as one of Boston's innkeepers. Neale's property, the Star Tavern, was at the intersection of Union and Hanover streets near the center of town, where he entertained the courts or other large groups.[21] The probate inventory of his estate, taken in 1684, listed a large number of dishes and cooking utensils: fifty-nine pewter dishes and forty-five plates, for example, along with fourteen pewter pots and several iron and copper pots, skillets, and kettles. The inventory also contained twenty-three pairs of sheets, four diaper tablecloths, eight other tablecloths, seven dozen napkins, two and a half dozen coarse napkins, and one and a half dozen coarse towels. The linens listed in this section of the inventory alone were valued at £25. The number of fancy cloths—the tablecloths and napkins in particular—indicate that Neale not only had room for large groups, but also entertained guests who expected finer accommodations than in a common tavern. Neale's occupation made him a fairly wealthy man. His estate totaled £835, of which £500 consisted of two houses and land, with £53 worth of silver plate.[22]

Because the inn was near the center of town, Neale's may have been a stopping place for merchants from the West Indies and Britain, particularly fellow members of the scs. John Borland and his brother Francis initially stayed at the inn when they moved to Boston in 1682, for instance. Shortly after Neale died in July 1684, his wife joined the revived Scots' Charitable Society. "Mrs. Neil, widow," was one of only two women who joined in their own names in the seventeenth century. Millicent Neale continued to run the inn, hiring David Kinbord (Campbell?), a Scot living in Cambridge, to help her, and presumably benefited by this ongoing association with the Atlantic merchant community.[23]

Thus the first society encompassed a wide range of families, from those who became wealthy and influential with extensive contacts throughout the Atlantic world, to those who had far more limited resources. Most of the early members, however, had recently been released from servitude when the scs was founded and were just beginning to establish themselves in Massachusetts. The 1684 society was quite different. Although several members toiled in low-status occupations, most of the men had settled into livings that enabled them to earn at least a competency. As a whole, they were far more closely connected to the Boston merchant class and to merchants trading in Atlantic markets than were earlier members.

The reorganization of the Scots' Charitable Society took place in 1684 within a different political context, discussed in the previous chapter. As noted there, by the 1680s the English government had established greater authority within Massachusetts, and royal officials and merchants challenged old Puritan families for leadership in the colony. These changes opened greater opportunities for new immigrants, and Scottish merchants, along with their non-Scottish colleagues, took advantage of them. This was also a time of increased Scottish activity in the sugar industry, which brought more Scots to the English colonies as a whole, and to Massachusetts in particular, given the colony's importance in the West Indies carrying trade. These wider connections among Scots were reflected in the preamble to the by-laws of the revived scs, approved in October 1684: "Wee are this day convened being Scottsmen & the sons of Scotts-men Inhabitants of Bostone and in the colony thairof with severall strangers of our Countriemen being of one accord most willing to renew the former good example [of providing charitable relief to indigent Scots in New England], and to give what the Lord shall enable and move us for this good work, that the poor strangers and families and children of our natione, when under this dispensatione may be the more ordourly and better relieved."[24] Clearly, Scots living in Boston, as well as their sons (and presumably daughters), still saw themselves as Scottish, as well as colonials. "Strangers" may have been countrymen, but they were not inhabitants of Massachusetts.

The charitable mission remained the stated primary focus of the second society. Following the model of charitable hospitals supported by merchant guilds in Scotland and the Royal Scottish Corporation in London, Boston Scots took it on themselves to provide relief for their countrymen as a religious, national, and civic duty. The society therefore crossed boundaries; it was a religious duty regardless of church membership or confessional affiliation, a national duty to aid countrymen and their families irrespective of place of birth, and a civic duty for Boston by keeping families off of public charity rolls. It also provided a forum for keeping problems within the community by encouraging the settlement of disputes among group members. The second society was better funded than the first, and it began dispensing aid immediately. In 1685, for example, the scs gave Alexander Grant ten shillings, and it helped Thomas Kelton and William Hamilton with five shillings each. The society paid for the funerals of indigent members, as well as for mourning fringes and gloves.[25]

In conjunction with the charitable motives of these men, the new organization also served to initiate and strengthen contacts among merchants throughout the Atlantic world. Membership in the scs was not restricted to merchants, but of forty-five members in Massachusetts from 1684 to 1690 for whom reliable information has been found, eleven identified themselves as merchants and ten as mariners. Several other men who described themselves as craftsmen were involved in overseas commercial activities. Thus almost half the members who can be clearly identified through Massachusetts records had direct connections with seaborne commerce. At least seven merchants lived in other colonies or in Scotland, and several more were probably overseas merchants, although no direct connection has yet been found.[26] Like the informal merchant networks established among Scots in Europe, the connections among merchants in the scs allowed the Scots to develop their markets in the Atlantic world. The scs was a more formal organization than the European mercantile networks, but like them it served to support commercial activities among Scots and maintain a Scottish identity in the Americas.[27]

The networks established by second-generation Scots in Boston can be illustrated through the life of John Ballantyne, the son of William and his wife, Hannah Hollard. Ballantyne was a Bostonian, born in 1653 and baptized in the First Church in 1661. He joined the First Church as an adult in 1675 and shortly thereafter his sons William and John were baptized. Ballantyne had trading interests throughout the Atlantic world, although when he joined the Scots' Charitable Society in 1684 he called himself a cooper, following the trade of his father. He participated in Boston town affairs by serving as constable in 1682/3; tithing man in 1680, 1681, and 1690; and as priser of grain in 1695/6. He also served as clerk of the Suffolk County court in the early 1700s. In 1690, Ballantyne was appointed to a committee of three to search for, seize, and bring before the court any gunpowder in the town. Thus John Ballantyne was closely involved in mercantile and public affairs in his native town. He also identified with the Scottish heritage of his father, even though he was New England–born, and participated in merchant networks that included men of many nationalities.[28]

In 1698, Ballantyne was listed, along with several other merchants, as owner of the sloop *William,* which had been captured from the French in 1696. Seven of the owners lived in Boston, and one, a Bridget Grafford (Crawford?), lived in Piscataqua, New Hampshire. The ship participated in the fish and timber trade along coastal New England and Newfoundland, and sailed to the West Indies and Europe. Later that year, he and two other Boston merchants claimed the ship *Good Speed.* In October 1699 he claimed partial ownership in the sloop *Dolphin,* along with prominent merchants Penn Townsend, Samuel Lillie, and Samuel Checkley, who had also been partners in the *William.* In November of the same year he was listed as partial owner of the sloop *Endeavour* of London, along with five London merchants and Jeremiah Tay of Boston. Ballantyne, then, was connected to the main centers of the New England trade, such as Newfoundland and the West Indies, and had ties to London. His primary business partners included English merchants in New England and London, and a few Scots. Yet he also desired the association with the Scottish community that came with membership in the SCS.[29]

Although one function of the society was to further mercantile connections throughout the Atlantic world, it also served to develop a Scottish identity in the English colonies. Many of the most prominent merchants in the colonies and in Scotland pledged themselves to help indigent countrymen in the Americas. Colonial-born sons of Scottish immigrants, many of whom married daughters of English, Irish, French, or Jersey families, or who were of mixed parentage themselves and apparently never visited Scotland, joined the society. And so, although many Scots and their descendants became active and even prominent members of colonial society, they did not see themselves solely through this lens. They were colonists, Massachusettsans, Bostonians, and Scots; John Ballantyne was all of these and probably identified with the English heritage of his mother as well. His close ties to London merchants may have been a legacy from the Hollard side of his family.

The formation of such an explicit "community of interest" was not the only method that non-English residents used to express national identities in

Massachusetts. As demonstrated in chapter 3, farmers and agricultural laborers continued to practice some of their cultural traditions. They retained a Scottish identity, addressing each other as "countrymen" (as did many of the Irish), and provided assistance for each other, even when being "countrymen" was the only link. John Upton, a Saugus ironworker, moved to Salem Farms when his indenture ended, and became a farmer and landowner. In 1665, he appeared before the Essex County court, charged with aiding and abetting Henry Spencer, a runaway servant from Boston, and for concealing clothes that Spencer had stolen from his master. Upton claimed that he met Spencer in Salem and, "being his countryman, brought him to his house and entertained him." Upton had a jury trial, but presented no defense of his actions except that he felt bound to help Spencer as a fellow Scot. The jury found him not guilty, although the magistrates did not agree. Any punishment that Upton may have received was not recorded.[30]

As another example, naming practices followed Scottish custom in many families in Massachusetts, wherein first sons were named for grandfathers rather than fathers. Brick burner Joseph Simpson, for instance, son of Alexander, named his eldest son Alexander. John Ballantyne, son of William, named his first son William. John and Sarah (Neale) Borland named their eldest son Andrew after her father, and their first daughter Beatrix after his mother. Their second son was named James, after John's maternal grandfather. This naming pattern follows the emphasis on collateral descent typical of Scottish society, rather than that of lineal descent common in England.[31]

Scots also brought a tradition of far-flung kinship and friendship networks with them to Massachusetts, and the communities formed by Scottish residents resembled their kinship ties at home. Rural Scots generally lived in small, scattered hamlets, known as "farmtouns," rather than the villages and farming communities more common to central and southern England. These touns were quite small, averaging only six to eight houses. Wealthy lords owned most of the land in Scotland; farmers were tenants or subtenants and held their farms on the sufferance of the landlord or primary tenant. Sizes of landholdings varied, but many subtenants and cottars had lots of only a few acres and a small house, or even just a small cottage and grazing rights.[32]

Social structures differed in various districts of Scotland, but in general the population below the landed class was highly mobile, moving from farmtoun to farmtoun, yet usually remaining within a region. Scottish communities therefore did not focus around a central place, but stretched across parish and county boundaries. Ned Landsman observes, "They [rural Scots] appear to have functioned within the confines of what might be called a regional community that transcended the bounds of the parish." Thus while families rarely lived in the same farmtoun, they did remain within a region, spreading kinship ties across geographical areas. Many such features can also be seen among Scots in Massachusetts, particularly in Essex County.[33] Although these patterns were altered by conditions in Massachusetts, such as the inability to establish churches and the lack of Scottish women to marry, and some characteristics may simply be those of rural people in the early modern world in general, the similarities still suggest a transfer of some Scottish traditions to "Puritan" Massachusetts.

Landsman's study of Scots in East New Jersey also provides several points of comparison for early Scottish residents of Massachusetts. He found that Scots in this region were highly mobile, moving up and down a corridor that stretched from Philadelphia to New York City. They usually moved to lands owned by other Scots, and settled in small villages with their countrymen. These settlements dotted the landscape of East New Jersey, and Scots moved in and out of them frequently. Yet land ownership was not necessarily a goal of many Scottish inhabitants of the area. Many men who arrived in the colony as servants never claimed their headright lands. Tenants and cottars in Scotland had few opportunities to acquire land and, as Landsman states, they "did not consider landowning to be the only measure of economic success."[34]

Conditions in Massachusetts differed from those in East New Jersey, of course. Scots did not have the opportunity to settle their own villages because the Massachusetts General Court tightly controlled the formation of towns. As demonstrated in chapter 3, however, after receiving their freedom many Scots settled on the edges of villages in small groups and frequently worked near one another in settlements resembling farmtouns. Essex County Scots, particularly ironworkers, were also highly mobile, moving from town to town following jobs in different iron foundries and forges. Kinship and social ties extended from Lynn to Salem, Reading, and Ipswich, and farther north into southern New Hampshire and south into Boston. Many Scottish families rented land or lived on very small lots with a few head of cattle or other livestock, much like cottars in Scotland. In 1661, Allester Mackmallen, for example, a former laborer at Saugus, purchased twenty rods of land, just over one-third of an acre, in Salem Village. This was not enough land to farm, but it certainly could contain a vegetable garden and small livestock, although the family's primary income still came from general labor.[35]

Social patterns similar to those in Scotland can be seen among Scottish residents of Essex County. Arzbell Anderson, a captive from Dunbar, worked at the Saugus ironworks. His indenture ended in the mid-1650s, but he remained at Hammersmith, chopping wood and raising livestock as a tenant on ironworks land. He did not own a house or land, but grazed livestock, worked as a laborer, and lived in a small community near other Scots. Anderson died at Saugus in 1661 and the administrators of his estate were two other Scots, blacksmith John Clarke and Allester Grime, both Dunbar captives. Oliver Purchase, who initially oversaw the estate, was the clerk of the ironworks, and Purchase, John Divan, and Edward Baker made the estate inventory. Divan and Baker also had long-standing connections to Hammersmith. Anderson owed debts to William Gibson, the shoemaker and merchant in Boston, and to Macam Downing and Rowland Mackfashion, also Scots associated with the ironworks. Anderson, in Massachusetts for only ten years, had forged ties with ironworkers and other Scots throughout the region, and the general outlines of his life in Essex County—a tenant grazing livestock on company land—resembled patterns from rural Scotland.[36]

A habit of living in small, clustered groups of houses, similar to farmtouns and the East New Jersey settlements, may have led many Scots to settle in these marginal areas of Essex County along with other non-English inhabitants, although they were not marginalized from town communities. Marginal areas such as Marblehead and Salem Farms were home to many non-Puritans, residents who arrived too late or with too few resources to obtain good farmland, thus forcing neighborhoods to develop in less desirable areas. In Salem Farms, also known as Salem Village (now Danvers), for instance, the land was not good enough for commercial farming, even though it was close to a major harbor, so the area attracted dissenters and outsiders of many kinds, particularly Quakers. The forty-acre farm purchased by John Upton in 1658, for instance, was surrounded by Quaker-owned farms. Conflicts were endemic in the area, since Salem Village farmers had been struggling with merchants in Salem for many years, particularly over establishing a separate church and, of course, as the site of the witchcraft outbreak in 1692.[37]

The relationships among Teague Brann, Allester Dugglas, and Macam Downing illustrate this tendency to settle in small clusters in Massachusetts. Brann, who died in the Battle of Black Point in 1677 during King Philip's War, owned a "dwelling house, a little out house or Hovell, with four acres of land, a small part of it orchard," located "[in] the woods," outside Lynn village. The rest of his estate consisted of livestock, farming tools, household implements, grain, and seed. Brann must have farmed his four acres, probably with the help of Allester Dugglas, who also lived on the property.[38] The disposition of his estate went primarily to Dugglas and Downing. Here then were three families, two of them Scottish, living near one another on land "in the woods," on the outskirts of a village, who probably shared the work and the ownership of tools, household goods, and the produce of the farm. Again, this follows the pattern for rural Scots in Scotland and in East Jersey of farming small tracts of land and living in rather isolated clusters.

Another small cluster of houses could be found in Reading, just over the Essex County line in Middlesex County, approximately ten miles west of Salem. The largest landowner among this group was John Upton. The former iron-worker had moved to Salem Farms after his service, purchased forty acres of land there in 1658, and then moved to Reading in the mid-1670s, although he kept his land in Salem. Upton had amassed 517 acres of land at his death in 1697, plus three other parcels worth £374 (no acreage was given for these parcels, although one tract was the most valuable of all his landholdings), making him the largest landowner and wealthiest man among the Scots who arrived in the 1650s. For all his wealth, however, Upton never held any town office or sat on a jury as far as the Essex County records show, and he was brought to court in 1675 for refusing to pay the minister and meetinghouse rates in Salem Village. He never joined the scs, but, as his encounter with Henry Spencer illustrates, he had a strong sense of his Scottish identity. Yet he also had ties to his non-Scottish neighbors in Salem and Reading, was admitted a freeman of the colony in 1691, and did not return to Scotland, although he had the means to do so. Upton's experiences illustrate the layers of association and identity that developed among non-English residents of Massachusetts. His Scottish heritage was important to him, and he lived within a small community of Scots. Although he had wealth, he never went back to Scotland, left no bequests to family there, and apparently had no communication with family overseas. He had made his home and life in Massachusetts, although he kept other aspects of his Scottish identity.[39]

James Hage, also a former Saugus ironworker from Scotland, lived close to and worked with Upton in Reading. The Hage and Upton families had lived near each other in Salem Village as well; Upton probably purchased forty acres from Hage in 1671. Although it is not known when Hage moved to Reading, it is clear that the families deliberately stayed close to each other. Out of an estate that totaled only five pounds at his death in 1682, Hage left Anne, John's daughter, "a Cow or mare," and named Upton as administrator. Hammer-smith collier Thomas Tower can also be associated with this group of families, since he took Hage's estate inventory. Tower's wife, Hannah Dastin, was born in Reading and the two kept their connections both to her family and his countrymen, even though they themselves moved throughout the region as he took work at new iron manufactories as they opened.[40]

It is probable that Irish residents of Massachusetts came overwhelmingly from rural areas and, like the Scots, had little tradition of holding land in fee simple or on long-term leases. Unfortunately, there is not enough information about the Irish to identify patterns from Ireland in Massachusetts. Some colonists, such as Philip Welsh, moved frequently, whereas others, such as Edward Nealand, owned land, and some, as with William Danford, held long-term leases. Although we cannot be certain where Irish settlers came from, many kidnapped servants may have come from southern Ireland, around Kinsale in County Cork, where a trade in servants to the West Indies and Chesapeake had existed since the 1620s. If so, many servants could have been Catholic and Gaelic, the predominant religion and ethnicity in southern Ireland.[41] In the original bill of sale in 1654 between George Dell, master of the *Goodfellow*, and magistrate Samuel Symonds of Ipswich, Philip Welsh was called "Edward"; a proviso added a week later states, "Upon his arrival in Ipswich such as do well understand his language doe say he owneth his name to be Philip." In the 1661 case, another servant testified that, upon the arrival of the Irishmen, he had asked William Downing what Welsh's name was and Downing told him that it was Philip. The implication, of course, is that Welsh did not speak English and so may have been from a Gaelic-speaking region of Ireland.[42]

In addition, John King, another servant from the *Goodfellow*, stated that he and others were taken "by some of the English soldiers," and John Downing claimed that he was taken "by the ship master or some one whom he hired."[43] The men, in other words, had been taken under the Elizabethan statute against "rogues and vagabonds" (39 Eliz., c. 4), and with the knowledge and authority of the English government. Although this does not prove that these servants were Catholic or Gaelic, it does mean that they were not from influential families, who could have protected them. Because Dell left port hurriedly to avoid having his cargo of servants freed "by the country," we can also assume that the general populace did not condone the actions of the English government or its agents.[44]

Other Gaelic or Catholic Irish also lived in coastal Massachusetts in the seventeenth century. As early as 1639, Dorman Mahoney came to Boston as a servant, and although he apparently spoke English and his religion is unknown, part of the agreement when his son Tege was indentured in 1643 to Joseph Armitage in Essex County was that Armitage would teach the boy "to read the English tongue."[45] Later, in 1681, Joane Suiflan (Sullivan?) petitioned the Essex County court to remove her from her indenture with Quaker Thomas Maule. She charged Maule and his wife with physical and emotional abuse and had the support of several neighbors, Quakers included, who confirmed her story. Maule denied the charges and claimed that Sullivan "could not speck one word of Inglesh . . . and [was] of bad caredge in langedg soe far as I understood her in Irish." Another deponent charged Sullivan with saying that Massachusetts "was a devilish place for thay did not goe to mast [mass]." Sullivan reportedly added that she would "stay out her time . . . and then goe whome to her one contry againe wher shee mit goe to mast."[46] The authorities made no response to this charge of Catholicism. In Boston, Goody Glover, an Irish Catholic servant of the Godwin family, was executed for witchcraft in 1688. The trial was conducted through interpreters, since Glover spoke Gaelic, making it very difficult to present her side of the story.[47]

Non-English immigrants did not transfer their social and economic patterns to Massachusetts wholesale. As Kerby Miller points out, an emphasis on persistence of traits undervalues the exchanges between donor and host societies. Some continued in traditional ways, and others took the opportunities for land ownership and economic independence that the colony offered. Many melded traditions and new opportunities, as they blended their families, creating new forms in the colonies.[48]

JERSEY COLONIALS IN EARLY MASSACHUSETTS

Jersey Islanders also participated in British communities yet retained non-English traits in Massachusetts. Many Jerseyans worked and lived within mixed-ethnicity communities, particularly in Marblehead and Salem Village, whereas others remained part of a close-knit community in Salem, centered around merchant Philip English. Men worked as general laborers, fishermen, or sailors, in close contact with their non-Puritan neighbors, and women usually worked as servants in Salem households. Peter Conney, for example, worked for blacksmiths William Curtis and Edward Humber in Salem Village, as did Scot Allester Grime. Peter LeCras lived near Ipswich and was servant to minister William Hubbard, and Thomas Baker lived in the same area and was servant to prominent landowner Nathaniel Wells.[49]

As noted above, by the middle of the seventeenth century the special commercial privileges that English monarchs had given the Channel Islands since at least the time of Henry VII, combined with the Channel Islanders' participation in the cod fisheries, opened an active trade between the islands and New England. Jersey ships entered Boston and Salem harbors with increasing frequency after 1650, loading fish, tobacco, and other commodities, and bringing more sailors, merchants, and fishermen to Massachusetts.[50] Jerseyans remained highly visible in the population of Essex County for many years because most spoke French as their first language and they tended to be clannish. In 1677, for instance, six letters were left in the shop of Ezekiel Cheever in Salem. He did not know the men to whom the letters were addressed and could not read the addresses because they were in French, but he knew that his landlord, a Jerseyan, would be able to deliver them. The landlord, Thomas Vealey, apparently was not literate, and took the letters to Mary Morall, another member of the Jersey community, to read. The letters eventually made it to their intended recipients, but this interaction gives the sense of a tightly knit community of French-speaking residents whose English-speaking neighbors were very much on the periphery. Their language and clannishness at times made them suspect in the eyes of their English-speaking neighbors. Yet, like other non-English colonists, these Jersey natives were not marginalized from the larger community and did participate in the development of a British society in coastal Massachusetts.[51]

Although fishing and trading contacts existed earlier, substantial emigration from the islands to Massachusetts did not begin until the 1660s, driven by the fisheries and, perhaps, by religious affinities. According to historian A. G. Jamieson, Channel Islanders were Calvinist Protestants and as such enjoyed closer sympathies with the Puritanism of New England than with the Arminianism of the Church of England. During the civil wars, Guernsey actively supported Parliament, and although the Jersey government was Royalist, the people were less than ardent in their support for the Stuarts. When Royalists regained control of the islands, they actively punished supporters of the Commonwealth. The Parliamentarian proclivities of many Jersey Islanders may have contributed to the increase in immigration to Massachusetts after the Restoration.[52] For many reasons, then, by the 1670s a thriving trade in fish, provisions, and servants had developed between Massachusetts and Jersey.

Jerseyans worked in many aspects of the fish trade and were well integrated into all levels of the industry. Many men were hired out for fishing voyages, filling spots on crews in which their masters had an interest. Thomas Nickels, a Jersey servant of Philip English, was sent by his master on a voyage with Edward Woodman that touched at Boston, Barbados, the Salt (Dry) Tortugas, Barbados again, and London. Woodman released Nickels in London without paying him, prompting an Essex County lawsuit by English.[53] Some men hired themselves out for fishing and merchant voyages, participating in both catching fish and selling them overseas. Benjamin Mazury, for example, worked as a fisherman, yet also sailed on merchant vessels to Bilbao, Spain, a major port in Salem's fish trade.[54] Other Jerseyans owned their ships, either privately or in partnership. Abraham Ketville owned the *Adventure* out of Marblehead with Andrew Tucker. The two men sailed with a mixed crew of English and Jersey sailors and sold their catch to English and Jersey merchants.[55] John Brock established himself at yet another level of the trade as a full or partial owner of several ketches, and acted as a factor for Jersey fishermen in Salem. Brock himself did not fish; he was accorded the title of "Mr." in the court records, sent "his men" to serve his turn at the watch, and met with Bristol merchants in Salem, presumably about the sale of fish.[56] Jerseyan John Petherick was shore man for, and probably partial owner of, a shallop commanded by his countryman John Searle, but whose crew included Richard Goodly, an English servant of fisherman Andrew Tucker. Jerseyans, then, were an integral part of the Essex County fish trade. Although, as Daniel Vickers has shown, fishing was a marginal occupation, the fish trade was an important component of the region's economy, demonstrating that even non-Puritan residents in peripheral livelihoods played a role in shaping the region.[57]

Channel Islanders frequently clashed with Massachusetts authorities and were viewed with some suspicion by their English-speaking neighbors. These immigrants faced a mixed reception in eastern Massachusetts, one that reflected the time of their arrival and the political problems of the period. The labor shortage that led to the importation of Scottish and Irish captives in the 1650s had eased, and with no pressing economic need for French-speaking "strangers," cultural differences between English speakers and French speakers created tensions within society. In addition, fears of both growing French influence with Indians on the northern borders of New England and Catholic influence over the later Stuart monarchs led many in Massachusetts to harbor a general distrust of Channel Islanders. The heavy involvement of Jerseyans in the fishing industry also highlighted their differences from Puritan farmers. Thus many Essex County residents looked askance at Jersey Islanders because of their language, clannishness, and business practices, which gave merchants a reputation for sharp dealing.

Unlike Scottish and Irish residents of Essex County, Jersey Islanders sued each other and their non-Jersey neighbors frequently. In the Jersey legal system, creditors had to take debtors to court quickly or risk taking on the entire debt of an estate if the debtor declared bankruptcy. Because commercial transactions in the seventeenth century depended on long-term credit, these laws encouraged merchants from Jersey to resort to lawsuits much more quickly than other merchants.[58] Philip English, for example, brought eight suits for debt against Essex County residents between 1674 and 1690. Three of these suits were against his brother-in-law Richard Hollingsworth. English also appeared in court as a defendant several times in these years. John Balaine of Jersey sued Philip English in Essex County, and English and his countryman Benjamin Mazury sued and countersued each other several times, as did merchant Daniel Janverin and shipwright Abraham Murrell. Because Jerseyans had little compunction about suing their family and friends, they violated an unwritten code followed by many early modern peoples. Although Massachusetts society as a whole was highly litigious in the seventeenth century, this quick recourse to the law gained Jerseyans in Massachusetts a poor reputation. The general suspicion accorded these French-speaking settlers emerged in slurs recorded in the court records.[59]

Fish merchant John Brock, for instance, entered into an altercation with constable John Waldron of Marblehead in 1672. Waldron and Brock argued about Brock's refusal to stand watch and to pay his minister's rates. During this altercation, the constable called Brock a "Jersey cheater" and "knave, cheater and French dog." Later that evening, the quarrel resumed at Christopher Lattimore's public house. Waldron accused Brock of being drunk, refusing a turn at the watch, insulting him, and "scoffing at [his] authority." In 1673, Thomas Baker reported being called "base rogue and French dog" by his master Nathaniel Wells. In a 1681 dispute between Jersey fisherman Abraham Ketville and his English partner Andrew Tucker, Tucker's wife agreed to have a mediator settle the problem, as long as the mediator was not "a Jarsey man."[60]

A few miscreants tried to take advantage of this reputation by blaming Jerseyans for instigating their crimes. John Collier, for example, when convicted of stealing pewter from merchant Gershom Browne, tried to throw blame on Thomas and Mary Vealey, claiming that the Vealeys knew about the thefts, encouraged them, and hid the items from the constable. John Best accused Jerseyan Nathaniel Beadle of receiving stolen money from "Black Dick," the slave of merchant William Browne, when, in fact, Dick claimed that it was Best who had encouraged him to steal from his master. The courts rarely accepted these excuses and, as with other non-English residents, the decisions did not discriminate against Jerseyans. In the dispute between John Brock and John Waldron, for instance, most of the deponents, English and Jersey alike, supported Brock's account of the incident, and many accused Constable Waldron of being drunk. Thus, even though Jerseyans had reputations for resisting authority and were frequently suspected of partiality toward countrymen, if not outright dishonesty, disputes did not necessarily create divisions along national lines, which is similar to the experiences of other non-English settlers.[61]

Many other Jerseyans were hauled before the court and charged with disrespect for religion, stealing from their masters, and "unseemly behavior" toward women. For instance, Thomas Baker, servant to Nathaniel Wells, was accused in 1678 of laughing during minister William Hubbard's sermon, for which he was "admonished." Abel Osier was presented for "carry[ing] himself very lasciviously" toward two of his fellow servants in magistrate Bartholomew Gedney's household. Perhaps these men were simply young and unwilling to accept local standards of conduct, or as servants in prominent households their masters were more likely to report misbehavior. Yet for all of these incidents, Jerseyans also participated in the larger community—Osier, for instance, died fighting in King Philip's War.[62]

Jerseyans also tended to be less willing than other non-English residents to accept the authority of Massachusetts officials. They appeared in court frequently for contempt of authority and reviling religion; such cases constituted almost a third of the court actions involving residents from Jersey that were not related to debt (as compared to composing about 15 percent of the court actions against Scottish and Irish residents).[63] Constables in particular seemed to offend natives of Jersey, especially with their power to collect taxes, close the pubs at night, and order fulfillment of watch duty. Many Jersey Islanders appeared in court for attacking constables in the course of their duties, for refusing to accept their authority, and for using "opprobrious" or "reviling" language toward them. In addition to the altercation between John Brock and John Waldron, Edward Feveryeare had "use[d] many aprobious vilifying speeches" to constable William Lake when he asked for the minister's rate in 1674. Likewise, in 1679 Nathaniel Beadle called constable William Curtis a "pitifull Cur" and "foole" when Curtis asked him to pay his minister's rate, and made "scornfull speeches" when Curtis tried to warn him out of the tavern later that evening. Beadle was also accused of helping Nicholas and Jacob Manning avoid arrest by John Williams, the marshal's deputy, in 1680.[64]

Nevertheless, like other non-English residents of Essex County, Jerseyans served on juries and even as constables, participating in the activities of the larger community. Brothers Nathaniel, Samuel, and Thomas Beadle served as constables in 1677 and on juries eight times from 1672 to 1685, and Edward Feveryear served on juries twice in the 1680s. In addition, Samuel and Thomas Beadle served in King Philip's War, where Samuel was injured so badly that he could not resume his trade as a turner and successfully petitioned the court to allow him to keep a tavern as compensation. Benjamin Mazury, Abel Osier, Thomas Baker, John Vowden, and Thomas Vealey also served in the war. For all the mistrust that characterized their relations with some of their neighbors, Jerseyans, like other non-English, were not outcast or marginalized.[65]

FRENCH COLONIALS IN EARLY MASSACHUSETTS

French residents also began to settle in Massachusetts at a relatively early date, and increased their presence dramatically after the revocation of the Edict of

Nantes in 1685. These immigrants largely settled in Boston or in separate agricultural villages on the frontier. The frontier towns were quite clearly an attempt to maintain a separate French identity in the English colony, but Huguenots in Boston also expressed aspects of their religion and culture. A brief examination of these French refugees illustrates some important distinctions between the Huguenot reception in seventeenth-century Massachusetts and the experiences of other non-English groups.

Huguenots settled Frenchtown in the Narragansett country in 1686, purchasing their land from the Atherton Company. The company consisted of Massachusetts and Connecticut merchants and political leaders who speculated in land and had been in a long dispute with Rhode Island over ownership of the territory. Rhode Island and Connecticut both claimed the land, but the proprietors preferred that it be governed by Connecticut, knowing that they would receive special treatment. The dispute raged for many years before finally being referred to the Crown for a decision. In 1687, Sir Edmund Andros, governor of the Dominion of New England, awarded the land to Rhode Island, thereby invalidating titles sold by the Atherton Company. Huguenot immigrants were caught in the middle of this dispute, one about which they knew little. Many of the most prominent men in Boston and Connecticut—including Fitz-John and Waitstill Winthrop, the sons of John Winthrop, Jr.; merchants Daniel Dennison, Edward and Elisha Hutchinson, Richard Wharton, and Simon Lynd; former Massachusetts governor Simon Bradstreet; and Boston magistrate John Saffin—were stockholders in the company. These people were in the best position to help indigent refugees, but also held a vested interest in selling and settling this territory. Thus Huguenots were left with questionable land titles, many of which conflicted with titles held by Rhode Islanders.[66]

The Huguenots retained unchallenged possession of their property for a few years. By 1689, however, land disputes arose again, and the outbreak of King William's War led to increased problems for French residents of the Narragansett country. The local militia commander, Major Richard Smith, and French minister Ezekiel Carré reported to Boston, "That the Inhabitants of Greenwich [Rhode Island] do insult over and are intended to offer some Violence to the People of the said French Plantation in forcing their Armes from them, laying open their enclosures and destroying their meadows." The Council ordered Rhode Islanders to refrain from abusing French residents, on the grounds that the English government would disapprove of their actions, and it asked that any differences between the two communities be resolved through the courts. Suspicions grew, however, as the war raged on. The next year, the Rhode Island government required the French to take an oath of allegiance to the English government, which they did without hesitation. Even this did not alleviate the suspicions and, in 1691, inhabitants of Greenwich and Kingstown, disregarding French claims to the area, disrupted the settlement by repeatedly tearing down fences around agricultural land. The Huguenots soon dispersed to Boston and New York. The combination of long-standing land disputes, intercolonial arguments, and European wars led to the disintegration of this French settlement.[67]

War between England and France also destroyed the Huguenot settlement at Oxford, founded in 1687. Oxford was a frontier town in central Massachusetts, just south of Worcester, and thus was exposed to attack in times of trouble. The moving force behind this town was Gabriel Bernon, a prominent merchant and promoter who lived primarily in Boston but had extensive land holdings in the new settlement. Bernon arranged to purchase the town site from a group of proprietors that included former Council president and future governor Joseph Dudley, along with several other prominent men in Massachusetts. The settlement grew steadily, constructing a gristmill, sawmill, and church, and by 1690 the town housed twenty-five to thirty families.[68]

The settlement had the support of important leaders in Massachusetts, and because Bernon had close ties to the Boston merchant community, residents faced few of the problems that beset their countrymen in Rhode Island. As an exposed frontier town, however, Oxford became a target when the war between France and England intensified in the 1690s. In 1694, the daughter of one settler was killed and two other children were captured by a band of Native Americans from Canada. After this, hostile bands of French and Indians appeared in the area frequently. Residents began to desert the settlement, including Isaac du Tuffeau, Bernon's agent, and minister Daniel Bondet. After a concerted Indian attack in August 1696, most of the remaining settlers left Oxford. Many families initially fled to Boston, but most soon moved to New Rochelle in New York. In 1699, Huguenots tried to resettle Oxford, but the village was dispersed again by attacks from the French and Indians.[69]

The settlements of Frenchtown and Oxford set French Protestants apart from other non-English residents in Massachusetts. Most non-English settlers remained in the densely populated coastal sections of the colony, primarily near the large port towns of Boston and Salem, and kept communities together within Puritan society. Only Huguenots tried to retain their culture through separate settlements. This may have been because of the historic friction between France and England, even though persecuted Huguenots had received a generous welcome in England and its colonies, or because the migration occurred within a few short years and many émigrés arrived in family groups.

They may also have believed it would be easier to retain their church structure and liturgy away from the larger settlements and to maintain French culture and traditions uninfluenced by a more diverse population.

The French church in Boston also became a touchstone for Huguenot identity. Founded in 1685, the church struggled for many years. Because the congregation could not always pay them adequately, ministers came and went. Wealthy Huguenot merchants supported the French church, but the poverty of many refugees kept overall contributions low. By 1700, several leading families had left the colony, including Gabriel Bernon, David Bassett, and René Grignon, and many others joined English churches. Pierre Bowdoin, John Foy, and Thomas Mallet all gave money to build King's Chapel, although the absence of membership records for this period makes it difficult to know whether they were actually church members. James and Ann LeBlond joined Boston's Second Church in 1690, as did Solomon LeGare in 1695. In 1726, Ann LeBlond transferred her church membership to the Brattle Street congregation.[70]

The members of the French church received many marks of favor from the colony and residents of Boston. Because church members could not afford to build their own meetinghouse, the General Court allowed the congregation to meet at the Boston Latin School. The French church also used its own liturgy and celebrated holidays. The Massachusetts law against celebrating Christmas and other religious days, instituted in 1659 to control "unruly" elements who still wished to observe traditional festival days, had been grudgingly removed from the books in 1681 by order of the English government. Samuel Sewall noted an increase in Christmas keeping thereafter, and in 1699 reprimanded a Mr. Newman for "partaking with the French church on the 25 December on account of its being Christmas-day, as they abusively call it." Thus even though staunch Puritans rejected and disliked these ceremonies, they were practiced openly by the end of the century.[71]

Whereas the French church represented persistence in Huguenot identity, membership in English churches provided political and economic benefits. King's Chapel had the support of the English government and royal officials in Massachusetts, which made it politic for those hoping for preferment to give to the building construction fund or to attend services, if not join the church outright. Similarly, attending or joining a Congregational church strengthened ties with these communities. Although their control over Massachusetts government was declining, many Puritans still held substantial political and economic influence in the colony. Huguenots may also have chosen to attend these churches as a means of blending into the dominant population, a survival mechanism learned from their years of persecution in France. Whatever the personal, political, or commercial reasons that Huguenots had for attending King's Chapel or a Congregational church, many merchants also felt obligated to support the French congregation until the 1740s, when the church disbanded. Much like members of the Scots' Charitable Society, no matter how closely tied Huguenots became to mercantile society in Massachusetts, they also used certain cultural traditions to develop an identity as French colonials.[72]

For the welcome, charity, and acceptance accorded Huguenot refugees, many Massachusetts residents still harbored suspicions about them. In 1692, the General Court proposed to make Huguenots take an oath of allegiance to William and Mary. The Court also wanted to take an inventory of French arms and ammunition, arresting French residents who "do not give a satisfactory account of themselves." The outcome of this resolution is not known. In 1704, Samuel Sewall presented a memorial to the governor and Council suggesting that "all the French-men residing in this Province, be Registered, and . . . That if at any time after, they be convicted of holding Correspondence with the French & Indian Enemy, they may without dispute, be proceeded with as English-men. . . . And that all French Roman Catholics, be forthwith made Prisoners of War." Sewall also recommended that the governments of other New England colonies be pressed to pass similar laws. Sewall offered this petition shortly after the attack on Deerfield, and it is not clear if Huguenot settlers of many years' residence were among those required to register.[73]

At this same time, however, Huguenots began to be elected to town offices in Boston. John Barber was chosen constable in 1704, although he refused the post and another man was elected in his place. Andrew Faneuil served as constable the same year, and James LeBlond was elected to the office in 1707. In addition, Barber and LeBlond served as tithing men in 1706 and 1709, respectively. Although these were minor offices and not highly prestigious, non-English merchants were frequently elected to them, and they represented a first step into public or political service. If the community truly distrusted Huguenots, these men would not have been able to participate in public affairs.[74]

Thus Huguenots, like other non-English migrants to Massachusetts in the seventeenth century, followed their own path to inclusion in colonial society. Although Massachusetts society has generally been described as English or Puritan, it in fact encompassed many groups of Europeans, as well as Native Americans and Africans. All these peoples contributed to the development of Massachusetts and to a more heterogeneous colonial society than had existed earlier in the century. The Puritan beginnings of the Bay Colony gave the region's history a distinct flavor, but by 1700 Massachusetts society cannot be described simply as "Puritan." The government was controlled by royal appointees, the population reflected those in many parts of the Atlantic world, toleration of Trinitarian Protestant denominations was official policy, and even the Congregational churches had relaxed their membership standards. Massachusetts had become part of the English, soon-to-be British, colonial system.

CONCLUSION:
INTO THE EIGHTEENTH CENTURY

By the early eighteenth century, Massachusetts society had changed dramatically. Settled initially as a refuge from the corruptions of English society, Massachusetts had been transformed into an Atlantic entrepôt, home to people from Europe, Africa, and North America. The English remained the largest segment of the population, but the old Puritan families had been pressured to relinquish much of their power and influence to merchants and royal officials. Among these newly influential groups, as well as within the laboring population, were immigrants from Scotland, Ireland, the Channel Islands, France, and their colonial-born children. The integration of these diverse peoples with the pre-dominantly English population was not without friction, but it had happened largely without violence until 1689. Yet such accommodation had not resulted in assimilation. Many non-English residents of Massachusetts had forged new colonial meanings for old national identities as part of the mix of communities and identities that developed from conditions in the colonial world. Men and women in early Massachusetts apparently had few problems thinking of them-selves as English, Irish, or Scottish as well as colonials and New Englanders. Through their relationships with countrymen and -women, communities of interest, and public service, they expressed loyalty to both their old and new homes. In many cases, colonial-born children also showed evidence of loyalties to their parents' native countries as well as to their own.

The development of local communities and wider networks of non-Puritan residents was the mechanism through which most of these settlers integrated themselves into Massachusetts society. Ironworkers, agricultural laborers, and merchants had all constructed networks, accommodating people with a variety of interests and nationalities. People, communication, and goods traveled across these networks, whether those networks were composed of Atlantic traders or Essex County fishermen. Darrett Rutman calls such networks a "social web," and the image is useful.[1] Instead of linear relationships among discrete settlements, diverse peoples intersected with one another at many different points. Colonists were connected to one another within layers of relationships that spread throughout the colony and later into the Atlantic world. These interlocking ties gave rise to shared colonial identities that transformed Massachusetts into a British space by the turn of the century.

The ability of early modern peoples to think of themselves as members of many communities—or to hold several different identities—should not be a surprise. Most people belong to many communities of interest simultaneously: members of a scholarly community, a political group, a religious organization, and a nationality. At times, these identities come into conflict. Early modern peoples were no different in this respect. They, too, thought of themselves as adherents of a religion, as citizens of a nation, and as members of a craft guild or profession. They also must have experienced times when these identities clashed. Yet the perspective of history tends to blur such events. A paucity of data, through the loss of both personal and official records, makes it difficult to recover the complexities of peoples' lives, particularly those of the "lower sorts." They are therefore viewed through larger lenses—as Puritans or Englishmen, in the case of early New England—thereby losing some of their nuance. Although the presence of several thousand non-Puritan settlers in seventeenth-century Massachusetts may not have made a difference in the political arena, it is important to know that they were there. It changes the modern understanding of the texture of life in the past—it was not just Englishmen jousting among themselves over open- or closed-field farming, political position, or religious rights. Englishmen also had to learn how to live with their Scottish, Irish, and French-speaking neighbors. In short, early modern peoples faced many of the same issues that we face today. The resolution of these issues, however, was different: although dissent and diversity were not celebrated, they did learn to live with one another, a development that accelerated adoption of a British provincial identity in the eighteenth century.

Only European residents of the Bay Colony and their descendants were researched for this study, but Native Americans and African Americans also contributed to the diversity of the colony. The experiences of these groups differed greatly from those of other non-Puritan residents. Although many settlers from Europe arrived as servants, voluntarily and involuntarily, their status as indentured servants with formal contracts was not the same as the long-term servitude and slavery experienced by Indians and Africans. Colonists from Europe also had legal and political rights not held by slaves or Indians. Native Americans and Africans were seen as "Others" and most Europeans attempted to regulate and subjugate them. In short, cultural differences among Scots, Huguenots, and English were far less pronounced than those among Europeans, Indians, and Africans. The provincial identity that developed over the course of the seventeenth century was a European identity, one that excluded these Others. Yet, however limited this European-based identity, it was never simply English or Puritan.[2]

The diversity of European society in Massachusetts can be seen in the social organizations and political alignments of the late seventeenth and early eighteenth centuries. The Ancient and Honorable Artillery Company, for example, had been chartered by the Massachusetts government in 1639 and membership became a prized indicator of social status in Boston. By the last quarter of the century, the organization also included non-English settlers and their sons. In 1675, for example, William Gibson, a shoemaker-merchant and member of the Scots' Charitable Society (scs), joined the Artillery Company. In 1682, John Ballantyne, the Boston-born son of Scottish immigrant William Ballantyne, both of whom were members of the scs, also joined. Thomas Mallet, who joined the company in 1685, was a Huguenot linen draper. Duncan Campbell became a member in 1686. A bookseller-merchant, postmaster, and member of the scs, Campbell cultivated royal appointments as well as friendships with supporters of the old charter government. John Borland, a prominent merchant originally from western Scotland, joined in 1692. James Fowle, who joined in 1693, was a tailor from Scotland. He arrived in Boston in 1681 and joined the Scots' Charitable Society in 1684. All these men also held many town offices in Boston.[3]

Second- and third-generation Massachusettsans of non-English descent also became members of the Artillery Company. John Ballantyne, Jr., the son and grandson of John and William, joined the company in 1694. He served as scavenger in Boston several times in the 1710s, was appointed justice of the peace in 1724, and sat in the Massachusetts legislature in 1726, as well as holding military commissions. He also married Mary, the daughter of Adam Winthrop, thereby joining one of New England's first families. David and Sampson Dewer, the sons and grandsons of merchants Sampson and Thomas, became members of the company in 1695 and 1718, respectively. All four men were members of the Scots' Charitable Society. John Buchanan (admitted in 1695) was the Boston-born son of John and Moer Bowhanno, Scottish and Irish servants who came to Massachusetts before 1658. Grafton Feveryear (1717) was descended from a Jersey Island family in Salem. Andrew and Nathaniel Cunningham, the sons of Andrew and Sarah Gibson Cunningham (the daughter of William Gibson), joined the company in 1720, and both men held prestigious town and colony offices throughout their lives. Andrew Cunningham served as a captain in the militia, and as constable and collector of taxes. Nathaniel was also a militia captain and constable, and served on many committees appointed by the Boston selectmen to regulate the marketplace. In 1739, he was a representative to the General Court. Moses DeChamps, a member of the company in 1737, was the son or grandson of Huguenot refugee Moses DeChamps.[4]

Most of these men served in town and colony offices throughout the late seventeenth and early eighteenth centuries. Although, as we have seen, non-Puritan settlers had served in minor offices since the late 1640s, political changes in England and New England after 1660 made the participation of non-Puritan settlers in local and colonial government more commonplace. After the Restoration, merchants from England, Scotland, France, and the Channel Islands began moving to Boston to take advantage of commercial opportunities. These merchants were joined by an ever-increasing number of political appointees sent by the English government to ensure colonial acquiescence to imperial rule. Merchants saw a chance, by supporting the royal government and its officers, to break the hold of the old Puritan elite on Massachusetts institutions. Although political changes occurred slowly between 1660 and 1685, the imposition of the Dominion of New England in 1686 hastened the transition. Political events after 1686—the installation of the Dominion government, its overthrow during the Glorious Revolution, the return to charter rule, and finally royal government under the new charter of 1691—brought new alliances to Massachusetts.[5]

Political coalitions shifted frequently in the final years of the century, uniting, however briefly, men of different backgrounds and religious denominations. Richard Johnson characterizes these "parties" as "a country persuasion suspicious of the ways of royal government and two fluid groups of office seekers distinguished from each other more by the fact of their success or failure than by their attachment to ideological issues."[6] Even the "country party" came to accept the fact of royal government and learned to work within the system to further its own policies. Thus members of old Puritan families and non-Puritan merchants and politicians can be found on all sides of the issues.

In 1686, magistrates, deputies, merchants, and landowners split into two primary factions. One group opposed the restructuring of government and the loss of colonial boundaries implicit in the Dominion of New England. The other group recognized the advantages of working within the new political structure and developing closer ties to England. When the Dominion fell in 1689, the first faction advocated the reestablishment of the old charter government, whereas the second group wanted to work with William and Mary to develop a more representative government. Yet in neither case did these factions break down along Puritan and non-Puritan lines. Members of old Puritan families, such as Joseph Dudley, joined later arrivals led by Richard Wharton to establish royal government in the colony. Waitstill and Fitz-John Winthrop, representatives of an old Puritan family, initially supported the Dominion but switched their allegiance to the charter party by the early 1690s. Non-Puritan residents also fell on all sides of the political divides. Scottish merchant Mungo Crawford was among those arrested and jailed for supporting Edmund Andros, governor under the Dominion, whereas fellow Scots Archibald Ferguson of Marblehead and John Ballantyne of Boston supported the overthrow of the Dominion and the reestablishment of the old charter government. Huguenot Pierre Bowdoin supported the arrest of Andros, but not government under the old charter.[7]

The careers of English merchants and officials offer similar evidence of shifting alliances at the turn of the century. Nathaniel Byfield was the son of a dissenting minister in England and came to New England in 1674. He held minor offices in Bristol County (on the Massachusetts–Rhode Island border) under the Dominion, but by 1692 had moved to Boston to join his brother-in-law Jahleel Brenton, the customs collector. As a member of the House of Representatives, Byfield opposed governor William Phips and supported Joseph Dudley in his attempt to regain the governorship in the 1690s. He fell out with Dudley in 1710 and soon thereafter went to England to obtain the governorship for himself. This attempt failed, and Dudley stripped Byfield of his offices. Byfield later made an alliance with Elisha Cooke, Jr., a member of the opposition, or "country," party in the House.[8]

In the latter half of the century, many new immigrants to Boston, such as Byfield, continued to take advantage of their contacts with England to further their interests in New England. Peter Lidget moved from Barbados to Boston around 1650 and became heavily invested in the mast trade. He had extensive connections with London merchants and naval office officials. His son Charles, born in Boston in 1650, became very active in Massachusetts politics and supported the Dominion government. Charles also was a founder of King's Chapel. Yet through marriages with the Usher and Shrimpton families, the Lidgets became connected to many of the old Puritan families in the colony, including the Hutchinsons, Stoddards, and Tyngs.[9]

Merchant Francis Foxcroft followed a similar path. Foxcroft arrived in Boston in 1665, and later joined the Anglican church and supported the Dominion government. He signed a petition in 1690 asking William and Mary to reestablish .royal government in the colony, but then, as a member of the House of Representatives, opposed governor William Phips. Yet he married the daughter of former old-charter governor John Danforth and later settled on Danforth's Cambridge estate. Foxcroft was reappointed to public office by Joseph Dudley.[10]

One last example of the mixing of political, social, and religious allegiances at the turn of the century comes from the experiences of Giles Dyer. Dyer arrived in Boston before 1673 and, like many post-Restoration merchants, joined the Anglican church when it was founded. He also served as an officer in the militia, and as tithing man, assessor, selectman, and sheriff. He supported the Dominion government, holding several of his offices during this period, and petitioned for the continuation of royal government after its fall. He, too, opposed William Phips and later was restored to office by Joseph Dudley. At Dyer's death in 1713, his family asked Samuel Sewall to be a pallbearer. Sewall agonized over his decision, but finally declined the honor because he could not bring himself to enter King's Chapel for the service, although he did walk in the funeral procession and accepted the family's gift of gloves. Lidget, Foxcroft, and Dyer were members of the Ancient and Honorable Artillery Company, as were Elisha Cooke, Jr., Nathaniel Byfield, Joseph Dudley, and Samuel Sewall.[11]

Non-Puritan settlers and their descendants continued to serve town and colony in numerous offices. Scot and scs member Archibald Ferguson became a selectman of Marblehead (in 1689 and later) and member of the House of Representatives. Francis Borland (son of John) served as a constable in Boston (in 1719 and later), as did Huguenots Daniel Johonnot (in 1717 and later) and Andrew Sigorney (in 1720 and later). Grafton Feveryear moved to Boston from Salem and became a clerk of the market (in 1715 and later). John Buchanan, son of John and Moer Bowhanno, held several offices in Boston, such as tithing man, scavenger, and constable from 1700 onward, as did Benjamin Gibson, son of William (tithing man, constable, and clerk of the market from 1706). Solomon Kneeland, son of John, served as tithing man, clerk of the market, and constable from 1706, and William Webster, son of John and Mary (Hay) Webster, a Scottish and Irish family, held the offices of constable, tithing man, viewer of shingles, and measurer of planks and timber from 1709. John Ballantyne was appointed to a committee that drafted a Charter of Incorporation for Boston in 1708, and began serving as register for the Suffolk County Court in 1715.[12]

For all their participation in local affairs, however, most non-English merchants distanced themselves from the political troubles of the final two decades of the seventeenth century, generally avoiding positions in colonial govern-ment.[13] By the 1720s and 1730s, however, non-English colonists and their sons and grandsons served in a wide variety of colonial offices. James Bowdoin and William Foy, from Huguenot and Jersey families, respectively, became members of the Governor's Council in the mid-1700s, and Foy served as treasurer of the colony. Bowdoin's descendants became governors of Massachusetts and New Hampshire. Like the sons and daughters of immigrants in later centuries, these men and women were fully part of the social and political structure that their parents helped create.[14]

Thus in 1693, when William Phips lost his temper and declared that French sailors were "as good or better Englishmen" than Jahleel Brenton, the New England–born collector of customs, his words captured the changes that had occurred in Massachusetts over the course of the past sixty years of European settlement. Phips most likely used the phrase in an imperial sense, which is to say that Huguenot merchants and colonial-born royal officials were equally good subjects of the English government. As we have seen, however, non-Puritan residents had also become full members of Massachusetts society.

Phips's statement also reflected the expectations of non-English residents of Massachusetts by the end of the century. Benjamin Faneuil approached the governor on equal terms in defense of a French ship and crew. He received Phips's acquiescence, and the ship's captain was allowed to dock and unload the cargo. As a Boston merchant, Faneuil expected the support of the Massachusetts government regardless of his place of birth. Opposition came from the New England–born royal official, Jahleel Brenton, who was charged with enforcing the Navigation Acts. Thus foreign-born residents of the English colonies saw themselves as good imperial subjects and upstanding inhabitants of the colony. Over the course of sixty years, non-English residents had demonstrated that they had much to contribute to the old Puritan Commonwealth.

The confrontation between Phips and Brenton illustrates one of the over-riding divisions in Massachusetts society at the end of the seventeenth century. These men behaved in ways that supported their personal interests, whether those were colonial, imperial, or commercial. National or religious background had little to do with these interests. Faneuil was as French as the ship's crew in terms of birth and culture. As for his religion, he attended the Anglican King's Chapel but supported the Calvinist Huguenot church in Boston. Phips, a New England native, had been appointed governor by William and Mary, but only at the behest of Increase Mather, a Puritan minister who nevertheless saw the need to work with the English government. Phips was pulled between his loyalty to Massachusetts and to the Crown. Brenton, who came from Rhode

Island, also held a royal appointment, but his primary allegiance was to the English government.[15]

By 1700, Massachusetts did not look all that different from England's other North American colonies. The Bay Colony had a royal government, a diverse population, and economic and social stratification. Puritanism colored the colony's institutions and social values, but Massachusetts had ceased to be the "Puritan Commonwealth." Historians have found many reasons for these changes: political pressure from England, the rise of commerce, and declension from the religious standards of the founders. This study has examined one other cause—the presence of non-Puritan residents in the colony. These settlers brought badly needed skills and capital to the colony, and thus were able to negotiate with Puritan leaders to maintain some of their cultural traditions and social ideals. They did not assimilate into Puritan society and they were not marginalized. They participated in the social and political institutions of the colony, but did not necessarily accept Puritan ideology. In this way, these non-Puritan residents helped to shape Massachusetts society.

Appendix

POPULATION ESTIMATES

The following population estimates for non-Puritan residents in coastal Massachusetts (Suffolk, Essex, and Middlesex counties) were compiled from many records, including those of the Essex County Quarterly Courts, the published volumes of the *Boston Town Records*, the Suffolk Files at the Massachusetts Archives, the Middlesex County (Pulsifer Transcript) collection at the Massachusetts Archives, the two published volumes of the Suffolk County Quarterly Courts records, and various town records, vital statistics, and local histories. All these sources are cited in the text and in the bibliography.

Although non-Puritans represent a small proportion of the population of the colony, the figures below are conservative estimates. They include only those people that I can directly link to one of the communities discussed in the book (and therefore do not include fishermen or religious dissenters; see the introduction for these groups). There are many others in the colony whom I suspect were not English or Puritan, but I do not have enough information to be certain. I am also certain that I have not identified all non-English, non-Puritan residents. The first number in the non-Puritan list is the actual count; the number in parentheses is a family count, using six as the multiplier (see Greene and Harrington, *American Population Before the Federal Census of 1790*, xxiii).

Population (Europeans only)		
	Population Totals	Non-Puritans
Massachusetts in 1654	approx. 16,000	
Massachusetts in 1690	approx. 50,000	approx. 313 (1,878)
Suffolk County in 1690	approx. 10,700	approx. 95 (570)*
Boston in 1674	approx. 4,000	
Boston in 1690	approx. 6,000	approx. 91 (546)
Braintree in 1690	approx. 695	approx. 2 (12)

Population (Europeans only) (*continued*)

	Population Totals	Non-Puritans
Essex County in 1690	approx. 7,225	approx. 175 (1,050)
Ipswich in 1690	approx. 875	approx. 15 (90)
Lynn in 1690 (including Saugus)	approx. 600	approx. 87 (522)
Marblehead in 1690		
(not including fisher families)	approx. 1,030	approx. 5 (30)
Newbury in 1690	approx. 1,000	approx. 6 (36)
Salem in 1678	approx. 1,200	
Salem in 1690	approx. 2,000	approx. 48 (288)
Topsfield in 1690	approx. 375	approx. 6 (36)
Wenham in 1690	approx. 350	approx. 6 (36)
Middlesex County in 1690	approx. 9,320	approx. 32 (192)
Cambridge in 1688	approx. 764	approx. 9 (54)
Charlestown in 1690	approx. 980	approx. 14 (70)
Reading in 1690	approx. 375	approx. 3 (18)
Woburn in 1690	approx. 710	approx. 3 (18)
Plymouth Colony in 1690	approx. 6,960	approx. 4 (24)
Taunton in 1684	approx. 264	approx. 3 (18)

* Several towns in each county had only one non-Puritan identified. These have been included in the county totals but not listed separately.

Sources for overall population figures: Evarts B. Greene and Virginia D. Harrington, *American Population Before the Federal Census of 1790* (New York: Columbia University Press, 1932; reprint, Gloucester, Mass.: Peter Smith, 1966), 13–22; Richard P. Gildrie, "Salem Society and Politics in the 1680s," *Essex Institute Historical Collections* 114, no. 4 (1978): 185–206; and Edward M. Cook, Jr., *The Fathers of the Towns: Leadership and Community Structure in Eighteenth-Century New England* (Baltimore: Johns Hopkins University Press, 1976), 194–95.

Notes

NOTES TO INTRODUCTION

1. Sworn Statement of William Hill and Henry Franklin, 4 September 1694, Photostat Collection, Massachusetts Historical Society, Boston, Massachusetts (hereafter Photostat Coll., MHS); and Deposition of Benjamin Faneuil, 4 September 1694, Photostat Coll., MHS.

2. Richard R. Johnson, *Adjustment to Empire: The New England Colonies, 1675–1715* (New Brunswick: Rutgers University Press, 1981), 228–29, 278–82; and Emerson W. Baker and John G. Reid, *The New England Knight: Sir William Phips, 1651–1695* (Toronto: University of Toronto Press, 1998), 159–61, 227–29.

3. See, for example, Darrett Rutman, *Winthrop's Boston: A Portrait of a Puritan Town, 1630–1649* (Chapel Hill: University of North Carolina Press, 1965; reprint, New York: Norton, 1972), 184–86; and Francis J. Bremer, *John Winthrop: America's Forgotten Founding Father* (Oxford: Oxford University Press, 2003), 343–47. The French overtures, first by Charles de Saint Etienne de La Tour and then by Charles de Menon, Sieur d'Aulnay de Charnise, were part of their dispute over control of Acadia. Nevertheless, contact with French settlers in North America was established very early.

4. Nathaniel B. Shurtleff, ed., *Records of the Governor and Company of the Massachusetts Bay in New England* (Boston: William White, 1853; reprint, New York: Arno, 1968), 2:109 (hereafter *Mass. Recs.*).

5. Throughout this book, the term "non-Puritan" is used to denote involuntary or economic migrants who came to Massachusetts with little connection to the religious motives of the founding generation. Calvinist refugees, primarily from France but also from Scotland, are also included in this term. Although their religious beliefs were similar to those of the Puritans, they were seen as different because of their nationality. "Puritan," then, is used to refer to members of the old families, those who settled early in the colony's history. I do not use these terms explicitly to identify confessional loyalty. The distinction is more about family status than religious affiliation. The lines between Puritan and non-Puritan cannot always be clearly defined, which underscores the argument of this study about the complexity of early Massachusetts society.

6. M. Halsey Thomas, ed., *The Diary of Samuel Sewall* (New York: Farrar, Straus and Giroux, 1973), 1:406, 494; 2:1000. Anglicans also celebrated Christmas, a trend that gained acceptance among Congregational churches by the early eighteenth century, and which deeply disturbed Samuel Sewall. For Christmas celebrations, see Stephen Nissenbaum, *The Battle for Christmas* (New York: Knopf, 1997), 3–26.

7. See chapter 2 for more on the Saugus ironworks. See also James E. McWilliams, *Building the Bay Colony: Local Economy and Culture in Early Massachusetts* (Charlottesville:

University of Virginia Press, 2007), 63–74. McWilliams writes, "Not only did foreigners work in the local economy without undermining Puritanical values but they helped Puritan pioneers to continue their traditional communal habits while interacting with one another on a more routine basis" (74).

8. T. C. Smout, *Scottish Trade on the Eve of Union, 1660–1701* (Edinburgh: Oliver and Boyd, 1963), 90–115.

9. See James H. Kettner, *The Development of American Citizenship, 1608–1870* (Chapel Hill: University of North Carolina Press, 1978), 16–28, 68–69, 86–87; Brian P. Levack, *The Formation of the British State: England, Scotland, and the Union, 1603–1707* (Oxford: Oxford University Press, 1987), 51–53, 183–84; and James S. Hart and Richard J. Ross, "The Ancient Constitution in the Old World and the New," in *The World of John Winthrop: Essays on England and New England, 1588–1649*, ed. Francis J. Bremer and Lynn A. Botelho (Boston: Massachusetts Historical Society, 2005), 237–89.

10. Robert Emmet Wall, Jr., "The Decline of the Massachusetts Franchise, 1647–1666," *Journal of American History* 59, no. 2 (1972): 303–10; T. H. Breen, "Who Governs: The Town Franchise in Seventeenth-Century Massachusetts," *William and Mary Quarterly* 27, no. 3 (1970): 460–74; and Stephen Foster, "The Massachusetts Franchise in the Seventeenth Century," *William and Mary Quarterly* 24, no. 4 (1967): 613–23.

11. For modern syntheses discussing the diversity of the population, see, for example, Joseph A. Conforti, *Saints and Strangers: New England in British North America* (Baltimore: Johns Hopkins University Press, 2006); and Richard Archer, *Fissures in the Rock: New England in the Seventeenth Century* (Hanover: University Press of New England, 2001). As early as 1936, scholars noted the presence of non-English residents in late seventeenth- and early eighteenth-century New England. See, for example, Clifford Shipton, "Immigration to New England, 1680–1740," *Journal of Political Economy* 44, no. 2 (1936): 225–39. Shipton argues that most seventeenth-century immigrants assimilated into Puritan culture and played little role in the development of society. His study focuses on the early eighteenth century, though, when immigration, particularly from Ireland and Scotland, had increased noticeably and led to tension in the colony. In the 1730s and 1740s, economic conditions in Massachusetts deteriorated, and the treatment of non-English immigrants worsened as well. In 1938, Carl Bridenbaugh noted the increase in immigration to Boston in the early 1700s and the rise of nativist sentiment. Carl Bridenbaugh, *Cities in the Wilderness: The First Century of Urban Life in America, 1625–1742*, 2d ed. (New York: Knopf, 1960), 250. As we shall see, the situation for non-Puritan laborers in the last half of the seventeenth century was rather different.

12. Daniel Vickers, *Farmers and Fishermen: Two Centuries of Work in Essex County, Massachusetts, 1630–1850* (Chapel Hill: University of North Carolina Press, 1994), 156; Christine Leigh Heyrman, *Commerce and Culture: The Maritime Communities of Colonial Massachusetts* (New York: Norton, 1984), 45, 223; Richard P. Gildrie, "Salem Society and Politics in the 1680s," *Essex Institute Historical Collections* 114, no. 4 (1978): 188–89; and Richard P. Gildrie, *Salem, Massachusetts, 1626–1683: A Covenant Community* (Charlottesville: University Press of Virginia, 1975), 163. Proper observation of the Sabbath, according to Puritans, included minimal work—only necessary chores—and attendance at formal services. Puritans rejected the reading of set services, such as those required by the Church of England, making it unlikely that captains regularly read services to their crews.

13. For non-Puritan mercantile families, see chapter 4; Bernard Bailyn, *The New England Merchants in the Seventeenth Century* (Cambridge: Harvard University Press,

1955); David Thomas Konig, "A New Look at the Essex 'French': Ethnic Frictions and Community Tensions in Seventeenth-Century Essex County, Massachusetts," *Essex Institute Historical Collections* 110, no. 3 (1974): 167–80; and Phyllis Whitman Hunter, *Purchasing Identity in the Atlantic World: Massachusetts Merchants, 1670–1780* (Ithaca: Cornell University Press, 2001).

14. See Neil Kamil, *Fortress of the Soul: Violence, Metaphysics, and Material Life in the Huguenots' New World, 1517–1751* (Baltimore: Johns Hopkins University Press, 2005); J. F. Bosher, "Huguenot Merchants and the Protestant International in the Seventeenth Century," *William and Mary Quarterly* 52, no. 1 (1995): 77–102; and Jon Butler, *The Huguenots in America: A Refugee People in New World Society* (Cambridge: Harvard University Press, 1983). The international connections of Protestant merchants attracted many non-Puritan, yet Calvinist, families to Massachusetts. This point is developed further in chapter 4. See also chapter 5 for more on the agricultural villages in central Massachusetts and Rhode Island.

15. See chapters 3 and 5 for more about these families.

16. Although African slaves were far more common in the Chesapeake colonies and the West Indies in the seventeenth century, and thus slavery in these regions has received far more attention from historians, many scholars have discussed slavery in early New England. See, for example, Lorenzo J. Greene, *The Negro in Colonial New England, 1620–1776* (New York: Columbia University Press, 1942; reprint, Port Washington, N.Y.: Kennikat, 1966); Robert C. Twombly and Robert H. Moore, "Black Puritan: The Negro in Seventeenth-Century Massachusetts," *William and Mary Quarterly* 24, no. 2 (April 1967): 224–42; Winthrop D. Jordan, *White over Black: American Attitudes Toward the Negro, 1550–1812* (Chapel Hill: University of North Carolina Press, 1968); A. Leon Higginbotham, *In the Matter of Color: Race and the American Legal Process: The Colonial Period* (Oxford: Oxford University Press, 1978); William D. Piersen, *Black Yankees: The Development of an Afro-American Subculture in Eighteenth-Century New England* (Amherst: University of Massachusetts Press, 1988); and Joann P. Melish, *Disowning Slavery: Gradual Emancipation and "Race" in New England, 1780–1860* (Ithaca: Cornell University Press, 1998).

17. William Wood, *New England's Prospect* (London, 1634; reprint, Boston: Prince Society, 1865), 86; John Josselyn, "An Account of Two Voyages to New England" (London, 1675; reprint, *Collections of the Massachusetts Historical Society*, 3d ser., 3 [1833]: 211–354), note about Africans, 231; Emanuel Downing to John Winthrop, August 1645, *Winthrop Papers* (Boston: Massachusetts Historical Society, 1943–47), 5:38–39; *Mass. Recs.*, 3:397; Thomas, *Diary of Samuel Sewall*; and Richard S. Dunn, James Savage, and Laetitia Yeandle, eds., *The Journal of John Winthrop, 1630–1649* (Cambridge: Harvard University Press, 1996), 347. Population figures for Europeans in seventeenth-century Massachusetts are difficult to compile, and those for Africans even more so. See, however, the numbers compiled by Lorena Walsh, "The African American Population of the Colonial United States," in *A Population History of North America*, ed. Michael R. Haines and Richard H. Steckel (Cambridge: Cambridge University Press, 2000), 191–239; and John J. McCusker, "Colonial Statistics," in *Historical Statistics of the United States: Earliest Times to the Present*, ed. Susan B. Carter et al. (Cambridge: Cambridge University Press, 2006), 5:627–772, especially 651–53. John Gorham Palfrey quotes a letter by Simon Bradstreet in 1679 claiming that about 120 Africans lived in Massachusetts, and McCusker cites 170. Bradstreet also said that this equaled the number of Scots in the colony and was about twice as large as the number of

Irish. The numbers of Scots and Irish were considerably larger than this, as shall be shown below. John Gorham Palfrey, *History of New England* (Boston: Little, Brown, 1858; reprint, New York: AMS, 1966), 3:334–35.

18. For Native Americans and New England settlers, see, for example, Neal Salisbury, "Red Puritans: The 'Praying Indians' of Massachusetts Bay and John Eliot," *William and Mary Quarterly* 31, no. 1 (1974): 27–54; S. F. Cook, *The Indian Population of New England in the Seventeenth Century* (Berkeley and Los Angeles: University of California Press, 1976), 9; Neal Salisbury, *Manitou and Providence: Indians, Europeans, and the Making of New England, 1500–1643* (Oxford: Oxford University Press, 1982), for Plymouth's actions at Wessagusset, see 125–34; Edward Byers, *The Nation of Nantucket: Society and Politics in an Early American Commercial Center, 1660–1820* (Boston: Northeastern University Press, 1987); Jean M. O'Brien, *Dispossession by Degrees: Indian Land and Identity in Natick, Massachusetts, 1650–1790* (Cambridge: Cambridge University Press, 1997); Jill Lepore, *The Name of War: King Philip's War and the Origins of American Identity* (New York: Knopf, 1999); William S. Simmons, "Conversion from Indian to Puritan," in *New England Encounters: Indians and Euroamericans, c. 1600–1850*, ed. Alden T. Vaughan (Boston: Northeastern University Press, 1999), 181–204; Ann Marie Plane, *Colonial Intimacies: Indian Marriage in Early New England* (Ithaca: Cornell University Press, 2000); and Jenny Hale Pulsipher, *Subjects unto the Same King: Indians, English, and the Contest for Authority in Colonial New England* (Philadelphia: University of Pennsylvania Press, 2005). This list is by no means exhaustive.

19. Carla Gardina Pestana, *Quakers and Baptists in Colonial Massachusetts* (Cambridge: Cambridge University Press, 1991); and Carla Gardina Pestana, "The Social World of Salem: William King's 1681 Blasphemy Trial," *American Quarterly* 41, no. 2 (1989): 308–27. Quaker presentments appear throughout the Essex County Quarterly Court records as well. Salem was, of course, the earliest Puritan settlement in Massachusetts and had established its church before the Great Migration began in 1630. This church was always rather independent, attracting Roger Williams, George Burroughs, and other slightly unorthodox ministers. Christine Heyrman also connects several witchcraft accusations in 1692 to associates and family members of Quakers (although the accused were not Quakers themselves), indicating the depth of suspicion of Quakers throughout the seventeenth century. Heyrman, *Commerce and Culture*, chapter 3; and Heyrman, "Specters of Subversion, Societies of Friends: Dissent and the Devil in Provincial Essex County, Massachusetts," in *Saints and Revolutionaries*, ed. David D. Hall, John M. Murrin, and Thad W. Tate (New York: Norton, 1984), 38–74. The suspicion of Quakers also illustrates the permeability of the boundaries between Puritans and non-Puritans, since many Quakers converted from orthodox Puritanism. Religious conversion changed their status in society even though most were English.

20. Pestana, *Quakers and Baptists in Colonial Massachusetts*, 44, 49–50.

21. As can be seen in the footnotes above, many excellent books and articles have been written about fishermen, Quakers, Baptists, Native Americans, and Africans. This book therefore focuses on early economic immigrants from Britain, Ireland, and Europe, who have in general received far less attention from scholars. Although a large literature on Huguenots does exist, they are included here because they were so highly integrated into the mercantile economy of the late seventeenth century.

22. Karen Ordahl Kupperman, "Thomas Morton, Historian," *New England Quarterly* 50, no. 4 (1977): 660–64; Jack Dempsey, *Thomas Morton of Merrymount: The Life and Renaissance of an Early American Poet* (Stoneham, Mass.: Jack Dempsey, 2000);

Philip F. Gura, "The Radical Ideology of Samuel Gorton: New Light on the Relation of English to American Puritanism," *William and Mary Quarterly* 36, no. 1 (1979): 78–100; and Philip F. Gura, *A Glimpse of Sion's Glory: Puritan Radicalism in New England, 1620–1660* (Middletown: Wesleyan University Press, 1984), 276–303. Gura argues that Gorton helped shape the New England Way by taking some beliefs to an extreme, thereby allowing less radical Puritans to define orthodoxy.

23. Emery Battis, *Saints and Sectaries: Anne Hutchinson and the Antinomian Controversy in the Massachusetts Bay Colony* (Chapel Hill: University of North Carolina Press, 1962); and Michael P. Winship, *The Times and Trials of Anne Hutchinson* (Lawrence: University Press of Kansas, 2005). Roger Williams maintained a correspondence with John Winthrop over the years. Winthrop even warned Williams of his impending arrest and banishment to England, giving him time to leave the colony for Narragansett Bay. Bremer, *John Winthrop*, 251–52.

24. Margaret E. Newell, "Robert Child and the Entrepreneurial Vision: Economy and Ideology in Early New England," *New England Quarterly* 68, no. 2 (1995): 223–56.

25. John J. Waters discusses some of these issues in "Hingham, Massachusetts, 1631–1661: An East Anglian Oligarchy in the New World," *Journal of Social History* 1, no. 4 (1968): 351–70. Many differences existed between East Anglian and West Country settlers in the town, yet these groups largely agreed on a Presbyterian-style church structure. Many Hingham settlers supported Robert Child in his dispute with colony leaders in Boston. Peter Hobart, minister of the Hingham church, also tended toward Presbyterianism and was used as an example by Edward Winslow to defend Massachusetts against the charges of Samuel Gorton. Edward Winslow, *Hypocrisie Unmasked* (London, 1646; reprint, New York: Burt Franklin, 1968), 99–100.

26. Shipton, "Immigration to New England," 226; Stephen Innes, *Creating the Commonwealth: The Economic Culture of Puritan New England* (New York: Norton, 1995), especially chapter 6; and David Thomas Konig, *Law and Society in Puritan Massachusetts: Essex County, 1629–1692* (Chapel Hill: University of North Carolina Press, 1979), 70. Although many early church records in Essex County have been lost, extant records, as well as those for Boston churches, indicate that although some non-Puritan immigrants joined Congregational churches, apparently most did not. Shipton focused mainly on upper-status immigrants, and, as we shall see, merchants after 1680 joined churches in greater numbers than did laborers of the 1640s and 1650s. By this time, church membership, whether Congregational or Anglican, brought important political and economic benefits.

27. Butler, *Huguenots in America*, 71. Huguenots were Calvinist, as were Puritans, and so their religious doctrines were similar, which aided the accommodation of French Protestants in Massachusetts. For political and economic reasons, however, many Huguenot merchants ended up supporting the Anglican King's Chapel after its founding 1686.

28. Konig, "A New Look at the Essex 'French,'" 167–80; and Konig, *Law and Society*, chapter 3. Massachusetts settlers were litigious to begin with, but Konig notes that Jersey bankruptcy laws encouraged a quick resort to the legal system to protect mercantile investments. See "A New Look," 173–74. For the development of the legal system in Massachusetts, see John M. Murrin, "The Legal Transformation: The Bench and Bar of Eighteenth-Century Massachusetts," in *Colonial America: Essays in Political and Social Development*, 2d ed., ed. Stanley A. Katz (Boston: Little, Brown, 1971), 415–49; and William E. Nelson, *Americanization of the Common Law: The Impact of Legal Change on Massachusetts Society, 1760–1830* (Cambridge: Harvard University Press, 1975), 36–45.

29. Williams was banished in 1635 for many reasons, including questioning the legality of the Massachusetts charter, advocating separation from the Church of England, criticizing clerical meetings as incipient Presbyterianism, and objecting to civil enforcement of religious doctrine, all of which undermined the New England Way. For a concise description of the events, see Bremer, *John Winthrop*, 249–51. Anne Hutchinson was banished in 1637 for her belief in free grace, for preaching to mixed assemblies of men and women, and for challenging the religious and civil leadership of Massachusetts. See Winship, *Times and Trials of Anne Hutchinson*.

30. For a general discussion of heterodoxy in Massachusetts, see Gura, *A Glimpse of Sion's Glory*; and Stephen Foster, *The Long Argument: English Puritanism and the Shaping of New England Culture, 1570–1700* (Chapel Hill: University of North Carolina Press, 1991). For the Ward quote, see Perry Miller, *The New England Mind: From Colony to Province* (Cambridge: Harvard University Press, 1953), 123. For William Pynchon, see Philip F. Gura, "'The Contagion of Corrupt Opinions' in Puritan Massachusetts: The Case of William Pynchon," *William and Mary Quarterly* 39, no. 3 (1982): 469–91; and Stephen Innes, *Labor in a New Land: Economy and Society in Seventeenth-Century Springfield* (Princeton: Princeton University Press, 1983), especially 14–16. A few ministers, such as Thomas Parker, James Noyes, and Peter Hobart instituted less restrictive (or "Presbyterical") membership requirements for their churches, but were allowed to keep their pulpits. See Harry Stout, *The New England Soul: Preaching and Religious Culture in Colonial New England* (Oxford: Oxford University Press, 1986), 52.

31. Darrett B. Rutman, "The Social Web: A Prospectus for the Study of Early American Community," in *Insights and Parallels: Problems and Issues of American Social History*, ed. William L. O'Neill (Minneapolis: Burgess Publishing, 1973), 57–89.

32. "Scotch Prisoners Sent to Massachusetts in 1652, by Order of the English Government," *New England Historical and Genealogical Register* 1 (1847): 377–80. Surname analysis can be useful for large-scale population estimates when figures are sketchy at best, but can be very misleading in a study like this one. I wanted to understand how non-Puritans of European descent shaped the development of Massachusetts; thus I had to be sure that the people I presented were either clearly not English, or if English, not Puritan. The English and the Scots share surnames, particularly in the border regions, and spelling cannot be a guide, given the lack of standardization in the seventeenth century. For English non-Puritans, I could not depend on status, such as servants, because of the emphasis that early settlers placed on obtaining godly servants. I therefore focused on ironworkers because New Englanders and their supporters in England considered most ironworkers licentious at best, and usually completely irreligious. For a discussion of surname analysis, see Forrest McDonald and Ellen Shapiro McDonald, "The Ethnic Origins of the American People, 1790," *William and Mary Quarterly* 37, no. 2 (1980): 179–99; Thomas L. Purvis, "The European Ancestry of the United States Population, 1790," *William and Mary Quarterly* 41, no. 1 (1984): 85–101; Donald H. Akenson, "Why the Accepted Estimates of the Ethnicity of the American People, 1790, Are Unacceptable," *William and Mary Quarterly* 41, no. 1 (1984): 102–19; and Thomas L. Purvis, Donald H. Akenson, Forest McDonald, and Ellen Shapiro McDonald, "Commentary," *William and Mary Quarterly* 41, no. 1 (1984): 119–35.

33. Common sailors, probably the most diverse group of people, also developed transatlantic networks, but are extremely difficult to trace in the seventeenth century. Extant records simply do not allow us to build any coherent picture about the lives of individual sailors in the way that merchants or captains can be followed.

NOTES TO CHAPTER 1

1. See Philip F. Gura, "The Radical Ideology of Samuel Gorton: New Light on the Relation of English to American Puritanism," *William and Mary Quarterly* 36, no. 1 (1979): 78–100; Philip F. Gura, *A Glimpse of Sion's Glory: Puritan Radicalism in New England, 1620–1660* (Middletown: Wesleyan University Press, 1984); Stephen Foster, *The Long Argument: English Puritanism and the Shaping of New England Culture, 1570–1700* (Chapel Hill: University of North Carolina Press, 1991); Janice Knight, *Orthodoxies in Massachusetts: Rereading American Puritanism* (Cambridge: Harvard University Press, 1994); and Michael P. Winship, *The Times and Trials of Anne Hutchinson* (Lawrence: University Press of Kansas, 2005).

2. Francis J. Bremer, *John Winthrop: America's Forgotten Founding Father* (Oxford: Oxford University Press, 2004), 197, 211–18, 245, 349, 351–52; and Darrett B. Rutman, *Winthrop's Boston: A Portrait of a Puritan Town, 1630–1649* (Chapel Hill: University of North Carolina Press, 1965; reprint, New York: Norton, 1972), 119–23, 167–69.

3. Louise A. Breen, *Transgressing the Bounds: Subversive Enterprises Among the Puritan Elite in Massachusetts, 1630–1692* (Oxford: Oxford University Press, 2001).

4. Bremer, *John Winthrop*, 238–39.

5. For critiques of the traditional imagery, see Stephen Nissenbaum, "New England as Region and Nation," in *All over the Map: Rethinking American Regions*, ed. Edward L. Ayres, Patricia Nelson Limerick, Stephen Nissenbaum, and Peter S. Onuf (Baltimore: Johns Hopkins University Press, 1996), 38–61; Joseph Wood, *The New England Village* (Baltimore: Johns Hopkins University Press, 1997); and Joseph A. Conforti, *Imagining New England: Explorations of Regional Identity from the Pilgrims to the Mid-Twentieth Century* (Chapel Hill: University of North Carolina Press, 2001). The outpouring of community studies from the late 1960s to the early 1980s dispelled many of these myths, although the structure of these studies reinforces the linkage between community and town. See, for example, Sumner Chilton Powell, *Puritan Village: The Formation of a New England Town* (Middletown: Wesleyan University Press, 1963); Kenneth A. Lockridge, *A New England Town: The First One Hundred Years*, expanded ed. (New York: Norton, 1970); Philip Greven, *Four Generations: Population, Land, and Family in Colonial Andover* (Ithaca: Cornell University Press, 1970); Stephen Innes, *Labor in a New Land: Economy and Society in Seventeenth-Century Springfield* (Princeton: Princeton University Press, 1983); and Christine Leigh Heyrman, *Commerce and Culture: The Maritime Communities of Colonial Massachusetts, 1690–1750* (New York: Norton, 1984).

6. A few of the regional studies have concentrated on counties, such as Daniel Vickers, *Farmers and Fishermen: Two Centuries of Work in Essex County, Massachusetts, 1630–1850* (Chapel Hill: University of North Carolina Press, 1994); and David Thomas Konig, *Law and Society in Puritan Massachusetts: Essex County, 1629–1692* (Chapel Hill: University of North Carolina Press, 1979), but the community studies generally focus on towns. See Thomas Bender, *Community and Social Change in America* (New Brunswick: Rutgers University Press, 1978; reprint, Baltimore: Johns Hopkins University Press, 1982), 11. Francis J. Bremer discusses similar ideas about community in terms of friendship and network theory in *Congregational Communion: Clerical Friendship in the Anglo-American Puritan Community, 1610–1692* (Boston: Northeastern University Press, 1994), 9–16.

7. Faren R. Siminoff, *Crossing the Sound: The Rise of Atlantic American Communities in Seventeenth-Century Eastern Long Island* (New York: New York University Press, 2004), 62–63.

8. Counties also constituted communities, particularly in a legal sense. Massachusetts created counties in 1643 and based the court system on county jurisdiction. Yet few people identified themselves as residents of a county—their primary identity and allegiance was to the town or village. Representation in the House of Deputies at the General Court was also divided by town. To trace the formation of new towns, see John Frederick Martin, *Profits in the Wilderness: Entrepreneurship and the Founding of New England Towns in the Seventeenth Century* (Chapel Hill: University of North Carolina Press, 1991); and William Francis Galvin, *Historical Data Relating to Counties, Cities, and Towns in Massachusetts* (Boston: Secretary of the Commonwealth and the New England Historic Genealogical Society, 1997). See also John M. Murrin, "Review Essay," *History and Theory* 11, no. 2 (1972): 226–75; and Mark DeWolfe Howe, "The Sources and Nature of Law in Colonial Massachusetts," in *Law and Authority in Colonial America*, ed. George Athan Billias (Barre, Mass.: Barre Publishers, 1965), 1–16, for the importance of counties.

9. See, for example, Alexander Bravand's estate inventory in George F. Dow and Mary G. Thresher, eds., *Records and Files of the Quarterly Courts of Essex County, Massachusetts* (Salem, Mass.: Essex Institute, 1911–75), 7:145 (hereafter *ECR*). The Scots' Charitable Society is discussed in chapter 5.

10. Steve Murdoch, *Network North: Scottish Kin, Commercial, and Covert Associations in Northern Europe, 1603–1746* (Leiden: Brill, 2006), 50–73; and Darrett B. Rutman, "The Social Web: A Prospectus for the Study of Early American Community," in *Insights and Parallels: Problems and Issues of American Social History*, ed. William L. O'Neill (Minneapolis: Burgess Publishing, 1973), 57–89.

11. For discussions of exogamous marriage, see, for example, Joyce D. Goodfriend, *Before the Melting Pot: Society and Culture in Colonial New York City, 1664–1730* (Princeton: Princeton University Press, 1992), 95–99; and Jon Butler, *Huguenots in America: A Refugee People in New World Society* (Cambridge: Harvard University Press, 1983), 80–82. Ned C. Landsman, in *Scotland and Its First American Colony, 1683–1765* (Princeton: Princeton University Press, 1985), 32–34, 159–60, also discusses exogamous marriage as a method of establishing extensive communities. James I tried to encourage marriages between English and Scots as one way to bind his two kingdoms together; see below. Brian P. Levack, *The Formation of the British State: England, Scotland, and the Union, 1603–1707* (Oxford: Oxford University Press, 1987), 186–87.

12. In the eighteenth century, other charitable societies based on nationality developed, such as the Charitable Irish Society, which was formed in 1737. The charity was intended "for the Relief of Poor, aged, and infirm Persons, and such as have been reduced by Sickness, Shipwrack, and other accidental Misfortunes." The membership was to consist of "all Irish Men, or of Irish Extraction," thereby including men of mixed national parentage. Charitable Irish Society, *The Constitution and By-laws of the Charitable Irish Society of Boston* (Boston: James F. Cotter, 1876), 22. For charity in early Massachusetts in general, see Peter Richard Virgadamo, "Colonial Charity and the American Character: Boston, 1630–1775" (Ph.D. diss., University of Southern California, 1982); and Conrad Edick Wright, *The Transformation of Charity in Postrevolutionary New England* (Boston: Northeastern University Press, 1992). By the end of the century, there were political and economic benefits in attending King's Chapel, established in 1686. At times, members of old Puritan families also supported King's; see chapter 5.

13. In her study of colonial New York, Joyce Goodfriend also notes the permeability of ethnic boundaries. Goodfriend, *Before the Melting Pot*, 178–80.

14. For a good overview of the development of British identity, see Ned C. Landsman, *From Colonials to Provincials: American Thought and Culture, 1680–1760* (New York: Twayne, 1997), 6, 7.

15. Jenny Wormald, "James VI, James I, and the Identity of Britain," in *The British Problem, c. 1534–1707: State Formation in the Atlantic Archipelago*, ed. Brendan Bradshaw and John Morrill (New York: St. Martin's Press, 1996), 148–71. Wormald also argues (159) that James's commitment to "Britishness" may have been "a vast smokescreen," and rather than creating a unitary state, he was trying to incorporate England and Ireland into "his ancient kingdom of Scotland." See also Levack, *The Formation of the British State*, 179–97.

16. English and Scottish influence in Ireland began much earlier than the reign of James VI and I, of course. The "Old English" settled in Ireland in the 1300s, generally had remained Catholic during the Reformation, and had ties to many Gaelic Irish clans. The "New English" settled during the reign of Elizabeth or later, were largely Protestant, and established plantations in Munster. Scots in the western part of the country had long-standing ties and conflicts with the Irish, particularly in Ulster, due to proximity, shared Celtic culture, and, after the Reformation, religious and political differences. Karl Bottigheimer, *Ireland and the Irish: A Short History* (New York: Columbia University Press, 1982), 99; Nicholas Canny, *Making Ireland British, 1580–1650* (Oxford: Oxford University Press, 2001), 121–64, 165–242; and David Stevenson, *Scottish Covenanters and Irish Confederates: Scottish-Irish Relations in the Mid-Seventeenth Century* (Belfast: Ulster Historical Foundation, 1981), 1–41.

17. Nicholas Canny, "The Origins of Empire: An Introduction," in *The Origins of Empire: British Overseas Enterprise to the Close of the Seventeenth Century*, ed. Nicholas Canny (Oxford: Oxford University Press, 1998), 1–33; Canny, "Fashioning 'British' Worlds in the Seventeenth Century," in *Empire, Society, and Labor: Essays in Honor of Richard S. Dunn*, ed. Nicholas Canny, Gary B. Nash, Joe Illick, and William Pencak (University Park: Pennsylvania History, 1997), 26–45; and Canny, *Making Ireland British*, especially chapter 4.

18. Canny, "Origins of Empire," 14.

19. Canny, "Fashioning 'British' Worlds," 30.

20. John Livingstone to John Winthrop, Jr., 5 Jan 1634/5, *Winthrop Papers* (Boston: Massachusetts Historical Society, 1943–47), 3:187–88; and Richard S. Dunn, James Savage, and Laetitia Yeandle, eds., *The Journal of John Winthrop, 1630–1649* (Cambridge: Harvard University Press, 1996), 120. Livingstone was the father of Robert Livingston, who used his ties to New England to begin his commercial empire in New York.

21. Dunn, Savage, and Yeandle, *Journal of John Winthrop*, 159–60; see also Nathaniel B. Shurtleff, *Records of the Governor and Company of the Massachusetts Bay in New England* (Boston: William White, 1853; reprint, New York: Arno, 1968), 1:129. Sir John Clotworthy was from the southwest of England and migrated to Ireland as a young man. He eventually held estates in Ulster, Antrim, and Down with a largely Scottish tenantry. Through his landholdings and political connections, he sympathized with the Calvinist beliefs of Scottish Presbyterians. Canny, *Making Ireland British*, 236–37, 295. See also T. C. Barnard, *Cromwellian Ireland: English Government and Reform in Ireland, 1649–1660* (Oxford: Oxford University Press, 1975; reprint, 2000), 124–26.

22. Colin Kidd, *British Identities Before Nationalism: Ethnicity and Nationhood in the Atlantic World, 1600–1800* (Cambridge: Cambridge University Press, 1999), 1–6, 75–85, 123–27.

23. Linda Colley, *Britons: Forging the Nation, 1707–1837* (New Haven: Yale University Press, 1992), 5–6, 163–64; Linda Colley, *Captives* (New York: Pantheon Books, 2002), 4–12; and Kathleen Wilson, *The Island Race: Englishness, Empire, and Gender in the Eighteenth Century* (London: Routledge, 2003), 1–28.

24. John Guy, *Tudor England* (Oxford: Oxford University Press, 1988), 281–89; Bremer, *Congregational Communion,* 64–75; Alison Olsen, "The English Reception of the Huguenots, Palatines, and Salzburgers, 1680–1734: A Comparative Analysis," in *From Strangers to Citizens: The Integration of Immigrant Communities in Britain, Ireland, and Colonial America, 1550–1750,* ed. Randolph Vigne and Charles Littleton (Brighton, U.K.: Sussex Academic Press, 2001), 481–91; and J. F. Bosher, "Huguenot Merchants and the Protestant International in the Seventeenth Century," *William and Mary Quarterly* 52, no. 1 (1995): 77–102.

25. Extant church records rarely note attendees who were not members. It is therefore difficult to know who attended church regularly without joining, or those who did not attend. Scot Alexander Bravand, for example, apparently attended the Wenham church, since he left a bequest to the minister, but was not a member and does not appear in the church records. Bravand Estate Inventory, ECR, 7:145; William Blake Trask, "Records of the Congregational Church in Wenham, Mass.," *New England Historical and Genealogical Register* 61 (October 1907): 330–38 (hereafter NEHGR); and William Blake Trask, "Records of the Congregational Church in Wenham, Mass.," NEHGR 62 (January 1908): 34–48.

26. Many scholars believe that Puritans tried to institute a "traditional" social model in New England that may have existed in only a few places in England. They argue that Puritans deliberately rejected the modernizing forces at work in seventeenth-century England in their attempt to establish a society in opposition to English trends. Although this may have been the conscious intent of Massachusetts's founding generation, the society that developed, particularly in the last forty years of the century, became modern—seen as a shift from a communitarian and homogeneous society to a more commercial and diverse one—in more ways than the original settlers could have anticipated. Carl Bridenbaugh, *Cities in the Wilderness: The First Century of Urban Life in America, 1625–1742,* 2d ed. (New York: Knopf, 1960), 30–31; Jack P. Greene, *Pursuits of Happiness: The Social Development of Early Modern British Colonies and the Formation of American Culture* (Chapel Hill: University of North Carolina Press, 1988), 8, 28–36; and Bremer, *John Winthrop,* 51–61.

27. T. H. Breen and Stephen Foster, "The Puritans' Greatest Achievement: A Study of Social Cohesion in Seventeenth-Century Massachusetts," *Journal of American History* 40, no. 1 (1973): 5–22.

NOTES TO CHAPTER 2

1. John Frederick Martin, in *Profits in the Wilderness: Entrepreneurship and the Founding of New England Towns in the Seventeenth Century* (Chapel Hill: University of North Carolina Press, 1991), 111–17, 121–23, discusses expansion in early New England, primarily in terms of land use. For economic development, see also Margaret Ellen Newell, *From Dependency to Independence: Economic Revolution in Colonial New England* (Ithaca: Cornell University Press, 1998); and James E. McWilliams, *Building the Bay*

Colony: Local Economy and Culture in Early Massachusetts (Charlottesville: University of Virginia Press, 2007).

2. Mixed communities also developed in maritime industries, but, as noted in the introduction, several excellent studies of fishing communities have been published. This book, therefore, does not specifically focus on fishermen.

3. See, for example, Richard S. Dunn, James Savage, and Laetitia Yeandle, eds., *The Journal of John Winthrop, 1630–1649* (Cambridge: Harvard University Press, 1996), 24, 96.

4. David Cressy, *Coming Over: Migration and Communication Between England and New England in the Seventeenth Century* (Cambridge: Cambridge University Press, 1987), 53–58. Richard Dunn gives a similar estimate, writing that "even in New England, servants constituted about a third of the initial work force." Dunn, "Servants and Slaves: The Recruitment and Employment of Labor," in *Colonial British America: Essays in the New History of the Early Modern Era*, ed. Jack P. Greene and J. R. Pole (Baltimore: Johns Hopkins University Press, 1984), 157–94, quote 160. See also Richard Archer, "New England Mosaic: A Demographic Analysis for the Seventeenth Century," *William and Mary Quarterly* 47, no. 4 (1990): 477–502.

5. Daniel Vickers, "Competency and Competition: Economic Culture in Early America," *William and Mary Quarterly* 47, no. 1 (1990): 3–29; and Daniel Vickers, *Farmers and Fishermen: Two Centuries of Work in Essex County, Massachusetts, 1630–1850* (Chapel Hill: University of North Carolina Press, 1994), 14–23.

6. Dunn, Savage, and Yeandle, *Journal of John Winthrop*, 102.

7. Ibid., 342.

8. Ibid., 323–24; William Fiennes, Lord Saye and Sele, to John Winthrop, 9 July 1640, *Winthrop Papers* (Boston: Massachusetts Historical Society, 1943–47), 4:263–68; Karen Ordahl Kupperman, *Providence Island, 1630–1641: The Other Puritan Colony* (Cambridge: Cambridge University Press, 1993), 146–47, 320–25; April Lee Hatfield, *Atlantic Virginia: Intercolonial Relations in the Seventeenth Century* (Philadelphia: University of Pennsylvania Press, 2004), 114–23; and Susan Hardman Moore, *Pilgrims: New England Settlers and the Call of Home* (New Haven: Yale University Press, 2007), 50–51, 54–73.

9. Dunn, Savage, and Yeandle, *Journal of John Winthrop*, 345.

10. See, for example, John Noble, ed., *Records of the Court of Assistants of the Colony of the Massachusetts Bay, 1630–1692* (Boston: Suffolk County, 1901–28; reprint, New York: Arno, 1973), 2:105, 106, 135–36 (hereafter *Court of Assistants Records*); and Nathaniel B. Shurtleff, *Records of the Governor and Company of the Massachusetts Bay in New England* (Boston: William White, 1853; reprint, New York: Arno, 1968), 2:180–81 (hereafter *Mass. Recs.*).

11. Dunn, Savage, and Yeandle, *Journal of John Winthrop*, 573.

12. For servants in general, see Richard Archer, *Fissures in the Rock: New England in the Seventeenth Century* (Hanover: University Press of New England, 2001), 106–7, 125–27; Archer, "New England Mosaic," 487–88; Cressy, *Coming Over*, 52–63; Dunn, "Servants and Slaves," 157–64; Lawrence W. Towner, "'A Fondness for Freedom': Servant Protest in Puritan Society," *William and Mary Quarterly* 19, no. 2 (1962), 201–19; and Abbott Emerson Smith, *Colonists in Bondage: White Servitude and Convict Labor in America, 1607–1776* (Chapel Hill: University of North Carolina Press, 1947; reprint, Gloucester, Mass.: Peter Smith, 1965), 53–55.

13. George F. Dow and Mary G. Thresher, eds., *Records and Files of the Quarterly Courts of Essex County, Massachusetts* (Salem, Mass.: Essex Institute, 1911–75), 1:231 (hereafter ECR).

14. Dorothy Crane to Richard Crane, 15 March 1638/9, *Winthrop Papers*, 5:105–6.

15. Indenture of Catherine Lemon, May 1649, *Winthrop Papers*, 5:339.

16. Lucy Downing to Margaret Winthrop, 20 January 1640/1, *Winthrop Papers*, 4:306–7. Lucy and Emanuel Downing had settled in Ipswich, Massachusetts, in 1638 (they returned to England in the early 1640s), and Margaret Winthrop lived in Boston. Although this was an exchange of servants within the colony, the young woman's credentials from England followed her. Francis J. Bremer, *John Winthrop: America's Forgotten Founding Father* (Oxford: Oxford University Press, 2003), 248.

17. Archer, *Fissures in the Rock*, 105–8; Bremer, *John Winthrop*, 162–64; and Dunn, Savage, and Yeandle, *Journal of John Winthrop*, 18. See Thomas Motte to John Winthrop, 13 June 1629, *Winthrop Papers*, 2:97; John Winthrop to Margaret Winthrop, 20 October 1629, *Winthrop Papers*, 2:160–61; and John Sampson to John Winthrop, 12 January 1629/30, *Winthrop Papers*, 2:185, for examples of letters from and about potential migrants.

18. Dunn, Savage, and Yeandle, *Journal of John Winthrop*, 109, 93.

19. See, for example, Mary Dudley to Margaret Winthrop, 28 March 1636, *Winthrop Papers*, 3:239. This is not to imply that all servants were unruly or that all unruly servants were not from godly families. Nor should we assume that servants, both godly and not, or non-Puritans in general were the only offenders to appear before the courts. Presentments for improper behavior cut across the social spectrum.

20. Emanuel Downing to John Winthrop, August 1645, *Winthrop Papers*, 5:38–39; and Bremer, *John Winthrop*, 312–15.

21. William Wood, *New England's Prospect* (London, 1634; reprint, New York: Burt Franklin, 1968), 86; John Josselyn, "An Account of Two Voyages to New England" (London, 1675; reprint, *Collections of the Massachusetts Historical Society*, 3d ser., 3 [1833]: 211–354), notation about slaves at 2 October 1639, 231; Bremer, *John Winthrop*, 312–14; and Alden T. Vaughan and Virginia Mason Vaughan, "England's 'Others' in the Old and New Worlds," in *The World of John Winthrop: Essays on England and New England, 1588–1649*, ed. Francis J. Bremer and Lynn A. Botelho (Boston: Massachusetts Historical Society, 2005), 57.

22. *Mass. Recs.*, 2:152

23. Robert E. Moody, ed., *The Saltonstall Papers, 1607–1815*, 2 vols., in *Collections of the Massachusetts Historical Society* (Boston: Massachusetts Historical Society, 1972–74), 80:117; and E. N. Hartley, *Ironworks on the Saugus* (Norman: University of Oklahoma Press, 1957), 45–46, 48, 54.

24. Dunn, Savage, and Yeandle, *Journal of John Winthrop*, 345.

25. Samuel Eliot Morison makes a similar point about fishermen in Marblehead, writing, "Marblehead obeyed or not the laws of the Great and General Court, as suited her good pleasure; but as long as she 'made fish,' the Puritan magistrates did not interfere." Morison, *The Maritime History of Massachusetts, 1783–1860* (Boston: Houghton Mifflin, 1921; reprint, Cambridge, Mass.: Riverside, 1961), 13. Stephen Innes, in *Labor in a New Land: Economy and Society in Seventeenth-Century Springfield* (Princeton: Princeton University Press, 1983), xvii, also notes this trend. Given the return rate of settlers, estimated by Susan Hardman Moore at 16 percent to 24 percent of the population of New England in the 1640s, colonial leaders needed to encourage any potential settlers to remain. Moore, *Pilgrims*, 55–56.

26. Stephen Innes, *Creating the Commonwealth: The Economic Culture of Puritan New England* (New York: Norton, 1995), 242.

27. Hartley, *Ironworks on the Saugus*, 174; Joshua Foote to John Winthrop, Jr., 20 September 1643, *Winthrop Papers*, 4:415–16; and Rolf Loeber, "Preliminaries to the Massachusetts Bay Colony: The Irish Ventures of Emanuel Downing and John Winthrop, Sr.," in *"A Miracle of Learning": Studies in Manuscripts and Irish Learning: Essays in Honour of William O'Sullivan*, ed. T. C. Barnard, Dáibhí Ó Cróinín, and Katharine Simms (Aldershot, U.K.: Ashgate, 1998), 164–99.

28. Hartley, *Ironworks on the Saugus*, 53.

29. Robert C. Black, *The Younger John Winthrop* (New York: Columbia University Press, 1966), 111, 116–18; and Hartley, *Ironworks on the Saugus*, 55–56. John Winthrop, Jr., had a deep interest in alchemy, which drove his search for metals and minerals, and he combined an interest in economic development with alchemical experimentation. He shared these interests with a few other early residents of Massachusetts, most notably Dr. Robert Child and Richard Leader. Child is best known for his participation in the Remonstrance in 1646, which objected to many aspects of Massachusetts's political and religious governance. Leader followed Winthrop as the manager of the Saugus ironworks. In addition, at least one of the ironworkers, miner Richard Post, may also have had an interest in alchemical metallurgy. Little is known about Post, but he left Saugus for Winthrop's New Haven ironworks in the mid-1650s, hired specifically to test ore. Walter William Woodward, "Prospero's America: John Winthrop, Jr., Alchemy, and the Creation of New England Culture, 1606–1676" (Ph.D. diss., University of Connecticut, 2001), 40–41, 98–100. See also John L. Brooke, *The Refiner's Fire: The Making of Mormon Cosmology, 1644–1844* (Cambridge: Cambridge University Press, 1996), 36–37. For Post, see ECR, 1:157; 4:221, 304, 344; and Hartley, *Ironworks on the Saugus*, 280.

30. Black, *Younger John Winthrop*, 117; and Hartley, *Ironworks on the Saugus*, 65–78.

31. *Mass. Recs.*, 3:81–82, 125–28, 185–86, quotes 127, 128.

32. Ibid., 3:185–86, quote 186. See Hartley, *Ironworks on the Saugus*, 99; and Innes, *Creating the Commonwealth*, 250–52, for the reputation of ironworkers. See Moore, *Pilgrims*, 54–57, for ministers returning to England.

33. Hartley, *Ironworks on the Saugus*, 100–103, 125–26.

34. My summary of the European context for and technology of the Saugus ironworks is based on Hartley, *Ironworks on the Saugus*, chapter 9.

35. At least four, and perhaps six, of the twenty-four known investors—in particular Sir Lionel Copley, John Becx, Dr. Robert Child, and Joshua Foote, the men most involved with operations—had been involved in other iron-production facilities in England and Ireland. Family, religious, and alchemical associations also gave Winthrop, and thus probably the primary investors, access to other sources of information and experience. Loeber, "Preliminaries to the Massachusetts Bay Colony," 182–84; and Woodward, "Prospero's America," 73, 107, 164–66.

36. Hartley, *Ironworks on the Saugus*, 11, 12, 176. The General Court also insisted that the plants use indirect processing, since the privileges that they granted the Undertakers depended on the construction of both furnaces and forges to ensure finished products for Massachusetts residents. In indirect processing, a blast furnace reduced the iron ore to molten metal, which was cast into sows and pigs (smaller, more workable units of cast iron), as well as utilitarian hollowware. The cast-iron bars were then turned into wrought iron in the forge. The Walloon process complicated this second stage by requiring the use of two hearths—the finery and the chafery—to finish the iron. In this

method, the finery melted the pigs to remove carbon and other impurities from the metal, and through the use of a huge, water-powered machine hammer brought the iron to a semifinished stage. At the chafery, wrought iron was heated and placed under the hammer once again in order to remove any remaining carbon. The iron was then finished and drawn into bars for use at the rolling and slitting mill or for sale. According to modern experts, the bog ore in the region could easily have been processed into usable iron by using a simple bloomery, in which the furnace and a one-hearth forge processed ore into cast and then wrought iron. Later ironworks in colonial Massachusetts used this simplified process.

37. For fishermen, see Vickers, *Farmers and Fishermen*, especially chapter 3; and Christine Leigh Heyrman, *Commerce and Culture: The Maritime Communities of Colonial Massachusetts, 1690–1750* (New York: Norton, 1984). See also Innes, *Creating the Commonwealth*, 250–51.

38. Robert Child to John Winthrop, Jr., 27 June 1643, *Winthrop Papers*, 4:395; and Joshua Foote to John Winthrop, Jr., 20 September 1643, *Winthrop Papers*, 4:415.

39. Promoters of the Ironworks to John Winthrop, Jr., 13 March 1647/8, *Winthrop Papers*, 5:209.

40. English law provided precedents for protecting workers from unreasonable dismissals, which also may have kept Massachusetts courts from prosecuting workers too harshly. See Richard B. Morris, *Government and Labor in Early America* (New York: Octagon Books, 1965), 17–35. Darrett B. Rutman also discusses the disconnect between ideal and reality in Massachusetts society. Such slippage created the spaces where "disruptive" and "dysfunctional" non-Puritans could live within a seemingly homogeneous Puritan society. Rutman, "The Mirror of Puritan Authority," in *Law and Authority in Colonial America*, ed. George Athan Billias (Barre, Mass.: Barre Publishers, 1965), 149–67.

41. ECR, 1:133; Hartley, *Ironworks on the Saugus*, 189; and ECR, 8:201; 2:196; 3:83. Saugus was also called Hammersmith, after the ironworks near London.

42. ECR, 1:133, 134, 135, 138. In May 1648, an Elizabeth Pinnion was acquitted in the Court of Assistants on two counts of adultery, although she was sentenced to be whipped at Boston and Lynn for "her evill & adulterous behavior & swearing." The name Elizabeth is most likely a mistake, and the case refers to Esther, since there were no other Pinnions in Essex County, and Esther and Nicholas did not have a daughter named Elizabeth. *Mass. Recs.*, 2:243. The irony of Russell being charged for spending the Sabbath drinking with the man who suspected him of having an affair with his wife apparently did not occur to the magistrates.

43. ECR, 1:173.

44. ECR, 1:271, 272; and *Mass. Recs.*, 1:126, 183, 274; 2:84; 3:243–44, 261. Other members of ironworks families fined include the wife of Joseph Jenks, Jr.; John Gorum; John Parker; and "Sarah, daughter-in-law of Francis Perrie."

45. ECR, 1:414; 2:195, 196; 3:83.

46. The General Court passed several sumptuary laws beginning in the 1630s. These laws applied to all residents, but were repealed in 1644. The 1651 law, however, set specific limits. Families with estates under two hundred pounds could not wear silk, lace, "greate bootes," or other specified items. Several presentments in the Essex County courts that accused residents of violating the sumptuary laws were eventually dismissed because the defendants proved that they had the requisite estates. The General Court expressed "our utter detestation & dislike that men or women of meane condition, educations, & callinges should take uppon them the garbe of gentlemen." Many other residents

were also presented for breaking the sumptuary laws at about this time. The 1651 law was in effect only for a few years. *Mass. Recs.*, 1:126, 183, 274; 2:84; 3:243–44, 261.

47. Although the issue of unconverted adult children had troubled the churches since at least the publication of the Cambridge Platform in 1648, in 1656 Connecticut called for a synod to resolve the dilemma in response to problems in Hartford. Massachusetts agreed to meet (although Plymouth and New Haven did not), and ministers and lay elders convened in Boston in 1657. The resolution, which, after another synod in 1662, resulted in the Halfway Covenant, continued to roil the churches for several decades. Harry Stout, *The New England Soul: Preaching and Religious Culture in Colonial New England* (Oxford: Oxford University Press, 1986), 58–61; Stephen Foster, *The Long Argument: English Puritanism and the Shaping of New England Culture, 1570–1700* (Chapel Hill: University of North Carolina Press, 1991), 186–87; and James F. Cooper, Jr., *Tenacious of Their Liberties: The Congregationalists in Colonial Massachusetts* (Oxford: Oxford University Press, 1999), 90–91. Ironworkers Thomas Beale and Joseph Jenks were also presented for absence from meeting in March 1656. *ECR*, 1:414.

48. Innes, *Creating the Commonwealth*, especially chapter 6.

49. Gail Sussman Marcus, "'Due Execution of the Generall Rules of Righteousnesse': Criminal Procedure in New Haven Town and Colony, 1638–1658," in *Saints and Revolutionaries: Essays on Early American History*, ed. David D. Hall, John M. Murrin, and Thad W. Tate (New York: Norton, 1984), 99–137; and John M. Murrin, "Magistrates, Sinners, and a Precarious Liberty: Trial by Jury in Seventeenth-Century New England," in Hall, Murrin, and Tate, *Saints and Revolutionaries*, 152–206.

50. Many of the cases against workers in this period are grouped together in the records, and a comment at the end of a presentment in 1647 notes that the case was "referred to next sitting at the Iron Works." *ECR*, 1:137.

51. The Essex County Quarterly Court records are full of presentments for ironworkers in the 1640s and early 1650s, but by 1653, with the bankruptcy of the ironworks, these cases decline. Innes, *Creating the Commonwealth*, chapter 6.

52. Franklin Bowditch Dexter, ed., *New Haven Town Records* (New Haven, Conn.: New Haven Colony Historical Society, 1917–19), 2:117–23, 134, 148–51, 159–62 (hereafter *New Haven Town Records*). Moran was a Scot who had probably worked at Hammersmith before moving to New Haven. Although his name never appeared in the records with the other Scottish prisoners, in an unrelated custody decision Moran was identified as having been a servant of Oliver Purchase, the clerk at Hammersmith. He therefore may have arrived in New England in the early 1650s, and was sold to Purchase personally rather than for the ironworks. Ruth Pinnion was eventually executed by Connecticut for infanticide. See Mary Beth Norton, *Founding Mothers and Fathers: Gendered Power and the Forming of American Society* (New York: Knopf, 1996), 27–38, for more on the Pinnion family. See also Innes, *Creating the Commonwealth*, 260–63.

53. *New Haven Town Records*, 2:146. The Pinnions were the worst troublemakers, although they frequently appeared in the records associated with the Ralph Russell family, also ironworkers. Although Russell was fairly reputable, his children were less so. Also appearing in the records associated with these families was John Ross (also spelled Rose), who may have been a Scot formerly from Massachusetts. The Pinnions remained in New Haven; Esther died there in the late 1660s and Nicholas in the mid-1670s. Their son Thomas became a proprietor of New Haven in 1685 and a freeman of the town by 1702/3. See *New Haven Town Records*, 2:117–23, 134, 148–51, 222–23; 3:56, 92, 196, 321; and Norton, *Founding Mothers*, 36, 420n19.

54. The proprietors of the New Haven ironworks struggled, as did those at Saugus, through much of the plant's productive life. The strictness of the New Haven magistrates and the difficulty in finding skilled workers contributed to the financial difficulties faced by the proprietors. Production ended in 1680. See Hartley, *Ironworks on the Saugus*, 280–88.

55. ECR, 1:134, 136, 181, 184. See also Innes, *Creating the Commonwealth*, 256–60.

56. In Providence, the Prays became involved in a long struggle with the authorities to obtain a legal divorce. See Ann Marie Plane, "Colonizing the Family: Marriage, Household, and Racial Boundaries in Southeastern New England to 1730" (Ph.D. diss., Brandeis University, 1995), 331–38.

57. ECR, 1:130, 153, 159, 200; Hartley, *Ironworks on the Saugus*, 273–74; and *New Haven Town Records*, 1:73, 77, 81, 87. Although warnings out frequently were civil procedures by towns to declare certain people ineligible for poor relief, in this case the New Haven magistrates called Turner to court three times (in July, August, and September) after his initial warning in May 1651. Turner claimed that he could not leave because his wife was pregnant and could not get passage on a ship. In September, the magistrates allowed him "libertie to staye in the Towne till the next Court," provided that Thomas Jeffery, who provided his bond, would agree to continue it. Turner does not appear in the records after this, so it is unclear if or when he and Sarah left the colony.

58. *Mass. Recs.*, vol. 4, pt. 2:11, 38. Ballantyne and his wife, Hannah, petitioned several times to have parts of the sentence remitted; in the end, William kept his ear and the court allowed the fine to be paid in installments. Edward M. Cook, Jr., *The Fathers of the Towns: Leadership and Community Structure in Eighteenth-Century New England* (Baltimore: Johns Hopkins University Press, 1976), 25; and Robert Tarule, *The Artisan of Ipswich: Craftsmanship and Community in Colonial New England* (Baltimore: Johns Hopkins University Press, 2004), 70.

59. See Hartley, *Ironworks on the Saugus*, but especially chapter 13, for the families who left Essex County. There is no evidence that Lawrence and Sarah Turner went to New Haven to work for John Winthrop, Jr., although it might explain their presence in that colony.

60. *New Haven Town Records*, 2:44–45; ECR, 6:55, 258–59, 377; 7:399; George Madison Bodge, *Soldiers of King Philip's War* (Boston: George Madison Bodge, 1906; reprint, Baltimore: Genealogical Publishing, 1967), 138; Carole Doreski, ed., *Massachusetts Officers and Soldiers in the Seventeenth-Century Conflicts* (Boston: New England Historic Genealogical Society and Society of Colonial Wars in the Commonwealth of Massachusetts, 1982), 240; and Hartley, *Ironworks on the Saugus*, 188, 240, 280, 286, 299–302.

61. ECR, 4:221, 304; *Probate Records of Essex County* (Salem, Mass.: Essex Institute, 1920), 2:222.

62. Hartley, *Ironworks on the Saugus*, 296–97; Bodge, *Soldiers*, 264, 371; and Doreski, *Massachusetts Officers*, 153. For more on the Leonard family, see below. See also *New Haven Town Records*, 2:99.

63. For John Gifford, see ECR, 2:89. For Samuel Harte, see ECR, 5:2, 63, 183, 251; 7:332. For Oliver Purchase, see *Acts and Resolves, Public and Private, of the Province of Massachusetts Bay* (Boston: Wright and Potter, 1869–1922), 7:290, 337, 677, 715.

64. Hartley, *Ironworks on the Saugus*, 15, 179–80, 208–10; ECR, 2:215, 97–98; 8:228; and Middlesex Court Records, Pulsifer Transcript (microfilm), 3:21, Judicial Archives, Massachusetts Archives, Boston, Massachusetts (hereafter Middlesex Court Records, Judicial Archives).

65. Hartley, *Ironworks on the Saugus*, 274–76, 294–95. The third James Leonard married Mercy Crossman in 1743. She may have been a descendant of Saugus ironworker Robert Crossman. John A. Schutz, *Legislators of the Massachusetts General Court, 1691–1780* (Boston: Northeastern University Press, 1997), 273.

66. ECR, 1:174, 194; 5:170, 186, 230, 287, 290, 326, 351–55; 6:1–4, 34–35. The suits against Hannah Downing were withdrawn, although in Nathaniel Leonard's complaint, he defended himself by saying, "I being a singell man my fortten would be leveled with her owne which we trust shall prove is very mene." Even among non-Puritan communities, then, the upwardly mobile second generation wanted to distance themselves from those who were not upwardly mobile. For more on the career of Henry Leonard, see also Alonzo Lewis and James Newhall, *History of Lynn* (Lynn, Mass.: By the authors, 1865; reprint, Lynn, Mass.: G. C. Herbert, 1890), 206–7; Hartley, *Ironworks on the Saugus*, 129, 189, 272, 294–97; Paul Boyer and Stephen Nissenbaum, *Salem Possessed: The Social Origins of Witchcraft* (Cambridge: Harvard University Press, 1974), 123–26; and Innes, *Creating the Commonwealth*, 263–70.

67. The ironworks went bankrupt in 1653, which began more than twenty years of lawsuits in the Essex County courts. Several groups of local proprietors unsuccessfully attempted to operate the plant on a smaller scale. The works had been abandoned by 1680. Hartley, *Ironworks on the Saugus*, 265–66.

68. This consortium included John Gould. Animosity over the operation of the bloomery may account in part for his testimony against the Leonards, noted above. Hartley, *Ironworks on the Saugus*, 294–96.

69. ECR, 5:130–31, 173, 186, 196, 218, 230, 285; and *Court of Assistants Records*, 3:245–46. For the agricultural communities around Ipswich, see chapter 3. Daniel Black may have been Scottish. A Daniel Black appears on the *John and Sarah* list of captives in 1652, and a man by that name lived in Middlesex County in 1654. Charles Edward Banks claims that the "Daniel Black who came to York [Maine] from Topsfield in 1685 was a son of a Scotch prisoner who arrived in the *John and Sarah*." The Essex County Black, however, is never identified as Scottish in these records. "Scotch Prisoners Sent to Massachusetts in 1652, by Order of the English Government," *New England Historical and Genealogical Register* 1 (October 1847): 378; Middlesex Court Records, 1:68, Judicial Archives; and Charles Edward Banks, *History of York, Maine* (Boston: C. E. Banks, 1931–35; reprint, Baltimore: Regional Publishing, 1967), 1:210. The Carrell and Bridges families are discussed in chapter 3.

70. ECR, 5:130, 351–55; 6:1–4. See Darrett B. Rutman, "The Social Web: A Prospectus for the Study of Early American Community," in *Insights and Parallels: Problems and Issues of American Social History*, ed. William O'Neill (Minneapolis: Burgess Publishing, 1973), 57–88, for his discussion of the vertical and horizontal ties that held communities together in the early modern world.

71. Church, town, colony, and court records have been examined for all the people named here. These sources are listed in the bibliography.

72. The wars in Britain and Ireland during the 1640s and 1650s have generated many studies. See, for example, Conrad Russell, *The Causes of the English Civil War* (Oxford: Oxford University Press, 1990); and Russell, *The Fall of the British Monarchies, 1637–1642* (Oxford: Oxford University Press, 1991). General studies with good discussions of the events of the period include Christopher Hill, *God's Englishman: Oliver Cromwell and the English Revolution* (London: Dial, 1970); Brian Levack, *The Formation of the British State: England, Scotland, and the Union, 1603–1707* (Oxford: Oxford University Press, 1987);

and Mark Kishlansky, *A Monarchy Transformed: Britain, 1603–1714* (London: Penguin, 1996). For more detail about the later wars between Scotland and England, see John D. Granger, *Cromwell Against the Scots: The Last Anglo-Scots War, 1650–1652* (East Linton, U.K.: Tuckwell, 1997). Through the National Covenant (1638) and Solemn League and Covenant (1643) the Scots, with the cooperation of the English, hoped to establish Presbyterianism in Scotland, England, and Ireland. Charles II had to agree to these provisions before he was proclaimed king in Scotland upon the death of his father. See also David Stevenson, *Scottish Covenanters and Irish Confederates: Scottish-Irish Relations in the Mid-Seventeenth Century* (Belfast: Ulster Historical Foundation, 1981).

73. Granger, *Cromwell Against the Scots*, 29–56, 113–45; and Charles E. Banks, "Scotch Prisoners Deported to New England by Cromwell, 1651–1652," *Proceedings of the Massachusetts Historical Society* 61 (1927–28): 7–11, 17–19.

74. Granger, *Cromwell Against the Scots*, 56–58, 144–45; and Banks, "Scotch Prisoners," 12–13. Banks also notes that the number of men bound for New England is in question, because in September 1650 the Council ordered Haselrig to send 150 men to Samuel Clark for New England, along with 900 prisoners bound for Virginia. In October, this group was apparently on board a ship in the Thames waiting to sail. After this, the Council issued the November orders for 150 men to sail with Augustine Walker. Therefore, the number of Scots sent to New England in 1650 could range from 150 to 300 men. The Council of State also worried that sending too many prisoners to the colonies would destabilize colonial governments. After the Battle of Worcester, the Council ordered that only one Scottish minister was to be sent for every two hundred men. Banks, "Scotch Prisoners," 18. See also Diane Rapaport, "Scots for Sale: The Fate of the Scottish Prisoners in Seventeenth-Century Massachusetts," *New England Ancestors* (Winter 2003): 30–32; Rapaport, "Scots for Sale, Part II: Scottish Prisoners in Seventeenth-Century Maine and New Hampshire," *New England Ancestors* (Holiday 2004): 26–28; Rapaport, "Scottish Slaves in Colonial New England, Part I: 'Disposed of . . . For Our Best Advantage,'" *The Highlander* 42, no. 5 (2004), 10–18, 71; Rapaport, "Scottish Slaves in Colonial New England, Part II: 'A Pore Man . . . That Hath Nothing to Live by But His Labor,'" *The Highlander* 42, no. 6 (2004), 10–17; and Rapaport, "Scottish Slavery in Seventeenth-Century New England," *History Scotland* 5, no. 1 (2005): 44–52. Rapaport's use of the term "slave" to describe involuntary indentured servitude, as well as her insistence that the Scots were treated as second-class citizens, rather overstates the case. By seventeenth-century standards, the conditions for these prisoners once in New England were not bad.

75. Banks, "Scotch Prisoners," 12–13, 16. Sixty-two Scots were noted as being in Saugus on 24 December 1650, when an inventory of the assets of the company was taken. Because a normal voyage between London and Massachusetts lasted six to eight weeks in good weather, if these men came on the *Unity*, the ship made very good time. It is possible that two groups of Scots arrived in Boston during the winter of 1650. Saugus Inventory, *ECR*, 2:290. The Scots served from five to seven years in their indentures.

76. Banks, "Scotch Prisoners," 17–19.

77. Dunn, Savage, and Yeandle, *Journal of John Winthrop*, 120. See also John Livingstone to John Winthrop, Jr., 5 January 1634/5, *Winthrop Papers*, 3:187–88; and Lawrence H. Leder, *Robert Livingston and the Politics of Colonial New York* (Chapel Hill: University of North Carolina Press, 1961), 3–5. Livingstone was the father of Robert Livingston of New York. The younger man used his family and religious connections in the Netherlands, Scotland, and New England to begin his mercantile career.

78. John Becx to John Gifford, 26 April 1652, Lynn Iron Works Collection, Baker Library Historical Collections, Harvard Business School, Cambridge, Massachusetts (hereafter Lynn Iron Works Collection). Gifford became manager of the ironworks in 1650, taking over from Richard Leader. He was recruited from Gloucestershire, where he worked at ironworks in the Forest of Dean. Hartley, *Ironworks on the Saugus*, 139–40.

79. John Cotton to Oliver Cromwell, 28 July 1651, in *The Correspondence of John Cotton*, ed. Sergeant Bush, Jr. (Chapel Hill: University of North Carolina Press, 2001), 461.

80. *Mass. Recs.*, vol. 4, pt. 1:86. This 1652 law ordered Scots, Africans, and Native Americans living in the colony to report for militia training. In 1656, Africans and Native Americans were disarmed and exempted from training. *Mass. Recs.*, 3:397. Irish servants, discussed in chapter 3, were not listed in these laws. Presumably they were also required to serve, because the 1656 law states that "no other person," except Africans and Indians, "shall be exempted from training."

81. John Becx to John Gifford, 26 April 1652, Lynn Iron Works Collection; and ECR, 2:292.

82. ECR, 2:290; Undated Accounts, doc. 295, Lynn Iron Works Collection; and Hartley, *Ironworks on the Saugus*, 147. Coaling was one of the most expensive labor costs at the ironworks, costing 5s. 6d. per load. Master colliers were highly skilled craftsmen.

83. Deposition of William Emory, June 1658, ECR, 2:96.

84. For Arzbell Anderson, see ECR, 2:326; 3:16. For James Moore, see ECR, 2:192, 215–16. Because he was a collier, Moore's estate was probably larger, even though he died three years before Anderson (who worked as a general laborer).

85. Banks, *History of York*, 1:206–12, 261, 271–72; and Robert E. Moody, Charles T. Libby, and Neal W. Allen, eds., *Province and Court Records of Maine* (Portland: Maine Historical Society, 1928–75), 2:170, 345, 355. Banks lists Alexander Maxwell, Daniel Dill, and John Carmichael, for example, as land owners in York, whereas Daniel Livingston and James Jackson apparently did not have land. Banks, *History of York*, 1:210–12. See also Rapaport, "Scots for Sale, Part II," 26–28.

86. *New Haven Town Records*, 2:117–23.

87. For Clarke, see ECR, 9:338, 594. For Tower, see Hartley, *Ironworks on the Saugus*, 278, 294, 298; and ECR, 5:227.

88. ECR, 2:326, 338–39.

89. ECR, 2:224; 3:269; 4:200.

90. ECR, 9:46; 5:130; 3:274.

91. ECR, 3:21; *Town Records of Salem, Massachusetts* (Salem, Mass.: Essex Institute, 1911–34), 2:44; ECR, 4:97; 7:145; Richard D. Pierce, ed., *Records of the First Church in Salem, Massachusetts, 1629–1736* (Salem, Mass.: Essex Institute, 1974), 42, 165; and William Blake Trask, "Records of the Congregational Church in Wenham, Mass.," *New England Historical and Genealogical Register* 61 (October 1907): 330–38.

92. *Town Records of Salem*, 2:234, 243, 246; ECR, 7:145; and *Probate Records of Essex County*, 3:320. Very few Scots left wills or had probate inventories taken of their estates.

93. Will and Inventory of John Upton, Probate Docket No. 2326, Middlesex County, Judicial Archives; Essex County Land Records, 2:45, Essex County Registry of Deeds, Salem, Massachusetts; and ECR, 6:45–46.

94. Essex County Land Records, 3:170, 171; *Town Records of Salem*, 2:211; and ECR, 2:210.

95. Essex County Land Records, 3:22; and *Records of the Town Meetings of Lyn* (Lynn, Mass.: Lynn Historical Society, 1949–56), 2:3.

96. ECR, 2:71–72.

97. "Sarvants Appartayneinge Unto the Company" (1652–53), Lynn Iron Works Collection; and ECR, 8:195–203.

98. Hartley, *Ironworks on the Saugus*, 200–201; and ECR, 2:96.

99. Clarke's first wife is only identified in the records as "the daughter of Francis Perry." For John Clarke, see ECR, 2:215–16, 291; 9:338–39, 594; *Vital Records of Lynn, Massachusetts, to 1849* (Salem, Mass.: Essex Institute, 1905–6), 2:95; and *Probate Records of Essex County*, 1:354. For Francis and Jane Perry, see ECR, 1:56; *Mass. Recs.*, 1:90; *Vital Records of Salem*, 2:159–60; and Hartley, *Ironworks on the Saugus*, 195.

100. ECR, 2:192, 215; and *Vital Records of Lynn*, 2:255.

101. ECR, 2:326, 338–39; 3:16. See chapter 5 for more on traditional patterns from Scotland that can be seen in Massachusetts among the Scottish community.

102. These communities are discussed in greater detail in the next chapter. For Allester Dugglas, see *Vital Records of Lynn*, 2:238. For Macam Downing, see *Vital Records of Lynn*, 1:132, 133; 2:123; ECR, 5:351–55; *Vital Records of Ipswich, Massachusetts, to 1849* (Salem, Mass.: Essex Institute, 1910–19), 2:144; and *Vital Records of Salem*, 3:192. Both Chebacco Parish and Salem Village were marginal areas of Essex County; see chapter 3. As will be discussed below, although many of the non-Puritans presented here lived in Salem Farms (also known as Salem Village and, later, Danvers), none was involved in the 1692 witchcraft outbreak.

103. For Teague (Thaddeus) Brann, see ECR, 6:383–85. The pattern of small groups of families living closely together and sharing labor and equipment is discussed in chapter 5.

104. Adams Family Genealogy, http://www.renderplus.com/hartgen/htm/adams_2.htm (accessed 24 August 2004); ECR, 9:309; and *Vital Records of Salem*, 3:184. For Peter Twist, see, for example, ECR, 6:295; 8:372. He later lived in Salem Farms, along with many other "strangers." See chapter 3 for Salem Farms.

105. ECR, 2:35–36; 6:173, 359–61; and *Town Records of Salem*, 2:211, 297; 3:139. Philip and Hannah Welsh, in fact, tie together many of the non-Puritan communities in Essex County. See chapter 3 for more on them and a discussion of marginal areas.

106. For dissenters of many kinds in Massachusetts, see Michael P. Winship, *The Times and Trials of Anne Hutchinson* (Lawrence: University Press of Kansas, 2005); Archer, *Fissures in the Rock*; and Louise A. Breen, *Transgressing the Bounds: Subversive Enterprises Among the Puritan Elite in Massachusetts, 1630–1692* (Oxford: Oxford University Press, 2001).

NOTES TO CHAPTER 3

1. The classification of non-English residents into status categories is largely subjective. Extant tax records are too spotty to allow quantitative analysis, and many of the people studied here do not appear in those records that have survived. For my purposes, "lower status" denotes day laborers or people seen as poor by their neighbors, either by receiving public charity, being warned out so as not to be charged to the town, or being called poor in court testimony. "Middling status" are those inhabitants who owned land or were long-term tenants or craftsmen. These men frequently served on petty juries and held minor town offices. Rarely did the non-Puritan residents presented in this chapter move into the upper strata, denoted by large landholdings or prestigious town or colony offices, such as selectman, justice of the peace, magistrate, or deputy.

Large landholdings are those of more than one hundred acres, which was much more than the average family could reasonably expect to farm in a year. See Percy Wells Bidwell and John I. Falconer, *History of Agriculture in the Northern United States, 1620–1860* (Washington, D.C.: Carnegie Institute of Washington, 1925; reprint, New York: Peter Smith, 1941), 38–39. Stephen Innes estimates that a farming family of seven needed approximately sixty acres of land to survive. Innes, *Labor in a New Land: Economy and Society in Seventeenth-Century Springfield* (Princeton: Princeton University Press, 1983), 48. The status of offices comes from Edward M. Cook, Jr., *The Fathers of the Towns: Leadership and Community Structure in Eighteenth-Century New England* (Baltimore: Johns Hopkins University Press, 1976), 25–27.

2. Very few women were identified as Scottish in the seventeenth-century records; a greater number of women were described as Irish. For discussions of ethnicity and marriage patterns, see Joyce D. Goodfriend, *Before the Melting Pot: Society and Culture in Colonial New York City, 1664–1730* (Princeton: Princeton University Press, 1992), 95–99; Jon Butler, *Huguenots in America: A Refugee People in New World Society* (Cambridge: Harvard University Press, 1983), 81–84; and Ned C. Landsman, *Scotland and Its First American Colony, 1683–1765* (Princeton: Princeton University Press, 1985), 32–33, 159–60. Nicholas Canny notes that many early Scottish tenants on estates in Ireland tried to maintain Scottish communities (through marriage and contacts with home) but over time were "forced to become more cosmopolitan than their countrymen at home." A similar process occurred in Massachusetts, where ethnic boundaries among European settlers were quite porous. Nicholas Canny, "Fashioning 'British' Worlds in the Seventeenth Century," in *Empire, Society, and Labor: Essays in Honor of Richard S. Dunn*, ed. Nicholas Canny, Gary B. Nash, Joe Illick, and William Pencak (University Park: Pennsylvania History, 1997), 39. See also Steve Murdoch, *Network North: Scottish Kin, Commercial, and Covert Associations in Northern Europe, 1603–1746* (Leiden: Brill, 2006), 14–27.

3. For the development of the local economy in Massachusetts, see James E. McWilliams, *Building the Bay Colony: Local Economy and Culture in Early Massachusetts* (Charlottesville: University of Virginia Press, 2007).

4. As discussed in chapter 1, Massachusetts residents did not identify themselves as "British" in the seventeenth century. Their communities, however, resemble British communities in Ireland.

5. Innes, *Labor in a New Land*, 143–44, quote 143.

6. In 1690, Massachusetts supported a population of around 50,000, whereas Essex County contained 7,225 residents. For population figures, see Evarts B. Greene and Virginia D. Harrington, *American Population Before the Federal Census of 1790* (New York: Columbia University Press, 1932; reprint, Gloucester, Mass.: Peter Smith, 1966), 13–22; and Cook, *The Fathers of the Towns*, 194–95. Cook explains his typology in chapter 7. Topsfield is the only town of those discussed above that Cook also studied; without conducting a full analysis of the political structure of these towns, it is difficult to say exactly where the smaller towns fit. See the appendix for more population estimates.

7. Court cases were extracted from the nine published volumes of the Essex County Quarterly Court records and include all incidents that can be definitely attributed to a member of one of the non-Puritan families studied here. Of the ten cases noted above, six involved the Leonard family and three involved William Paterson, a Scottish merchant from the West Indies who lived in Salem for several years. Thus the majority of cases can be attributed to two families. George F. Dow and Mary G. Thresher, eds., *Records and Files of the Quarterly Courts of Essex County, Massachusetts* (Salem, Mass.:

Essex Institute, 1911–75) (hereafter ECR). For the function of the court system within New England society, see John M. Murrin, "Magistrates, Sinners, and a Precarious Liberty: Trial by Jury in Seventeenth-Century New England," in *Saints and Revolutionaries: Essays on Early American History*, ed. David D. Hall, John M. Murrin, and Thad W. Tate (New York: Norton, 1984), 152–206; and David Thomas Konig, *Law and Society in Puritan Massachusetts: Essex County, 1629–1692* (Chapel Hill: University of North Carolina Press, 1979), 107–16.

8. In a petition to the Court of Assistants in 1655, during an appeal of a case decided in Middlesex County, James Rosse, a Scot, asked permission "to goe home with his master, John Ruddocke, on his humble acknowledgement of his fault and promise of his good behaviour." Two years later, John Jephson asked the Assistants "for releife in respect of a Scottish servant, which is burdensome by reason of disease." The court refused to allow Jephson to abandon his responsibilities to his ill servant. Nathaniel B. Shurtleff, ed., *Records of the Governor and Company of the Massachusetts Bay in New England* (Boston: William White, 1853; reprint, New York: Arno, 1968), 4:244; 3:428 (hereafter *Mass. Recs.*).

9. Konig, *Law and Society*, 107–16.

10. ECR, 3:264–66; 2:197–98, 294–97.

11. The "New English" settled in Ireland during the reign of Elizabeth or later and were mainly Protestant. "Old English" families had been in Ireland since the 1300s and had generally remained Catholic, developing alliances with the Gaelic Irish, although tensions between these groups continued to exist. Karl Bottigheimer, *Ireland and the Irish: A Short History* (New York: Columbia University Press, 1982), 99. See also John Livingstone to John Winthrop, Jr., 5 January 1634/5, *Winthrop Papers* (Boston: Massachusetts Historical Society, 1943–47), 3:187–88.

12. T. C. Barnard, *Cromwellian Ireland: English Government and Reform in Ireland, 1649–1660* (Oxford: Oxford University Press, 1975; reprint, 2000), 1–15.

13. Bottigheimer, *Ireland and the Irish*, 123–28; and Nicholas Canny, *Making Ireland British, 1580–1650* (Oxford: Oxford University Press, 2001), 275–98. See also David Stevenson, *Scottish Covenanters and Irish Confederates: Scottish-Irish Relations in the Mid-Seventeenth Century* (Belfast: Ulster Historical Foundation, 1981), for the continued fighting and political intrigues in Ireland in the 1640s.

14. Bottigheimer, *Ireland and the Irish*, 129–31; John W. Blake, "Transportation from Ireland to America, 1653–1660," *Irish Historical Studies* 3 (1942–43): 267–81; and Abbot Emerson Smith, *Colonists in Bondage: White Servitude and Convict Labor in America, 1607–1776* (Chapel Hill: University of North Carolina Press, 1947; reprint, Gloucester, Mass.: Peter Smith, 1965), 162–74.

15. As noted above, "Irish" is a geographical term that could refer to people from very different religious and ethnic backgrounds. The Massachusetts records do not distinguish between Gaelic Irish, Old English, New English, or Ulster Scots. In general, I believe that most Ulster Scots were probably identified as Scottish, since some of the merchants discussed in chapter 4 were born of Scottish parents in Ulster but were considered Scots. For those described as "Irish," it is simply not possible to be more specific about their religion or ethnicity. See chapter 5 for the few clues that do exist.

16. *Mass. Recs.*, 3:291, 294; and ECR, 2:294–97, 310–11. Although only Philip Welsh, William Downing, John Downing, and John King (or Ring) claim to have been kidnapped, many other Irish men and women arrived about the same time as these men, as indicated in later depositions and marriage records.

17. *Mass. Recs.*, 3:291; and Smith, *Colonists in Bondage*, 166–67. For "Irish bloud" comment, see ECR, 4:179.

18. Petition of Alexander Gordon, 3 February 1653/4, Middlesex County Court Records, Pulsifer Transcript, Judicial Archives, Massachusetts Archives, Boston, Massachusetts (hereafter Middlesex Court Records, Judicial Archives); and *Mass. Recs.*, 3:381.

19. John Winthrop, Jr., of course, was the eldest son of governor John Winthrop. He served as an assistant and was the leading scientist and intellectual in early New England. John Endicott led the initial Puritan settlement at Salem in 1628 and served variously as assistant, deputy governor, and governor. Emanuel Downing was the husband of Lucy Winthrop, the sister of the elder John Winthrop. The Downings returned to England in the 1640s. Samuel Symonds established himself in Ipswich in the early 1630s and became one of the leading magistrates and landowners in the region. Symonds's second wife, Martha, was the sister of Elizabeth, the wife of John Winthrop, Jr. Through his first wife, Symonds was also related to the Harlakendens of Essex, England, a powerful Puritan family. David Cressy, *Coming Over: Migration and Communication Between England and New England in the Seventeenth Century* (Cambridge: Cambridge University Press, 1987), 279–84. Richard Dummer served as an assistant, magistrate, and treasurer of the colony before being disarmed for his and his wife's fervent support of Anne Hutchinson. Emery Battis, *Saints and Sectaries: Anne Hutchinson and the Antinomian Controversy in the Massachusetts Bay Colony* (Chapel Hill: University of North Carolina Press, 1962), 305. For examples of these land grants, see John Noble, ed., *Records of the Court of Assistants of the Colony of the Massachusetts Bay, 1630–1692* (Boston: Suffolk County, 1901–28; reprint, New York: Arno, 1973), 2:24–25, 42–43 (hereafter *Court of Assistants Records*).

20. ECR, 4:393; 2:294–97.

21. Daniel Vickers, "Working the Fields in a Developing Economy," in *Work and Labor in Early America*, ed. Stephen Innes (Chapel Hill: University of North Carolina Press, 1988), 49–69, quote 64. See also Vickers, *Farmers and Fishermen: Two Centuries of Work in Essex County, Massachusetts, 1630–1850* (Chapel Hill: University of North Carolina Press, 1994), 77–82.

22. Innes, *Labor in a New Land*, 49–53, quote 49; and ECR, 2:274–75. In the 1670s, Richard Dummer had at least two other non-Puritan tenants, Robert Robinson and Duncan Stewart. ECR, 6:65–66.

23. Landsman, *Scotland and Its First American Colony*, 20–22, quote 21; R. A. Butlin, "Land and People, c. 1600," in *A New History of Ireland*, vol. 3, *Early Modern Ireland, 1534–1691*, ed. T. W. Moody, F. X. Martin, and F. J. Byrne (Oxford: Oxford University Press, 1976), 153–55; and R. F. Foster, *Modern Ireland, 1600–1972* (London: Penguin, 1988), 18–19.

24. ECR, 7:292; and *Probate Records of Essex County* (Salem, Mass.: Essex Institute, 1920), 1:418. Many Starkweathers lived in the area at this time; I have not been able to identify Thomson's master.

25. *Probate Records of Essex County*, 1:368; and ECR, 4:223; 7:89.

26. ECR, 2:274–75; 3:430. The terms of Grasier's lease were common in coastal Massachusetts for undeveloped land. See Vickers, *Farmers and Fishermen*, 79–81.

27. ECR, 3:325–26; 8:151–52.

28. ECR, 2:243; 3:192–94; 5:130, 227; 7:338.

29. ECR, 2:197–98; 4:86; 5:425; 6:192; 7:154; 9:581.

30. In addition, a search of the Early American Imprints database for the seventeenth century, using terms such as "foreigner," "stranger," and various nationalities,

revealed no extended comments about non-Puritan laborers in sermons or other printed materials.

31. See, for example, ECR, 2:67, 180; 4:86, 289; 5:215, 221; 7:1, 271.

32. Violence was rare but not unknown, with the 1681 case between Joan Sullivan and Thomas Maule, wherein Sullivan accused Maule and his wife of physical and emotional abuse, as the most obvious incident (see chapter 5). ECR, 8:222–26. Sailors probably suffered the most abuse, but these cases rarely came before the quarterly courts. Maritime laborers were protected by admiralty laws administered after 1674 by the Court of Assistants, and after 1696 by the Vice-admiralty Court erected in Massachusetts. See L. Kinvin Wroth, "The Massachusetts Vice-admiralty Court," in Law and Authority in Colonial America, ed. George Athan Billias (Barre, Mass.: Barre Publishers, 1965), 32–73.

33. "Scotch Prisoners Sent to Massachusetts in 1652, by Order of the English Government," New England Historical and Genealogical Register 1 (1847): 377–80 (hereafter NEHGR); ECR, 7:292; 2:189; Vital Records of Ipswich, Massachusetts, to 1849 (Salem, Mass.: Essex Institute, 1910–19), 2:126, 199; and Probate Records of Essex County, 1:368–70.

34. ECR, 1:74, 229; 3:384; and Vital Records of Ipswich, 2:423. Davison's will and inventory can be found at an online genealogy site, at http://www.gencircles.com/users/ brons/3/dab/2351.html. I have not yet found the document in the Essex County records, but internal evidence indicates that this indeed is the Scottish Daniel Davison. His total estate was worth £720.

35. ECR, 2:242–43; 4:222–23, 289; 6:445, 451; 7:37, 271; and Carole Doreski, ed., Massachusetts Officers and Soldiers in the Seventeenth-Century Conflicts (Boston: New England Historic Genealogical Society and the Society of Colonial Wars in the Commonwealth of Massachusetts, 1982), 67.

36. See, for example, ECR, 2:242–43; 3:448; 4:5–7, 98; 5:375; 6:234; 8:287, 404–5. Deere may have been a turner as well as a farmer. See Robert Tarule, The Artisan of Ipswich: Craftsmanship and Community in Colonial New England (Baltimore: Johns Hopkins University Press, 2004), 81.

37. ECR, 2:22; 3:278; 4:135; 5:158; 7:22; and Vital Records of Ipswich, 2:370, 659. John Ring and John King, the Irish servant of Samuel Symonds, may be the same man, although no direct correlation between the two has been found. Neither Ring nor Deere joined the Topsfield church. John H. Gould, "Early Records of the Church in Topsfield," Essex Institute Historical Collections 3 (1888): 181–205.

38. ECR, 2:22; 3:278; 4:135; 5:158; 7:22; Vital Records of Ipswich, 2:370, 659; and Kerby A. Miller, Emigrants and Exiles: Ireland and the Irish Exodus to North America (Oxford: Oxford University Press, 1985), 27–28, 152.

39. ECR, 2:180; 3:325–26; 8:151–52, 165–66, 404–5.

40. For examples of depositions in disputes not directly related to Nealand, see ECR, 4:3–4; 9:112, 211, 191. For service as marshal's deputy, see ECR, 9:426. For service in the militia, see ECR, 5:31–32; Bodge, Soldiers of King Philip's War, 155, 283, 370; and Doreski, Massachusetts Officers, 174. In 1701/2, Nealand received payment for the militia service of his servant, John Graves, in 1696. Acts and Resolves, Public and Private, of the Province of the Massachusetts Bay (Boston: Wright and Potter, 1869–1922), 7:325.

41. His name has not been found in the extant church records. ECR, 5:375; and George Francis Dow, History of Topsfield, Massachusetts (Topsfield, Mass.: Topsfield Historical Society, 1940), 47.

42. ECR, 2:275, 280; 3:430–31, 438; 4:106, 148; 5:375; 7:293, 361. Although Grasier was forced to leave Ipswich after the dispute with Colburne, both he and Morrill had

remained in the area for six years after their initial warnings out. Warning out was frequently a legal issue, putting the colony on notice that the town did not claim an indigent person or family for the purposes of charity. Even when a warning out came from a judicial matter, as with Grasier, families were not always forced to leave immediately. Non-English residents were not warned out more frequently than other residents. Only Morrill, Grasier, and Welsh had such actions taken against them.

43. Thomson probably did have many ties to Wenham families, since the Haggets, his in-laws, lived there. See the Bravand Will, ECR, 7:145. See also William Blake Trask, "Records of the Congregational Church in Wenham, Mass.," NEHGR 61 (October 1907): 323–38; William Blake Trask, "Records of the Congregational Church in Wenham, Mass.," NEHGR 62 (January 1908): 34–48; and Frederick Lewis Weis, *The Colonial Clergy and the Colonial Churches of New England* (Lancaster, Mass.: Society of the Descendants of the Colonial Clergy, 1936), 277.

44. ECR, 5:261; *Acts and Resolves*, 7:326; *Vital Records of Wenham, Massachusetts, to the End of the Year 1849* (Salem, Mass.: Essex Institute, 1904), 145; and Trask, "Records of the Congregational Church in Wenham, Mass." (October 1907), 330–38.

45. "Scotch Prisoners," 379; ECR, 3:118; 9:299; and Trask, "Records of the Congregational Church in Wenham" (October 1907), 330–38.

46. *Vital Records of Ipswich*, 1:318–21; ECR, 5:124; Bodge, *Soldiers in King Philip's War*, 374, 375; Middlesex Court Records, 1:96, Judicial Archives; and David Dobson, *Directory of Scottish Settlers in North America, 1625–1825* (Baltimore: Genealogical Publishing, 1984–86), 2:177.

47. For example, in a 1681 case involving William Danford and William Longfellow for killing another man's steer, "Robin Robinson, a Scotchman," received twenty shillings for some pigs lost in the incident. This is probably Robert Robinson, who appears two other times in the records, with the birth of his son in Newbury and as a tenant of Richard Dummer, yet he was another non-Puritan who lived in the area but barely surfaces in the official records. ECR, 3:468; 6:66; 8:95–96.

48. For examples of services, see ECR, 2:222; 4:98; 6:234; 8:233 (juries of inquest); ECR, 3:21; 9:426 (marshal's deputy); *Town Records of Salem, Massachusetts* (Salem, Mass.: Essex Institute, 1911–34), 2:44 (hog reeve); ECR, 6:290; 9:149 (constable); and ECR, 9:1; *Town Records of Salem*, 2:298–99 (other services). Daniel Davison was a member of the Wenham church, as were most of his children. Alexander Mackmallen may have been a member, but the records are not clear. Trask, "Wenham Church Records" (October 1907), 330–38.

49. ECR, 2:197–98, 294–97; Blake, "Transportation from Ireland to America," 267–81; and Smith, *Colonists in Bondage*, 162–74.

50. ECR, 2:197–98, 294–96.

51. ECR, 3:384; 4:294; 5:425; and Bodge, *Soldiers in King Philip's War*, 167. See also Kyle Zelner, "Essex County's Two Militias: The Social Composition of Offensive and Defensive Units During King Philip's War, 1675–1676," *New England Quarterly* 72, no. 4 (1999): 577–93. Zelner argues that Gardner's troop was composed of the "rabble of Essex"—poor men with little status in the county—noting that "one of the strongest indicators of commitment to the community in mid-seventeenth-century Massachusetts was church membership" (584). Although the poverty and lack of social status cannot be denied, Zelner uses traditional definitions of community (as a place) and commitment to community (as a function of religious affiliation), which his description of the activities of the unit itself might seem to question. Impressed or not, these men served in a dangerous campaign to protect their families and communities.

52. *ECR*, 6:192; 7:360, 336, 8:179, 286; 9:581. Welsh's ties to other Irish settlers are described above.

53. As noted in chapter 2, he may have been a Scottish prisoner of war, but no direct link has been made between this man and the Daniel Black identified as a Scot in Middlesex County.

54. *ECR*, 5:130, 227; 3:430.

55. See chapter 2 for more on the Leonard/Downing case. See also *ECR*, 5:130, 227, 351–55.

56. *ECR*, 2:22, 242–43; 3:192–94; 5:133.

57. Gould, "Early Topsfield Church Records," 181–205. Although they did not give depositions, Irishmen and non–church members Anthony Carrell and Edward Nealand had helped Faith Black at various times when she and Daniel were fighting.

58. Even Rhode Islanders, with their long-standing grievances against Plymouth, Massachusetts, and Connecticut, took the "English" side in the war, much to the confusion of many Native Americans. See Jenny Hale Pulsipher, *Subjects unto the Same King: Indians, English, and the Contest for Authority in Colonial New England* (Philadelphia: University of Pennsylvania Press, 2005), 108–10.

59. As noted above, however, extant records do not allow us to make these distinctions among the "Irish" in early Massachusetts.

60. *ECR*, 4:179–80, 445, 449, 453.

61. The substance of the depositions was not recorded. This John Clarke is not the blacksmith in Lynn. *ECR*, 3:438, 469; and Jane Kamensky, *Governing the Tongue: The Politics of Speech in Early New England* (Oxford: Oxford University Press, 1997), 18–19.

62. *ECR*, 7:360–62.

63. *ECR*, 9:580–84. See also Richard P. Gildrie, *The Profane, the Civil, and the Godly: The Reformation of Manners in Orthodox New England* (University Park: Pennsylvania State University Press, 1994), xi–xiii, for further discussion of the charivari.

64. *ECR*, 8:95–96.

65. Kenneth A. Lockridge, *A New England Town: The First Hundred Years*, expanded ed. (New York: Norton, 1985), 4–16.

66. John Frederick Martin, *Profits in the Wilderness: Entrepreneurship and the Founding of New England Towns in the Seventeenth Century* (Chapel Hill: University of North Carolina Press, 1991), 52–53, 137–38.

67. Margaret Newell, *From Dependency to Independence: Economic Revolution in Colonial New England* (Ithaca: Cornell University Press, 1998), 72–83.

NOTES TO CHAPTER 4

1. The classic work on merchants in New England is Bernard Bailyn, *The New England Merchants in the Seventeenth Century* (Cambridge: Harvard University Press, 1955). It is in the final chapters of the book that Bailyn discusses the role of English merchants in changing Massachusetts society. This chapter therefore focuses on non-English merchants in order to add another dimension to these events.

2. Irish merchants did not immigrate to New England in noticeable numbers during the seventeenth century, because the Navigation Acts restricted Irish trade with North America until 1731. The trade that did exist between Ireland and North America in the seventeenth century was mostly directed to the West Indies. Thomas Truxes, *Irish-American*

Trade, 1660–1783 (Cambridge: Cambridge University Press, 1988), 7–28; and R. C. Nash, "Irish Atlantic Trade in the Seventeenth and Eighteenth Centuries," *William and Mary Quarterly* 42, no. 3 (1985): 329–56.

3. Brian P. Levack, *The Formation of the British State: England, Scotland, and the Union, 1603–1707* (Oxford: Oxford University Press, 1987), 8, 182–83, 220; and James H. Kettner, *The Development of American Citizenship, 1608–1870* (Chapel Hill: University of North Carolina Press, 1978), 16–24.

4. Bailyn, *New England Merchants*, 82–86, 110–11, 114–17; and Stephen Innes, *Creating the Commonwealth: The Economic Culture of Puritan New England* (New York: Norton, 1995), 272–73, 301–7. Samuel Maverick was also a member of the Carr Commission of 1664; his hostility to Massachusetts is apparent in the reports that he sent to England.

5. The earliest and best explication of the role of merchants in the transformation of Massachusetts is Bailyn, *New England Merchants*. More recently, James E. McWilliams, *Building the Bay Colony: Local Economy and Culture in Early Massachusetts* (Charlottesville: University of Virginia Press, 2007); Louise A. Breen, *Transgressing the Bounds: Subversive Enterprises Among the Puritan Elite in Massachusetts, 1630–1692* (Oxford: Oxford University Press, 2001); Phyllis Whitman Hunter, *Purchasing Identity in the Atlantic World: Massachusetts Merchants, 1670–1780* (Ithaca: Cornell University Press, 2001); and Innes, *Creating the Commonwealth*, have explored other aspects of this argument.

6. Bailyn, *New England Merchants*, 119–26, 129–31, 132–34. See L. Kinvin Wroth, "The Massachusetts Vice-admiralty Court," in *Law and Authority in Colonial America*, ed. George Athan Billias (Barre, Mass.: Barre Publishers, 1965), 32–73, for the establishment of admiralty courts. See also Jenny Hale Pulsipher, *Subjects unto the Same King: Indians, English, and the Contest for Authority in Colonial New England* (Philadelphia: University of Pennsylvania Press, 2005), 51–69.

7. Perry Miller, *The New England Mind: From Colony to Province* (Cambridge: Harvard University Press, 1953), 4.

8. Bailyn, *New England Merchants*, 20–21.

9. Bernard Bailyn, "The Apologia of Robert Keayne," *William and Mary Quarterly* 7, no. 4 (1950): 568–87.

10. Richard Sheridan, *Sugar and Slavery: An Economic History of the British West Indies, 1625–1775* (Baltimore: Johns Hopkins University Press, 1973), 41–44. See also Nuala Zahedieh, "Overseas Expansion and Trade in the Seventeenth Century," in *The Origins of Empire: British Overseas Enterprise to the Close of the Seventeenth Century*, ed. Nicholas Canny (Oxford: Oxford University Press, 1998), 398–422; Hilary McD Beckles, "The 'Hub of Empire': The Caribbean and Britain in the Seventeenth Century," in Canny, *Origins of Empire*, 218–40; and Margaret Ellen Newell, *From Dependency to Independence: Economic Revolution in Colonial New England* (Ithaca: Cornell University Press, 1998), 78–79.

11. Bailyn, *New England Merchants*, 127, 148–50; and Zahedieh, "Overseas Expansion and Trade," 406.

12. T. C. Smout, *Scottish Trade on the Eve of Union, 1660–1707* (Edinburgh: Oliver and Boyd, 1963), 70; Smout, "The Development and Enterprise of Glasgow, 1556–1707," *Scottish Journal of Political Economy* 7 (1967): 209; Smout, "The Glasgow Merchant Community in the Seventeenth Century," *Scottish Historical Review* 47, no. 1 (1968): 57; John Borland to Andrew Russell, 11/21 August 1686, RH 15/106/583/1, National Archives of Scotland, Edinburgh, Scotland (hereafter NAS); John Borland to Andrew Russell, July–August 1688, RH 15/106/ 643/2–6, NAS; and Daniel Campbell to James Robison, 22

October 1696, 1:101, Shawfield Muniments, Mitchell Library, Archives and Special Collections, Glasgow, Scotland (hereafter Mitchell Library).

13. Smout, *Scottish Trade on the Eve of Union*, 144–46; M. Lynch, "Continuity and Change in Urban Society, 1500–1700," in *Scottish Society, 1500–1800*, ed. R. A. Houston and I. D. Whyte (Cambridge: Cambridge University Press, 1989), 105–6.

14. F. D. Dow, *Cromwellian Scotland, 1651–1660* (Edinburgh: John Donald, 1979), 43–44, 71; Ian D. Whyte, *Scotland Before the Industrial Revolution: An Economic and Social History, 1050–1750* (London: Longman, 1995), 281, 284; and Julia Buckroyd, *Church and State in Scotland* (Edinburgh: John Donald, 1980), 7–11. See also Ian B. Cowan, *The Scottish Covenanters, 1660–1688* (London: Victor Gollancz, 1976); and David Stevenson, *Scottish Covenanters and Irish Confederates: Scottish-Irish Relations in the Mid-Seventeenth Century* (Belfast: Ulster Historical Foundation, 1981), for more on the religious divisions of the period.

15. Historians have not considered Scottish merchants as an important part of the colonial trade in the seventeenth century. Little research has been done on Scottish activity in the Americas before the Union of 1707, because commercial connections were slight when compared with the volume of trade in the eighteenth century. The evidence indicates, however, that Scottish merchants were more active in the seventeenth-century Atlantic world than many scholars realize. For Scotland and its connections with Europe and the Americas, see especially T. C. Smout, "The Early Scottish Sugar Houses, 1660–1720," *Economic History Review* 2d ser., 14 (1961–62): 240–53; Smout, *Scottish Trade on the Eve of Union*; Smout, "The Glasgow Merchant Community," 53–71; Gordon Jackson, "Glasgow in Transition, c. 1660–c. 1740," in *Glasgow*, vol. 1, *Beginnings to 1830*, ed. T. M. Devine and Gordon Jackson (Manchester: University of Manchester Press, 1995), 63–105; Ned C. Landsman, "Immigration and Settlement," in *Scotland and the Americas, 1600 to 1800*, ed. Michael Fry (Providence: John Carter Brown Library, 1995), 15–18; and Ned C. Landsman, "Nation, Migration, and the Province in the First British Empire: Scotland and the Americas, 1600–1800," *American Historical Review* 104, no. 2 (1999), 463–75. Jackson, in "Glasgow in Transition," 72, notes that trade between merchants in Scotland and the West Indies increased in spite of the Navigation Acts, and that "they were difficult to enforce when many emigrants were actually Scots."

16. Landsman, "Nation, Migration," 468.

17. Dewer left no indication of his motives for leaving Barbados. It could have been for commercial reasons, or, since he joined Boston's First Church in 1655, it is possible that he supported the Parliamentary faction in Barbados and was forced to leave when Royalists gained control of the government. Richard D. Pierce, ed., *Records of the First Church in Boston, 1630–1868*, Publications of the Colonial Society of Massachusetts (Boston: Colonial Society of Massachusetts, 1961), 39:60; and Beckles, "Hub of Empire," 238.

18. Letter, Thomas Dewer to Robert Scott, 22 May 16[67?], Suffolk Files 40:9, Judicial Archives, Massachusetts Archives, Boston, Massachusetts (hereafter Judicial Archives); Letter, Thomas Dewer to Robert Scott, 21 September 1667, Photostat Collection, Massachusetts Historical Society, Boston, Massachusetts (hereafter Photostat Coll., MHS); Letter, Thomas Dewer to Robert Scott, n.d. [September or October 1667], Photostat Coll., MHS; and Letter, Thomas Dewer to Robert Scott, 24 October 1667, Photostat Coll., MHS.

19. In addition to the letters noted above, see Letter, Thomas Dewer to Scott, 20 January 1667/8, Photostat Coll., MHS. For communication networks in the Atlantic, see Ian K. Steele, *The English Atlantic, 1675–1740* (Oxford: Oxford University Press, 1986).

20. *Boston Births, Marriages, and Deaths, 1630–1699*, Reports of the Records Commissioners 9 (Boston: Rockwell and Churchill, 1883), 3, 19, 38, 82 (hereafter *Boston Births*); and Pierce, *Records of the First Church in Boston*, 39:59.

21. Inventory of William Ballantyne, Probate Docket 7:4, Suffolk County, Judicial Archives.

22. Ibid. The whalebone is an interesting component of this inventory. Whalebone was a common trade item between Scotland and the Netherlands in the seventeenth century, although it rarely appears in Boston inventories. If not for local use, this may indicate that Ballantyne had connections to Scotland and Holland that have not yet been found. Smout, *Scottish Trade on the Eve of Union*, 104, 106, 194, 297. A kental, also spelled quintal, was a unit of measure equal to one hundred pounds.

23. For Scots and Huguenots, a common Calvinist religious ideology and international Protestant networks helped pave their way in New England. See Jon Butler, *The Huguenots in America: A Refugee People in New World Society* (Cambridge: Harvard University Press, 1983), 15, 74; Petition of Jacques Pepin, 4 August 1661, Suffolk Files 15A:9, Judicial Archives; and Sidney Perley, *The History of Salem, Massachusetts* (Salem, Mass.: Sidney Perley, 1926), 2:351. See also J. F. Bosher, "Huguenot Merchants and the Protestant International in the Seventeenth Century," *William and Mary Quarterly* 52, no. 1 (1995): 77–102.

24. Petition of Stephen Bellocque, 1665, Photostat Coll., MHS. One of the earliest contacts between Massachusetts and France occurred in the 1640s, when Charles d'Aulnay and Charles de la Tour struggled for control of Acadia. La Tour sought help from Massachusetts; John Winthrop allowed him to recruit volunteers, but would not supply official aid to one side or the other. Richard S. Dunn, James Savage, and Laetitia Yeandle, eds., *Journal of John Winthrop* (Cambridge: Harvard University Press, 1996), 440–51, 464–68, 473–74. No connection between these men and the French merchants of the 1650s and 1660s has been found.

25. J. H. Ingram, *The Islands of England: A Survey of the Islands Around England and Wales and the Channel Islands* (London: Batsford, 1932), 164–75; and A. G. Jamieson, ed., *A People of the Sea: The Maritime History of the Channel Islands* (London: Methuen, 1986), xxx.

26. J. C. Appleby, "Neutrality, Trade, and Privateering, 1500–1689," in Jamieson, *People of the Sea*, 59–105.

27. Appleby, "Neutrality," 69–74.

28. Perley, *History of Salem*, 2:358–59; and A. J. Jamieson, "The Channel Islands and Overseas Settlement, 1600–1900," in Jamieson, *People of the Sea*, 272. Brown was a respected merchant in Salem yet apparently did not participate in the life of the larger community by holding office, serving in the militia, or joining the church. He only appears in the court records in suits for debt, but these few records make clear that he was active in the mercantile community. George F. Dow and Mary G. Thresher, eds., *Records and Files of the Quarterly Courts of Essex County, Massachusetts* (Salem, Mass.: Essex Institute, 1911–75), 3:465; 7:354; 9:336 (hereafter ECR).

29. Perley, *History of Salem*, 2:372; and Jamieson, "Overseas Settlement," 269–89. Much has been written about Philip English. Perley mentions English throughout the last two volumes of his *History of Salem*. See also Ralph Bertram Harris, "Philip English," *Essex Institute Historical Collections* 67 (1930): 273–90; David Thomas Konig, *Law and Society in Puritan Massachusetts: Essex County, 1629–1692* (Chapel Hill: University of North Carolina Press, 1979), 70–74, 183–84; and Konig, "A New Look at the Essex

'French': Ethnic Frictions and Community Tensions in Seventeenth-Century Essex County, Massachusetts," *Essex Institute Historical Collections* 110, no. 3 (1974): 167–80. Brief but informative discussions about English also appear in Paul Boyer and Stephen Nissenbaum, *Salem Possessed: The Social Origins of Witchcraft* (Cambridge: Harvard University Press, 1974), 131–32; Bailyn, *New England Merchants*, 144–45; and Jamieson, "Overseas Settlement," 273–75.

30. For English's participation in Essex County affairs, see, for example, ECR, 5:115; 8:394; 9:149, 457, 193–99; John Noble, ed., *Records of the Court of Assistants of the Colony of the Massachusetts Bay, 1630–1692* (Boston: Suffolk County, 1901–28; reprint, New York: Arno, 1973), 1:30–31 (hereafter *Court of Assistants Records*); and "John Balaine v. Philip English," 6 September 1694, Photostat Coll., MHS.

31. Konig, "A New Look," 180; Boyer and Nissenbaum, *Salem Possessed*, 131–32, 181–82; Harris, "Philip English," 283–87; Carol Karlsen, *The Devil in the Shape of a Woman: Witchcraft in Colonial New England* (New York: Norton, 1987), 106–7; and Mary Beth Norton, *In the Devil's Snare: The Salem Witchcraft Crisis of 1692* (New York: Knopf, 2002), 144–46. Konig states that the Englishes were accused due to a general fear of French-speaking people during King William's War; Boyer and Nissenbaum note that English was politically connected to the Porter family, the antagonists of the Putnams, who, with their allies, were the primary accusers in Salem Village. Karlsen and Norton point out the previous accusations against Elinor Hollingsworth, who had taken control of her husband's estate after his death, which was mired in debt, and restored the family's fortunes. Other issues include the wealth and status of the Englishes, as well as Philip's connections to France and Essex County's French-speaking community. John A. Schutz, *Legislators of the Massachusetts General Court, 1691–1780* (Boston: Northeastern University Press, 1997), 215.

32. For witchcraft in New England, see Boyer and Nissenbaum, *Salem Possessed*; John Demos, *Entertaining Satan: Witchcraft and the Culture of Early New England* (Oxford: Oxford University Press, 1982); Christine Leigh Heyrman, *Commerce and Culture: The Maritime Communities of Colonial Massachusetts, 1690–1750* (New York: Norton, 1984), especially chapter 3; Heyrman, "Specters of Subversion, Societies of Friends: Dissent and the Devil in Provincial Essex County, Massachusetts," in *Saints and Revolutionaries: Essays on Early American History*, ed. David D. Hall, John M. Murrin, and Thad W. Tate (New York: Norton, 1984), 38–74; Karlsen, *The Devil in the Shape of a Woman*; and Norton, *In the Devil's Snare*. For an analysis of another witchcraft case in 1692, see Richard Godbeer, *Escaping Salem: The Other Witch Hunt of 1692* (Oxford: Oxford University Press, 2005).

33. Accused witch Sarah Osborne, who died in Boston's jail awaiting her trial, had been married to an Irishman, Alexander Osborne. She had many points of friction with the Salem community, however, including property disputes with male heirs and her marriage to Osborne, a younger servant. Alexander was dead by the time of the accusations. Perley, *History of Salem*, 2:31–33; and Karlsen, *Devil in the Shape of a Woman*, 262–63. Konig, in *Law and Society*, 184, notes three other accused women possibly associated with the Jersey community, and one accused woman who married a Welshman.

34. John Demos counts only four women accused of witchcraft (out of ninety-three cases where some kind of formal action was taken) throughout New England before 1692 who were "anomalous in their ethnic and/or religious heritage"; he concludes that "the witches seem to have been of solidly English stock and mostly 'Puritan' religion." Demos,

Entertaining Satan, 71, 402–9. For the ambiguous status of some accused witches, see Heyrman, "Specters of Subversion"; and Konig, *Law and Society*, 183–85.

35. John M. Murrin notes a connection between witchcraft and bestiality, the latter accusations afflicting men in the way that witchcraft tainted women. Yet here, too, only one bestiality accusation was levied against a non-English resident. In 1643, Irish servant Teagu Ocrimi was convicted of attempted buggery with a cow and was sentenced "to stand at the place of execution with a halter around his neck and to be severely whipped." Murrin, "'Things Fearful to Name': Bestiality in Early America," in *The Animal/Human Boundary: Historical Perspectives*, ed. Angela N. H. Creager and William Chester Jordan (Rochester: University of Rochester Press, 2002), 115–56, quote 132.

36. *Records of the Suffolk County Court, 1671–1680*, Publications of the Colonial Society of Massachusetts (Boston: Colonial Society of Massachusetts, 1974), 30:695, 747, 816, 924, 931–2, 1107 (hereafter *Suffolk Court Records*); Pierce, *Records of the First Church in Boston*, 39:60; *Boston Town Records, 1630–1660*, Reports of the Records Commissioners 2 (Boston: Rockwell and Churchill, 1877), 143, 154 (hereafter *Boston Town Records*, 2); *Boston Town Records, 1660–1701*, Reports of the Records Commissioners 7 (Boston: Rockwell and Churchill, 1881), 20, 125 (hereafter *Boston Town Records*, 7); and *Miscellaneous Papers*, Reports of the Records Commissioners 10 (Boston: Rockwell and Churchill, 1886), 70, 75, 76 (hereafter *Misc. Papers*). Fowle and Kincaid joined the Scots' Charitable Society in 1684.

37. *Vital Records of Salem, Massachusetts* (Salem, Mass.: Essex Institute, 1916), 3:337; and ECR, 6:115; 8:394; 9:149, 349, 457.

38. Pierce, *Records of the First Church in Boston*, 39:58, 73, 74; *Boston Town Records*, 7:30, 34, 59, 101, 116, 126, 173, 183, 196, 204; *Suffolk Court Records*, 29:447; *Boston Births*, 9:91; ECR, 3:16; Estate Inventory of Isaac Griggs, Probate Docket 16:436–39, Suffolk County, Judicial Archives; and Will of Ruth Johnson, Probate Docket 16:57–59, Suffolk County, Judicial Archives. Scottish merchants were more likely to join churches than their countrymen in Essex County. Many probably had left Scotland in the 1650s and 1660s due to the religious upheaval, and perhaps sympathized with the anti-Episcopalian stance of the Congregational churches. The economic and political benefits of church membership may also have been more important to them than their countrymen who were tenant farmers or agricultural laborers. For religious strife in Scotland after 1660, see Elizabeth Hannan Hyman, "A Church Militant, 1661–1690," *Sixteenth Century Journal* 26, no. 1 (1995): 49–74; Stevenson, *Scottish Covenanters and Irish Confederates*; Buckroyd, *Church and State in Scotland*; and Cowan, *Scottish Covenanters*.

39. Petition, 13 May 1662, Photostat Coll., MHS; and Petition, 24–26 October 1664, Photostat Coll., MHS.

40. George Hutchinson to John Pollock, 2 July 1675, Maxwells of Pollock Manuscripts, T-PM 113/572, Mitchell Library; and Hutchinson to Pollock, 28 September 1675, Maxwells of Pollock Manuscripts, T-PM 113/574, Mitchell Library.

41. Richard R. Johnson, *Adjustment to Empire: The New England Colonies, 1675–1715* (New Brunswick: Rutgers University Press, 1981), 44–52; and Bailyn, *New England Merchants*, 111, 168–70. Because non-English merchants in Massachusetts largely stayed out of colony politics at this time and left few personal documents, we do not know exactly where these men stood on the issue of the Dominion. As Calvinists and merchants, in general they probably opposed Andros and the Catholic sympathies of James II. Two of the men arrested and jailed with Andros, James Graham of New York and Mungo Crawford of Boston, however, were members of the Scots' Charitable Society.

42. Johnson, *Adjustment to Empire*, 232–34. For the development of provincial identity, see Ned C. Landsman, *From Colonials to Provincials: American Thought and Culture, 1680–1760* (New York: Twayne, 1997). Landsman notes that "American colonists did not identify with everything British," and that "Americans did not become culturally English so much as British" (3, 6). This holds true for seventeenth-century colonists as well.

43. Bailyn, *New England Merchants*, 143–48; and M. Halsey Thomas, ed., *The Diary of Samuel Sewall* (New York: Farrar, Straus and Giroux, 1973), 1:121.

44. Smout, *Scottish Trade on the Eve of Union*, 96–115, 239–56; and T. M. Devine, *Scotland's Empire, 1600–1815* (London: Penguin, 2003), 28–40. Continuing religious and political violence in the 1670s and early 1680s between Covenanters and Episcopalian supporters of Charles II also contributed to the decision of a few merchants to leave Scotland. Francis Borland discussed these issues as they related to his family. "Diary of Francis Borland," Microfilm Copy, Special Collections, Edinburgh University Library, Edinburgh, Scotland. See also Hyman, "A Church Militant"; Buckroyd, *Church and State in Scotland*; and Cowan, *Scottish Covenanters*, for the religious strife after 1660.

45. Butler, *Huguenots in America*, 14–27. See also Neil Kamil, *Fortress of the Soul: Violence, Metaphysics, and Material Life in the Huguenots' New World, 1517–1751* (Baltimore: Johns Hopkins University Press, 2005), 2–3; and Alison Olsen, "The English Reception of the Huguenots, Palatines, and Salzburgers, 1680–1734: A Comparative Analysis," in *From Strangers to Citizens: The Integration of Immigrant Communities in Britain, Ireland, and Colonial America, 1550–1750*, eds. Randolph Vigne and Charles Littleton (Brighton, U.K.: Sussex Academic Press, 2001), 481–91.

46. Jamieson, "Overseas Settlement," 271–73.

47. Landsman, "Nation, Migration," 468; see also Devine, *Scotland's Empire*, 34–35. Scots' Charitable Society, *Constitution and By-laws of the Scots' Charitable Society of Boston* (Cambridge, Mass.: Scots' Charitable Society, 1878). For more on the Scots' Charitable Society, see chapter 5. See also the discussion of the scs in Peter Richard Virgadamo, "Colonial Charity and the American Character: Boston, 1630–1775" (Ph.D. diss., University of Southern California, 1982), 159–93.

48. Clemy himself does not appear as a member of the Second Church, but Elizabeth joined in 1690 and their son Alexander was baptized there in 1693. Chandler Robbins, *History of the Second Church, or Old North, in Boston* (Boston: John Wilson and Son, 1852), 244. See also *Boston Births*, 9:63; 119; scs, *Constitution and By-laws*, 26, 95; Alexander Clemy, Inventory, Probate Docket 13:512, Suffolk County, Judicial Archives; and Alexander Clemy, Accounts and Distribution of Estate, Probate Docket 13:660, Suffolk County, Judicial Archives.

49. Alexander Clemy Accounts, Probate Docket 13:660, Suffolk County, Judicial Archives.

50. Alexander Cole settled in Salem, marrying Bethiah Pickman, the daughter of Essex County farmer Nathaniel Pickman (or Pitman). Bethiah's sister Tabitha married Jersey merchant Edward Feveryear of Salem. Cole joined the scs in 1684, but apparently did not hold local office or join the church. Will and Probate Inventory of Alexander Coal, Probate Docket 10:89, Suffolk County, Judicial Archives; ECR, 9:560; and scs, *Constitution and By-laws*, 94.

51. "Diary of Francis Borland," Edinburgh University. For Scottish-Dutch commerce, see Smout, *Scottish Trade on the Eve of Union*, 99–115, 185–93.

52. "Diary of Francis Borland," Edinburgh University. For his connections with Andrew Russell and the Moys, see the Andrew Russell Papers, GD 1/885, RH 15/106, RH

801, NAS. See also Smout, *Scottish Trade on the Eve of Union*, 107; and Ginny Gardiner, "A Haven for Intrigue: The Scottish Exile Community in the Netherlands, 1660–1690," in *Scottish Communities Abroad in the Early Modern Period*, ed. Alexia Grosjean and Steve Murdoch (Leiden: Brill, 2005), 279–80. Stevenson, in *Scottish Covenanters and Irish Confederates*, discusses the religious issues that alternately divided and brought together the many factions in Scotland and Ireland.

53. Cynthia A. Kierner, *Traders and Gentlefolk: The Livingstons of New York, 1675–1790* (Ithaca: Cornell University Press, 1992), 11; Smout, *Scottish Trade on the Eve of Union*, 101; and Steve Murdoch, *Network North: Scottish Kin, Commercial, and Covert Associations in Northern Europe, 1603–1746* (Leiden: Brill, 2006), 74–76.

54. Ships Licenses, Suffolk Files 7:93, 102, 120, 126, 127, 138, 141, 156, Judicial Archives. John Campbell will be discussed below. In addition, Francis Borland noted several ships in which John was a partner that arrived in Surinam when he was a minister there between 1685 and 1690. "Diary of Francis Borland," Edinburgh University.

55. Peirce, *Records of the First Church in Boston*, 39:81; and Thomas, *Diary of Samuel Sewall*, 1:386, 401, 409–10, 471, 549, 576–77, 582, 588; 2:647, 696, 698, 969. The activities of these men can be found throughout the *Boston Town Records*, particularly volume 8 of the Reports of the Records Commissioners series, as well as through the shipping records listed in the previous footnote. See also *Acts and Resolves, Public and Private, of the Province of Massachusetts Bay* (Boston: Wright and Potter, 1869–1922), 6:61–68, 8:181–95, 546, 593–95, 616. For the Darien Company, see James Samuel Barbour, *A History of William Paterson and the Darien Company* (Edinburgh: W. Blackwood and Sons, 1907), 12–15; George Pratt Insh, *The Company of Scotland Trading to Africa and the Indies* (London: Charles Scribner's Sons, 1932); David Armitage, "The Darien Venture," in Frye, *Scotland and the Americas*, 3–13; and Devine, *Scotland's Empire*, 40–45.

56. SCS, *Constitution and By-laws*, 96; Bill of Exchange, 23 September 1693; and Public Protest of Bill of Exchange, 24 November 1693; Letter, Daniel Campbell to Duncan Campbell, 5 March 1695, Shawfield Muniments, Mitchell Library.

57. *Boston Births*, 9:173, 179, 189, 221, 230, 246; *Miscellaneous Documents*, Reports of the Records Commissioners 1 (Boston: Rockwell and Churchill, 1876), 89, 117, 141, 150, 160 (hereafter *Misc. Docs.*); SCS, *Constitution and By-laws*, 94; Power of Attorney, William Gray of New York to Campbell, 22 August 1692, Miscellaneous Bound Collection, MHS; and Campbell to Fitz-John Winthrop, 1693–1702, Winthrop Papers, MHS. The Thwing Index at the Massachusetts Historical Society, a biographical index of early Boston residents, notes that a description of Campbell in 1686 said, "He is very industrious, dresses a la mode, and I am told a young lady of great fortune is fallen in love with him." Campbell's wife, Susanna, joined the Scots' Charitable Society in her own name in 1696, six years before Duncan's death. This may indicate that she was Scottish, and therefore that Campbell married into a Boston Scots family, but her background is not known. See also Isaiah Thomas, *The History of Printing in America* (New York: Weathervane Books, 1970), 188.

58. Carl Wilhelm Ernest, *Postal Service in Boston, 1639–1893* (Boston: Boston Public Library, 1975), 7–12; *American National Biography* (Oxford: Oxford University Press, 1999), 9:912–13, s.v. "Andrew Hamilton"; Letters, Duncan Campbell to Fitz-John Winthrop, 1693–1702, Winthrop Papers, MHS; and Petition, Duncan Campbell to William Stoughton, 26 February 1700/1, Suffolk Files 40:662, Judicial Archives. Campbell held no elected office in Boston or in the colonial legislature, although in his letter to Stoughton, he assures him "that I have been Ready by night or day, to doe what lay in my power to Serve the Publick."

His office as postmaster, however, carried a public stipend. Campbell apparently never joined a church, although he gave one pound for the construction of King's Chapel in 1689; his wife, Susanna, joined the Brattle Street Church in 1700. *The Manifesto Church: Records of the Church in Brattle Square, Boston* (Boston: Benevolent Fraternity of Churches, 1902), 102; Henry Wilder Foote, *Annals of King's Chapel* (Boston: Little, Brown, 1882), 1:89; and *Acts and Resolves*, 7:50, 429–34, 500–501; 8:18, 158, 198, 280–85, 562–63, 630–31.

59. John's relationship to Duncan is not clear. Although he has been identified as Duncan's son, it is more likely that they were brothers or cousins. Benjamin Franklin, ed., *Boston Printers, Publishers, and Booksellers, 1640–1800* (Boston: G.K. Hall, 1980), 69–70.

60. John Campbell, Thwing Index, MHS; SCS, *Constitution and By-laws*, 94; *Misc. Docs.*, 1:160; *Boston Births*, 9:221; and Thomas, *History of Printing*, 215. John Campbell's daughters married well (the Foys and Bowdoins are discussed below).

61. In general, Huguenots fled to England first, then came over to the colonies. In England, as Calvinists oppressed by a Catholic tyrant, they received a great deal of aid and support from earlier Huguenot immigrants, the English government, and the English public. Olsen, "English Reception," 481–91.

62. Request of the General Court, 15 June 1682, Suffolk Files 11:22A, Judicial Archives; and Letter from John Saffin and Elisha Hutchinson to Mr. Thomas Hinckley, 5 December 1686, Thomas Prince Papers, MHS. There was also a self-serving element, of course. Voluntary contributions allowed refugees to move to a permanent settlement and thus not become eligible for poor relief in Massachusetts towns. In general, however, charity was for religion's sake, being "for the credit of Religion that such strangers should be suitably" cared for. Request of the General Court, Suffolk Files 11:22A, Judicial Archives.

63. For more on these settlements, see chapter 5; and Charles Baird, *History of the Huguenot Emigration to America* (New York: Dodd, Mead, 1885), 2:255–81, 291–95, 300–309.

64. Butler, *Huguenots in America*, 78; and Foote, *Annals of King's Chapel*, 89. French-speaking merchants Thomas Mallet and John Foy also gave money to King's Chapel. Unfortunately, the records of the French church did not survive and so the full membership is not known. The membership and baptismal records for King's Chapel are also very spotty for the colonial period.

65. A. Holmes, "Memoir of the French Protestants Who Settled at Oxford, Massachusetts, A.D. 1686," *Collections of the Massachusetts Historical Society*, 3d ser., 2 (1830): 1–83; Baird, *History*, 2:205–7, 247–48; and Bond of Abraham Samuel, 7 May 1695, Photostat Coll., MHS. Duncan Mackfarland joined the Scots' Charitable Society in 1692. SCS, *Constitution and By-laws*, 95.

66. Butler, *Huguenots in America*, 78, 80, 85; Thomas, *Diary of Samuel Sewall*, 2:736; and Letter from John Oulton and Corner Walde to John Bowdoin, 23 April 1712, Miscellaneous Bound Collection, MHS.

67. Baird, *History*, 2:208–9, 213; *Misc. Docs.*, 1:154, 162; *Misc. Papers*, 10:110; Deposition of Benjamin Faneuil, 17 November 1694, Photostat Coll., MHS; and Orders for Captain John Jenkins, [1695?], Miscellaneous Bound Collection, MHS.

68. Shipping Licenses, 11 April 1698, Suffolk Files 7:104–5, 117, Judicial Archives. Baird, in *History*, 2:208, suggests that Andrew lived in Holland for a time, presumably to establish commercial connections there. Faneuil may have made initial contacts with Scottish merchants in Boston at this time. Robbins, *History of the Second Church*, 261.

69. Jamieson, "Overseas Settlement," 273; and Naval Office Shipping Lists for Massachusetts, 1686–1765, MHS.

70. ECR, 9:312, 323–25, 393–96. Brown had been involved in the New England trade since at least 1661; see above. Given his contacts Mudgett may also have been a Jerseyan, but no direct evidence linking him to Jersey has been found.

71. ECR, 9:323–25, 393–96. English's father-in-law, William Hollingsworth, had been declared dead in 1677 (lost at sea).

72. For the lives of merchant seamen, see Marcus Rediker, *Between the Devil and the Deep Blue Sea: Merchant Seamen, Pirates, and the Anglo-Atlantic Maritime World, 1700–1750* (Cambridge: Cambridge University Press, 1987), especially chapter 3.

73. LeBlond refused the office and paid a fine to avoid serving. He was later, however, elected tithing man and scavenger. Robert Francis Seybolt, *The Town Officials of Colonial Boston, 1634–1775* (Cambridge: Harvard University Press, 1939), 107, 115, 118, 121, 126, 129, 168, 169, 172. See also Butler, *Huguenots in America*, 78, 80; and Thomas, *Diary of Samuel Sewall*, 2:806, 866, 1011. Foy is also mentioned throughout Samuel Sewall's diary. See, for example, 1:47, 56, 75, 140, 154, 164, 18, 231–33.

NOTES TO CHAPTER 5

1. Other benevolent associations were founded in the eighteenth century: Anglicans formed the Episcopal Charitable Society in 1724, the Freemasons opened a chapter in Boston in 1733, Irish immigrants organized the Charitable Irish Society in 1737, and the Boston Marine Society, formed to aid indigent sailors, began in 1742. I have not found any reference to charitable societies associated specifically with French-speaking communities in early Massachusetts. Peter Richard Virgadamo, "Colonial Charity and the American Character: Boston, 1630–1775" (Ph.D. diss., University of Southern California, 1982), 213–20; and Charitable Irish Society, *The Constitution and By-laws of the Charitable Irish Society* (Boston: James F. Cotter, 1876).

2. Scots' Charitable Society, *Constitution and By-laws of the Scots' Charitable Society of Boston* (Cambridge, Mass.: Scots' Charitable Society, 1878), 28, 31.

3. The concept of ethnicity as developed for describing conditions in the nineteenth century cannot be applied directly to seventeenth-century Massachusetts. The English settlements were too new to be stable "host" societies in the nineteenth-century sense. Yet Miller's argument holds for the earlier period as well, in that the confluence of peoples— European, Native American, and African—shaped new identities for all. Kerby A. Miller, "Class, Culture, and Immigrant Group Identity in the United States: The Case of Irish-American Ethnicity," in *Immigration Reconsidered: History, Sociology, and Politics*, ed. Virginia Yans-McLaughlin (Oxford: Oxford University Press, 1990), 96–129, quote 98. See also Ned C. Landsman, "Pluralism, Protestantism, and Prosperity: Crèvecoeur's American Farmer and the Foundations of American Pluralism," in *Beyond Pluralism: The Conception of Groups and Group Identities in America*, ed. Wendy F. Katkin, Ned C. Landsman, and Andrea Tyree (Urbana: University of Illinois Press, 1998), 105–24.

4. Ned C. Landsman, *From Colonials to Provincials: American Thought and Culture, 1680–1760* (New York: Twayne, 1997), 1–7.

5. Colin Kidd, *British Identities Before Nationalism: Ethnicity and Nationalism in the Atlantic World, 1600–1800* (Cambridge: Cambridge University Press, 1999), 59–72, quote 64.

6. The court records for Suffolk County did not survive as well as those for Essex County, and thus information about early non-English residents of Boston is sketchy.

Scottish and Irish men and women do begin to appear in the marriage records in the late 1650s, however, the same time that indentured servants in Essex County began to marry. See *Boston Births, Marriages, and Deaths, 1630–1699,* Reports of the Records Commissioners 9 (Boston: Rockwell and Churchill, 1883) (hereafter *Boston Births*).

7. SCS, *Constitution and By-laws,* 25–26; Records of the Scots' Charitable Society, Microfilm, New England Historic Genealogical Society, Boston, Massachusetts (hereafter NEHGS). See also Virgadamo, "Colonial Charity," 112–15; and William Budde, "The Scots' Charitable Society of Boston, Massachusetts," in *A Cup of Kindness: The History of the Royal Scottish Corporation, a London Charity, 1603–2003,* by Justine Taylor (East Linton, U.K.: Tuckwell, 2003), 255–61.

8. SCS, *Constitution and By-laws*; and T. C. Smout, "The Glasgow Merchant Community in the Seventeenth Century," *Scottish Historical Review* 47, no. 1 (1968): 53–71, quote 58.

9. Taylor, *Cup of Kindness,* 25–27; and Ned C. Landsman, "Nation, Migration, and the Province in the First British Empire: Scotland and the Americas, 1600–1800," *American Historical Review* 104, no. 2 (1999): 463–75.

10. Landsman, "Nation, Migration," 468.

11. Scots did not form separate Presbyterian churches in Boston in the seventeenth century. The first mention of a ministerial appointment to a Presbyterian church in Boston was in 1730. Alexander Blaikie, *History of Presbyterianism in New England* (Boston: Alexander Moore, 1882), 59. See also Leonard J. Trinterud, *The Forming of an American Tradition: A Re-examination of Colonial Presbyterianism* (Philadelphia: Westminster, 1949); and Lefferts A. Loetscher, *A Brief History of the Presbyterians,* 4th ed. (Philadelphia: Westminster, 1978).

12. Patrick Griffin, in *The People with No Name: Ireland's Ulster Scots, America's Scots Irish, and the Creation of a British Atlantic World, 1689–1764* (Princeton: Princeton University Press, 2001), 3, makes a similar point about Scots in Scotland and Ulster.

13. Peter Grant falls into this category, for example. He worked at the Saugus ironworks in the early 1650s, after which the records become muddy. One Peter Grant appeared in Maine in the late 1660s, in 1698, and in 1704. Another Peter Grant lived in Boston at the same time. Neither of these men were specifically identified as Scottish, and not enough information about them has survived to guess at their identity. The only Peter Grant identified as a Scot after the 1650s was hanged as a pirate in 1675. Thus the Peter Grant from Saugus, the SCS member, and the pirate were all Scots, but were they all the same man? Or did Grant from Saugus move to Maine, eventually becoming a selectman of Berwick? For Grant in Maine, see Petition, n.d. [1669?], Suffolk Files 3:288, Judicial Archives, Massachusetts Archives, Boston, Massachusetts (hereafter Judicial Archives); Petition, 20 May 1698, Suffolk Files 11:127, Judicial Archives; and Kittery Rate List, 1704, Suffolk Files 3:418, Judicial Archives. For Grant in Boston, see *Boston Births,* 9:217; and *Miscellaneous Papers,* Reports of the Records Commissioners 10 (Boston: Rockwell and Churchill, 1886), 123 (hereafter *Misc. Papers*). For Grant the pirate, see John Noble, ed., *Records of the Court of Assistants of the Colony of the Massachusetts Bay, 1630–1692* (Boston: Suffolk County, 1901–28; reprint, New York: Arno, 1973), 1:34–39 (hereafter *Court of Assistants Records*).

14. Possible identifications, however, do exist for some of these men. For example, no information was found for Hercules Cosser, who joined the society in 1659. Yet in the 1680s, an Archelos Corser signed a petition in Lancaster. It is not possible to connect the two men directly. Another signatory of the same petition was Mordeca Makload,

who may also have been a Scot. Lancaster Petition, 28 May 1684, Suffolk Files 112:366, Judicial Archives.

15. See chapters 2 and 4 for the sources of information for the men discussed there. For this collective portrait, information was compiled from published primary records and archival sources for Essex and Suffolk counties. See my dissertation, "'As Good Englishmen': 'Strangers' in Seventeenth-Century Massachusetts" (Ph.D. diss., SUNY Stony Brook, 2001), for biographical sketches and complete bibliographical information for each of these men. A George Thompson also lived in Reading. His daughter Sarah married John Upton's eldest son, John, in 1680. It is not clear if the Boston or Reading Thompson is the SCS member, but nineteenth-century addenda to the microfilm records of the SCS at the New England Historical Genealogical Society list the man in Boston. *Vital Records of Reading to 1850* (Boston: Wright and Polter Printing, 1912), 461; and Will and Estate Inventory of George Thompson, Probate Docket No. 22452, Middlesex County, Judicial Archives.

16. When placed on a 1722 map of Boston, the earliest known map of the city, following the ward divisions of 1713, the fourth ward is near the commercial center of the town. The introduction to *Miscellaneous Documents,* Reports of the Records Commissioners 1 (Boston: Rockwell and Churchill, 1876), 14–15 (hereafter *Misc. Docs.*), states that in 1674 Boston was divided into eight militia companies. The description of the boundaries for these companies has not survived. Of the 1713 division of Boston into wards, the compilers state, "There is a certain probability that the first plan [1713] followed the lines then in use for the military companies, and that any changes would appear in the second plan [a 1715 redrawing of the ward boundaries]." I have thus superimposed the 1713 ward divisions onto the 1722 map as the best approximation of the divisions that might have existed in the seventeenth century. The tax lists on which this paragraph is based begin in 1674 and run intermittently until 1691, and include two lists of inhabitants of the town, one taken in 1688 and the other in 1695. Not all wards have returns for the same years. Tax lists are in volume 1 (*Misc. Docs.*) of the Reports of the Records Commissioners.

17. One family lived in ward 1, three in ward 2, three in ward 5, two in ward 7, and two in ward 8. The numbers of families do not add up to twenty-five because several families moved and so paid taxes in different wards.

18. See David Hancock, *Citizens of the World: London Merchants and the Integration of the British Atlantic Community, 1735–1785* (Cambridge: Cambridge University Press, 1995), 88, for the importance to merchants of living near the center of communication.

19. *Boston Town Records, 1660–1701,* Reports of the Records Commissioners 7 (Boston: Rockwell and Churchill, 1881), 52 (hereafter *Boston Town Records, 7*); *Misc. Docs.*, 1:76, 125, 144, 157, 169; Will of Alexander Simpson, Probate Docket 16:352, Suffolk County, Judicial Archives; and SCS, *Constitution and By-laws,* 25, 31. Mary Kneeland was probably the daughter of John, although his wife was also named Mary.

20. *Boston Births,* 9:176, 182, 197, 208, 223, 234, 249, 252, 253; *Misc. Docs.*, 1:125, 144, 169; Will of Joseph Simpson, Probate Docket 16:593, Suffolk County, Judicial Archives; and Inventory of Joseph Simpson, Probate Docket 17:57, Suffolk County, Judicial Archives. John and Mary Kneeland lived on Boston Neck on land that they rented from the town. Mary joined Boston's First Church in 1666. *Boston Town Records,* 7:211; and Richard D. Pierce, ed., *Records of the First Church in Boston, 1630–1868,* Publications of the Colonial Society of Massachusetts (Boston: Colonial Society of Massachusetts, 1961), 39:61.

21. SCS, *Constitution and By-laws,* 93; and *Boston Town Records,* 7:100. Neale purchased his property from Susannah Howlet in 1676. The ownership of the lot works

backward from Howlet to Sampson Sheafe, to Thomas Hawkins, to John Trotman, to John Davis as the original owner. The connection with John Courser is not clear, although he may have leased the tavern from any one of these previous owners. After Neale's death the property passed through his daughter Sarah to her husband, John Borland, and then to their son Francis. Samuel Adams Drake, *Old Boston Taverns and Tavern Clubs* (Boston: W. A. Butterfield, 1917), 120.

22. *Records of the Suffolk County Court, 1671–1680*, Publications of the Colonial Society of Massachusetts (Boston: Colonial Society of Massachusetts, 1933), 30:813, 920, 1020 (hereafter *Suffolk Court Records*); and *Misc. Docs.*, 1:72. In 1682, Neale was named one of ten innkeepers in Boston. In his will, Neale, like other members of the first SCS, did not acknowledge family in Scotland. *Boston Town Records*, 7:156; Inventory of Andrew Neale, Probate Docket 9:215, Suffolk County, Judicial Archives; and Will of Andrew Neale, Probate Docket 6:484–85, Suffolk County, Judicial Archives.

23. *Suffolk Court Records*, 30:1049, 1057; "Dairy of Francis Borland," Microfilm Copy, Special Collections, Edinburgh University Library, Edinburgh, Scotland; SCS, *Constitution and By-laws*, 94; and *Misc. Papers*, 10:60. See David Conroy, *In Public Houses: Drink and the Revolution of Authority in Colonial Massachusetts* (Chapel Hill: University of North Carolina Press, 1995), for a discussion of women as tavern keepers during this time period. Millicent Neale's membership in the SCS may indicate that she was from Scotland. If so, she would be one of the few Scottish women in Massachusetts before 1680. If she was not of Scottish descent, we would better understand just how malleable identity was in Massachusetts. Was she allowed to join because of her husband's Scottishness, or because of her children? Did her marriage to a Scot make her, in some sense, "Scottish"? Unless more information about her comes to light, we shall never know. Susanna Campbell, wife of Duncan, was the other woman to join the SCS. She became a member in 1696, six years before her husband died. (Duncan joined in 1686; see chapter 4.) A David Campbell, perhaps the employee of Millicent Neale, joined the SCS in 1686.

24. SCS, *Constitution and By-laws*, 28.

25. Records of the Scots' Charitable Society, NEHGS. Alexander Grant was a member of the first society and a ship's captain mentioned by Thomas Dewer in connection with Barbados merchants in the 1660s. Thomas Kelton arrived in Massachusetts in 1651 as a prisoner from Dunbar. He worked at Hammersmith until the mid-1650s. William Hamilton appears in a series of depositions taken in Boston in 1652. He was a servant at the time, and so may have arrived in Massachusetts as a prisoner of war. By the 1680s, Hamilton was a Boston shopkeeper and received the benevolence of the society from 1685 to the early 1690s. Deposition of William Hamilton, 2 August 1652, Photostat Collection, Massachusetts Historical Society, Boston, Massachusetts (hereafter Photostat Coll., MHS).

26. The total membership for the period was 135. Mariners included common sailors as well as masters of ships. Two men for whom no information was found described themselves as chapmen, traveling peddlers who would have had only peripheral connections to the Atlantic trading world. Many, if not most, members for whom no information was found probably did not live in New England and became connected with the society through seafaring activities. SCS, *Constitution and By-laws*, 93–97. Virgadamo argues that from 1690 to 1740, the SCS altered its financial and administrative structures, becoming more modern and professional in its operations. This argument fits well with my contention that the society fostered commercial networks. As merchants professionalized their commercial relationships, they would have transferred these new organizational ideas to the benevolent society that they ran. Virgadamo, "Colonial Charity," 159–93.

27. T. C. Smout, *Scottish Trade on the Eve of Union, 1660–1707* (Edinburgh: Oliver and Boyd, 1963); and Landsman, "Nation, Migration," 463–75.

28. *Boston Births*, 9:41, 82, 131, 136; *Misc. Docs.*, 1:70, 103, 105, 138, 150, 159; *Boston Town Records*, 7:140, 145, 159, 204, 222; and Pierce, *Records of the First Church in Boston*, 39:73, 77. Lydia, John's wife, joined the church in 1679. Their son John (born in 1677, the second child of this name) joined the Brattle Street Church around 1704. *The Manifesto Church: Records of the Church in Brattle Square, Boston* (Boston: Benevolent Fraternity of Churches, 1902), 127. For Ballantyne's position with the court, see, for example, Petition, 2 July 1695, Miscellaneous Bound Collection, M H S. The gunpowder commission was related to defense, since King William's War had just broken out and Bostonians were nervous about attacks by the French and their Native American allies. See also the petition circulated among Boston merchants at about the same time, asking the magistrates to secure all gunpowder in the town in one magazine away from the city center. Commission, Suffolk Files 36:120a, Judicial Archives; and Petition, Suffolk Files 70:513, Judicial Archives.

29. Ship Licenses, Suffolk Files 7:104, 125, 151, 154, Judicial Archives. The ownership of these ships was recorded as part of the oath taken by the master of the ship, or one or more of the owners, stating where and when the ship was built, its size, and its home port. Each listing also stated, "No forreigner directly or indirectly hath any share or part or interest therein." This statement, of course, was one provision of the Navigation Acts, codified in 1693, to insure that English and colonial goods were carried only in English- or colonial-owned ships.

30. George F. Dow and Mary G. Thresher, eds., *Records and Files of the Quarterly Courts of Essex County, Massachusetts* (Salem, Mass.: Essex Institute, 1911–75), 3:264–66 (hereafter E C R).

31. *Boston Births*, 9:136, 168, 182, 189; Ned C. Landsman, *Scotland and Its First American Colony, 1683–1765* (Princeton: Princeton University Press, 1985), 46–47; and John Borland, "Memoirs Relating to Our Family" (1701), Photostat Coll., M H S. In addition, although the name of William Ballantyne's father is not known, he named his first son John, perhaps after his father. Evidence of naming practices in other communities is not as abundant as among the Scots. The Irish men for whom this information is known named their eldest sons after themselves, as did the Jersey Islanders and the French. With French immigrants, however, because many moved in families, it is difficult to know the birth-order status of the children born in Massachusetts. See also Ian D. Whyte, *Scotland Before the Industrial Revolution: An Economic and Social History, 1050–1750* (London: Longman, 1995), 153.

32. The following description of Scottish society is based on Landsman, *Scotland and Its First American Colony*, 19–24. See also Whyte, *Scotland Before the Industrial Revolution*, 150–69.

33. Landsman, *Scotland and Its First American Colony*, 44–47, quote 34.

34. Ibid., 10, 135–40, quote 137.

35. Essex County Land Records, 3:22, Essex County Registry of Deeds, Salem, Massachusetts.

36. E C R, 2:338; 3:16. Grime was also Anderson's heir. Allester Mackmallen testified that Anderson and Grime were kinsmen and that the three families had lived near one another in Scotland, one of the few instances of a documented connection among non-English settlers in Massachusetts in their home country.

37. Essex County Land Records, 2:45; and Richard P. Gildrie, *Salem, Massachusetts, 1626–1683: A Covenant Community* (Charlottesville: University Press of Virginia, 1975), 117.

38. *Vital Records of Lynn, Massachusetts, to 1849* (Salem, Mass.: Essex Institute, 1905–6), 1:60, 74; 2:432, 440; and ECR, 6:383–85. Brann's nationality is unknown, but "Teague" suggests that he was Irish.

39. Essex County Land Records, 2:45; Will and Inventory of John Upton, Probate Docket No. 23261, Middlesex County, Judicial Archives; Essex County Land Records, 3:131; and ECR, 2:431; 5:53; 6:45–46. See also "List of Freemen," *New England Historical and Genealogical Register* 3 (October 1849): 352. Upton married Ellenor Stuart in the late 1650s; given her surname it is tempting to believe that she too was Scottish, but nothing else is known about her.

40. Inventory of James Hage, Probate Docket No. 10061, Middlesex County, Judicial Archives; and *Vital Records of Reading*, 66, 461. Ned Landsman, in *Scotland and Its First American Colony*, 36, suggests that mobility among tenant families in northeastern Scotland was based, in part, on "a reluctance . . . to part with what little autonomy the social order allowed." For non-Puritan colonists in Massachusetts, settlement on the edges of villages may have performed a similar function. John Brooke also found Baptists settling in small separate clusters in Worcester County in the early eighteenth century. John Brooke, *Heart of the Commonwealth: Society and Political Culture in Worcester County, Massachusetts, 1713–1861* (Amherst: University of Massachusetts Press, 1992), 88–89.

41. John W. Blake, "Transportation from Ireland to America, 1653–1660," *Irish Historical Studies* 3 (1942–43): 267–81; Abbot Emerson Smith, *Colonists in Bondage: White Servants and Convict Labor in America, 1607–1776* (Chapel Hill: University of North Carolina Press, 1947; reprint, Gloucester, Mass.: Peter Smith, 1965), 165–67; and Kerby Miller, *Emigrants and Exiles: Ireland and the Irish Exodus to North America* (Oxford: Oxford University Press, 1985), 139.

42. ECR, 2:294–97.

43. Ibid.

44. Blake, "Transportation from Ireland to America," 271–73; Smith, *Colonists in Bondage*, 165–67; Patrick J. Cornish, "The Cromwellian Regime, 1650–1660," in *A New History of Ireland*, vol. 3, *Early Modern Ireland, 1534–1691*, ed. T. W. Moody, F. X. Martin, and F. J. Byrne (Oxford: Oxford University Press, 1976), 362–63; and ECR, 2:296.

45. Thomas Lechford, *Notebook Kept by Thomas Lechford, 1638–1641*, in *Transactions and Collections of the American Antiquarian Society*, vol. 7 (Cambridge, Mass.: American Antiquarian Society, 1885), 251; John H. Edwards, "'Dorman Mahoone Alias Mathews': An Early Boston Irishman," *Proceedings of the Bostonian Society* (January 1917): 44–71; and ECR, 1:57. Although Tege Mahoney does not appear in the Saugus ironworks records, Joseph Armitage, a tailor, made clothing and did piecework for the company.

46. ECR, 8:222–26.

47. Carol Karlsen, *The Devil in the Shape of a Woman: Witchcraft in Colonial New England* (New York: Norton, 1987), 33–35. In this case, Glover's "strangeness" in nationality, language, and religion was clearly a factor in her indictment and execution. In the 1692 Salem witchcraft outbreak, such issues were not contributing factors; see chapter 4.

48. Miller, "Class, Culture, and Immigrant Group Identity," 97.

49. For Conney, see ECR, 4:170, 200. For LeCras, see ECR, 6:241–42. For Baker, see ECR, 5:232–33; 6:425.

50. A. G. Jamieson, "The Channel Islands and Overseas Settlement, 1600–1900," in *A People of the Sea: The Maritime History of the Channel Islands*, ed. A. G. Jamieson (London: Methuen, 1986), 269–89.

51. David Thomas Konig, "A New Look at the Essex 'French': Ethnic Frictions and Community Tensions in Seventeenth-Century Essex County, Massachusetts," *Essex Institute Historical Collections* 110, no. 3 (1974): 167–80; and ECR, 6:346–48.

52. Jamieson, "The Channel Islands and Overseas Settlement," 269–89.

53. ECR, 9:193–98.

54. ECR, 6:355–56; 7:328.

55. ECR, 8:193–95.

56. ECR, 5:90–92.

57. For the fishing community in Marblehead, see Daniel Vickers, "Work and Life on the Fishing Periphery of Essex County, Massachusetts, 1630–1675," in *Seventeenth-Century New England*, ed. David D. Hall and David Grayson Allen (Boston: Colonial Society of Massachusetts, 1984), 83–117; Vickers, *Farmers and Fishermen: Two Centuries of Work in Essex County, Massachusetts, 1630–1850* (Chapel Hill: University of North Carolina Press, 1994); and Christine Leigh Heyrman, *Commerce and Culture: The Maritime Communities of Colonial Massachusetts, 1690–1750* (New York: Norton, 1984). See also ECR, 9:309; 8:231–32.

58. Konig, "A New Look at the Essex 'French,'" 173–75.

59. The various suits among Jersey natives were extracted primarily from the published court records. See, for example, ECR, 4:176; 5:437; 6:346–48, 355–56; 7:349; 9:312, 323–25, 393–96; and *Balaine v. English*, 5 September 1694, Photostat Coll., MHS.

60. ECR, 5:90–92, 92, 232–33. Wells received a fine for his words against Baker, as well as for calling another man "old rogue, old witch and old wizard." ECR, 8:194. Tucker's wife Mary supervised the shore work of drying the catch and sold the fish to merchants in Salem and Boston.

61. For Vealey, see ECR, 9:284–87. For Beadle, see ECR, 9:110; 5:90–92.

62. See, for example, ECR, 2:280; 3:226–27; 5:141–42, 232; 6:175, 425–26; 7:331; and George Madison Bodge, *Soldiers of King Philip's War* (Boston: George Madison Bodge, 1906; reprint, Baltimore: Genealogical Publishing, 1967), 136.

63. Of the fifty-five cases in the published Essex County Quarterly Court records where natives of Jersey were either plaintiffs or defendants, twenty-six were for debt or some other issue relating to the exchange of goods or services, three were for breach of religion or slighting ministers, six for slighting authority or abusing constables, five for theft, four for fornication, two for slander or defamation, one each for rape, battery, and cursing, and six miscellaneous issues. The two slander or defamation cases relate to attempts to cast doubt on the honesty of Jerseyans.

In contrast, of the seventy-eight cases where Scottish or Irish residents of Essex County were plaintiffs or defendants, twenty-five were for debt or trespass, seven for abuse of constable or slighting authority or religion, one for theft, six for fornication, nine were language offenses, ten were alcohol related, four involved fighting, two were for lewd behavior, and fourteen were miscellaneous cases. These cases involved thirty long-term residents from Jersey and fifty-five Scots and Irish in Essex County. In addition, the Jersey cases span the years 1661 to 1690, and the Scots and Irish cases run from 1652 to 1691. Thus Jerseyans were brought to court slightly more often than other non-English residents, with more offenses against authority or religion.

64. ECR, 5:379; 7:246–47; 8:13–14.

65. For the Beadles, see ECR, 5:41, 168, 361; 6:73, 290; 7:246–47; 8:232, 237, 317–18, 372; 9:65, 271, 541, 571. For service by Daniel Bacon and Edward Feveryear, see ECR, 5:379,

444; 8:105; 9:41. For service in King Philip's War, see Bodge, *Soldiers of King Philip's War*, 58, 83, 136, 165, 222, 282; and Carole Doreski, ed., *Massachusetts Officers and Soldiers in the Seventeenth-Century Conflicts* (Boston: New England Historic Genealogical Society and the Society of Colonial Wars in the Commonwealth of Massachusetts, 1982), 11, 18, 172, 178, 240, 241. John LeGros and Thomas Beadle, sons of Jersey immigrants, also served in King William's War in the 1690s. Doreski, *Massachusetts Officers*, 18, 152. Some members of the Beadle, LeGros, and Mazury families joined the Salem church, mostly from the second generation. Richard D. Pierce, ed., *Records of the First Church in Salem, Massachusetts, 1629–1736* (Salem, Mass.: Essex Institute, 1974), 29, 31, 35, 39, 40, 41, 43, 44, 47, 55, 56, 57.

66. The Narragansett territory had been in dispute for many years. In 1664, the Carr Commission had been asked to settle the boundaries between Connecticut and Rhode Island. The commissioners had declared the land "the Kings Province," denying the validity of the Atherton Company's land titles, but the disputes continued. Andros made his decision in 1687 without settling the issue, and in 1703 a joint Connecticut–Rhode Island commission awarded the land to Rhode Island. Jenny Hale Pulsipher, *Subjects unto the Same King: Indians, English, and the Contest for Authority in Colonial New England* (Philadelphia: University of Pennsylvania Press, 2005), 55–56; Bernard Bailyn, *The New England Merchants in the Seventeenth Century* (Cambridge: Harvard University Press, 1955), 171–72; and Charles Baird, *History of the Huguenot Emigration to America* (New York: Dodd, Mead, 1885), 2:291–95. See also Jon Butler, *The Huguenots in America: A Refugee People in New World Society* (Cambridge: Harvard University Press, 1983), 60–63; and Richard R. Johnson, *Adjustment to Empire: The New England Colonies, 1675–1715* (New Brunswick: Rutgers University Press, 1981), 20, 374.

67. Huguenots appealed to the Council in Boston because the New England colonies had been incorporated into the Dominion of New England in 1686. Although the Dominion ended with the Glorious Revolution in England and the imprisonment of Edmund Andros in Massachusetts in 1689, and each colony had reinstituted its previous government, Huguenots probably believed that they had a better chance for restitution by appealing to the strongest and friendliest colony in the region. Baird, *History*, 2:305–9; and "To the Inhabitants of Greenwich in the Narragansett Country," 3 May 1689, Suffolk Files 11:45, Judicial Archives.

68. Baird, *History*, 2:255–66; and Butler, *Huguenots in America*, 63–64.

69. Baird, *History*, 2:263–81.

70. "The Humble Petition of the French Protestants in Boston," 21 June 1700, Suffolk Files 11:150, Judicial Archives; Henry Wilder Foote, *Annals of King's Chapel* (Boston: Little, Brown, 1882), 1:89; Chandler Robbins, *History of the Second Church, or Old North, in Boston* (Boston: John Wilson and Son, 1852), 261; and *Manifesto Church*, 103.

71. Petition of the French Congregation to Governor Andros, n.d., Suffolk Files 11:42, Judicial Archives; Nathaniel B. Shurtleff, ed., *Records of the Governor and Company of the Massachusetts Bay in New England* (Boston: William White, 1853; reprint, New York: Arno, 1968), 5:322; M. Halsey Thomas, ed., *Diary of Samuel Sewall* (New York: Farrar, Straus and Giroux, 1973), 1:90, 128, 406; and Stephen Nissenbaum, *The Battle for Christmas* (New York: Knopf, 1996), 3–26. As Nissenbaum notes, laws are made to control behavior that is already occurring, therefore many people must have tried to celebrate Christmas in the first two decades, and others, particularly in Marblehead and Salem Village, were presented for doing so even later in the century. None of the non-Puritans studied here, however, was involved in any of these incidents.

72. Neil Kamil, *Fortress of the Soul: Violence, Metaphysics, and Material Life in the Huguenots' New World, 1517–1751* (Baltimore: Johns Hopkins University Press, 2005), 1–10.

73. Baird, *History*, 2:304–5; Memorial, 20 April 1704, Photostat Coll., MHS.

74. *Boston Town Records, 1700–1728*, Reports of the Records Commissioners 8 (Boston: Rockwell and Churchill, 1883), 29, 31, 38, 41, 60. Butler, in *Huguenots in America*, 77–78, 80, discusses the early entry of Huguenot refugees into Boston politics as evidence of assimilation.

NOTES TO CONCLUSION

1. Darrett B. Rutman, "The Social Web: A Prospectus for the Study of Early American Community," in *Insights and Parallels: Problems and Issues of American Social History*, ed. William O'Neill (Minneapolis: Burgess Publishing, 1973), 57–89.

2. Several recent studies, most notably by Joann Melish, Jean O'Brien, and Ann Plane, have examined the processes by which Native Americans and African Americans were defined "out of existence" by nineteenth-century New Englanders of European descent. This created the image of a "free, white New England" in response to social pressures brought by the reform and abolition movements of that century, and has shaped modern perceptions of the region in the colonial period. Joann Melish, *Disowning Slavery: Gradual Emancipation and "Race" in New England, 1780–1860* (Ithaca: Cornell University Press, 1998); Jean M. O'Brien, *Dispossession by Degrees: Indian Land and Identity in Natick, Massachusetts, 1650–1790* (Cambridge: Cambridge University Press, 1997); and Ann Marie Plane, *Colonial Intimacies: Indian Marriage in Early New England* (Ithaca: Cornell University Press, 2000). The quoted phrases come from Melish, *Disowning Slavery*, 3. More recently, Joseph A. Conforti has integrated Africans and Indians into his discussion of strangers in colonial New England in *Saints and Strangers: New England in British North America* (Baltimore: Johns Hopkins University Press, 2006).

3. See chapter 4 for the offices held by the merchants. Oliver Ayer Roberts, *History of the Military Company of the Massachusetts, Now Called the Ancient and Honorable Artillery Company of Massachusetts, 1637–1888* (Boston: Alfred Mudge and Son, 1895), 1:236, 268, 275, 277, 292; and Louise A. Breen, *Transgressing the Bounds: Subversive Enterprises Among the Puritan Elite in Massachusetts, 1630–1692* (Oxford: Oxford University Press, 2001), 3.

4. The office of scavenger oversaw the removal of filth and public health hazards from the streets. Roberts, *History of the Military Company*, 1:275, 298, 303, 308, 397, 400, 404, 479; *Miscellaneous Documents*, Reports of the Records Commissioners 1 (Boston: Rockwell and Churchill, 1876), 82 (hereafter *Misc. Docs.*); *Boston Town Records, 1700–1728*, Reports of the Records Commissioners 8 (Boston: Rockwell and Churchill, 1883), 88, 95, 99 (hereafter *Boston Town Records*); *Miscellaneous Papers*, Reports of the Records Commissioners 10 (Boston: Rockwell and Churchill, 1886), 70 (hereafter *Misc. Papers*); and *Boston Births, Marriages, and Deaths, 1630–1699*, Reports of the Records Commissioners 9 (Boston: Rockwell and Churchill, 1883), 64 (hereafter *Boston Births*). Andrew Cunningham, Sr., was a glazier who arrived in Boston before 1684, when he joined the Scots' Charitable Society. Sarah Gibson Cunningham followed her parents into Boston's First Church in 1696. Carl Bridenbaugh describes Andrew Cunningham, Jr., as an "important personage, marrying and intermarrying into aristocratic circles." Scots' Charitable Society, *Constitution and By-laws of the Scots' Charitable Society* (Cambridge, Mass.:

Scots' Charitable Society, 1878), 94; Richard D. Pierce, ed., *Records of the First Church in Boston, 1630–1868*, Publications of the Colonial Society of Massachusetts (Boston: Colonial Society of Massachusetts, 1961), 39:95; Carl Bridenbaugh, *Cities in the Wilderness: The First Century of Urban Life in America, 1625–1742* (New York: Knopf, 1960), 252; and John A. Schutz, *Legislators of the Massachusetts General Court, 1691–1780* (Boston: Northeastern University Press, 1997), 156, 197.

5. Richard R. Johnson, *Adjustment to Empire: The New England Colonies, 1675–1715* (New Brunswick: Rutgers University Press, 1981), 296–98; and Bernard Bailyn, *The New England Merchants in the Seventeenth Century* (Cambridge: Harvard University Press, 1955), 174–77.

6. Johnson, *Adjustment to Empire*, 361.

7. For political turbulence in the 1680s and 1690s, see Johnson, *Adjustment to Empire*. Richard Dunn, in *Puritans and Yankees: The Winthrop Dynasty of New England, 1630–1717* (Princeton: Princeton University Press, 1962), discusses the political careers of the Winthrop brothers. See also W. H. Whitmore, ed., *Andros Tracts* (Boston: Prince Society, 1868; reprint, New York: Burt Franklin, 1968), 1:5, 2:239; and Robert E. Moody and Richard C. Simmons, eds., *The Glorious Revolution in Massachusetts: Selected Documents, 1689–1692*, Publications of the Colonial Society of Massachusetts (Boston: Colonial Society of Massachusetts, 1988), 64:105, 387, 418, 480.

8. See Johnson, *Adjustment to Empire*, 357–60, for more on Byfield's career. See also Rogers, *History of the Military Company*, 1:253–54, 317–18.

9. Bailyn, *New England Merchants*, 133–36; Rogers, *History of the Military Company*, 1:257; and Henry Wilder Foote, *Annals of King's Chapel* (Boston: Little, Brown, 1882), 1:89.

10. Bailyn, *New England Merchants*, 192; Johnson, *Adjustment to Empire*, 280–81; Rogers, *History of the Military Company*, 1:255; Foote, *Annals of King's Chapel*, 1:89; and Schutz, *Legislators*, 224.

11. Johnson, *Adjustment to Empire*, 280, 288, 386; Rogers, *History of the Military Company*, 1:260; Foote, *Annals of King's Chapel*, 1:89; and M. Halsey Thomas, ed., *Diary of Samuel Sewall* (New York: Farrar, Straus and Giroux, 1973), 2:724.

12. For Ferguson, see George F. Dow and Mary G. Thresher, eds., *Records and Files of the Quarterly Courts of Essex County, Massachusetts* (Salem, Mass.: Essex Institute, 1911–75), 9:592; Suffolk Files 35:301b, Judicial Archives, Massachusetts Archives, Boston, Massachusetts; and Schutz, *Legislators*, 218. For Borland, see *Boston Town Records*, 8:125. For Johonnot, see *Boston Town Records*, 8:123. For Sigorney, see *Boston Town Records*, 8:149. For Feveryear, see *Boston Town Records*, 8:117. For Buchanan, see *Boston Town Records*, 8:1, 30, 36, 43, 117. For Gibson, see *Boston Town Records*, 8:36, 42, 64, 109. For Kneeland, see *Boston Town Records*, 8:38, 42, 79, 100, 109, 123. For Webster, see *Boston Town Records*, 8:60, 100, 108, 117, 124, 129, 136. For Ballantyne, see *Boston Town Records*, 8:36, 56, 61, 75, 117.

13. Not all of them avoided political participation, of course. As we saw, Duncan Campbell solicited for appointive office, but non-English residents rarely stood for colony offices in the seventeenth century.

14. For Foy and Bowdoin, see chapter 4.

15. For more on Phips and Brenton, see Johnson, *Adjustment to Empire*, 274–84. See also Emerson W. Baker and John G. Reid, *The New England Knight: Sir William Phips, 1651–1695* (Toronto: University of Toronto Press, 1998), 223–31.

Bibliography

ARCHIVAL MATERIALS

Baker Library Historical Collections, Harvard Business School, Cambridge, Massachusetts
    Lynn Iron Works Collection
Essex County Registry of Deeds, Salem, Massachusetts
    Essex County Land Records
Judicial Archives, Massachusetts Archives, Boston, Massachusetts
    Middlesex Court Records, Pulsifer Transcript
    Probate Records, Middlesex County
    Probate Records, Suffolk County
    Suffolk Files
Massachusetts Historical Society, Boston, Massachusetts
    Miscellaneous Bound Collection
    Naval Office Shipping Lists for Massachusetts, 1686–1765
    Parkman Collection
    Photostat Collection
    Thomas Prince Papers
    Saltonstall Collection
    Sewall Collection
    Thwing Index
    Winthrop Papers
Mitchell Library, Archives and Special Collections, Glasgow, Scotland
    Shawfield Muniments
    Maxwells of Pollock Manuscripts
National Archives of Scotland, Edinburgh, Scotland
    Andrew Russell Papers
New England Historic Genealogical Society, Boston, Massachusetts
    Records of the Scots' Charitable Society, Microfilm
Phillips Library, Peabody Essex Museum, Salem, Massachusetts
    Records of the Essex County Quarterly Courts, Property of the Supreme Judicial
        Court, Division of Archives and Records Preservation
Special Collections, Edinburgh University Library, Edinburgh, Scotland
    "Diary of Francis Borland," Microfilm Copy

PRINTED PRIMARY MATERIAL

Acts and Resolves, Public and Private, of the Province of the Massachusetts Bay. 21 vols.
    Boston: Wright and Potter, 1869–1922.

Anderson, James R., ed. *The Burgesses and Guild Brethren of Glasgow, 1573–1750.* Edinburgh: J. Skinner, 1925.

Andrews, H. F. *List of Freemen, Massachusetts Bay Colony from 1630 to 1691.* Exira, Iowa: Exira Printing, 1906.

Baldwin, Thomas, ed. *Vital Records of Chelsea, Massachusetts to the Year 1850.* Boston: New England Historic Genealogical Society, 1916.

Boston Births, 1700–1800. Reports of the Records Commissioners 24. Boston: Rockwell and Churchill, 1894.

Boston Births, Marriages, and Deaths, 1630–1699. Reports of the Records Commissioners 9. Boston: Rockwell and Churchill, 1883.

Boston Marriages, 1700–1751. Reports of the Records Commissioners 28. Boston: Municipal Printing Office, 1898.

Boston Town Records, 1630–1660. Reports of the Records Commissioners 2. Boston: Rockwell and Churchill, 1877.

Boston Town Records, 1660–1701. Reports of the Records Commissioners 7. Boston: Rockwell and Churchill, 1881.

Boston Town Records, 1700–1728. Reports of the Records Commissioners 8. Boston: Rockwell and Churchill, 1883.

Charitable Irish Society. *The Constitution and By-laws of the Charitable Irish Society of Boston.* Boston: James F. Cotter, 1876.

Charlestown Land Records. Reports of the Records Commissioners 3. Boston: Rockwell and Churchill, 1878.

Dexter, Franklin Bowditch, ed. *New Haven Town Records.* 2 vols. New Haven, Conn.: New Haven Colony Historical Society, 1917–19.

Dorchester Births, Marriages, and Deaths to the End of 1825. Boston: Rockwell and Churchill, 1890.

Dorchester Town Records. Reports of the Records Commissioners 4. 2d ed. Boston: Rockwell and Churchill, 1883.

Dow, George F., and Mary G. Thresher, eds. *Records and Files of the Quarterly Courts of Essex County, Massachusetts.* 9 vols. Salem, Mass.: Essex Institute, 1911–75.

Dunn, Richard S., James Savage, and Laetitia Yeandle, eds. *The Journal of John Winthrop, 1630–1649.* Cambridge: Harvard University Press, 1996.

Gould, John H. "Early Records of the Church in Topsfield." *Essex Institute Historical Collections* 3 (1888): 181–205.

Hotten, John Camden, ed. *Original Lists of Persons of Quality . . . Who Went from Great Britain to the American Plantations, 1600–1700.* London, 1874. Reprint, Baltimore: Genealogical Publishing, 1986.

Hull, John. "Diaries of John Hull." *Transactions of the American Antiquarian Society* 3 (1857): 109–265.

Joslyn, Roger D., ed. *Vital Records of Charlestown, Massachusetts, to 1850.* Boston: New England Historic Genealogical Society, 1984.

Josselyn, John. "An Account of Two Voyages to New England." London, 1675. Reprint, *Collections of the Massachusetts Historical Society,* 3d ser., 3 (1833): 211–354.

Lechford, Thomas. *Notebook Kept by Thomas Lechford, 1638–1641.* In *Transactions and Collections of the American Antiquarian Society,* vol. 7 (Cambridge, Mass.: American Antiquarian Society, 1885).

"List of Freemen." *New England Historical and Genealogical Register* 3 (October 1849): 187–94, 239–47, 345–52.

The Manifesto Church: Records of the Church in Brattle Square, Boston. Boston: Benevolent Fraternity of Churches, 1902.

Miscellaneous Documents. Reports of the Records Commissioners 1. Boston: Rockwell and Churchill, 1876.

Miscellaneous Papers. Reports of the Records Commissioners 10. Boston: Rockwell and Churchill, 1886.

Moody, Robert E., ed. *The Saltonstall Papers, 1607–1815.* In *Collections of the Massachusetts Historical Society.* 2 vols. (80–81). Boston: Massachusetts Historical Society, 1972–74.

Moody, Robert E., Charles T. Libby, and Neal W. Allen, eds. *Province and Court Records of Maine.* 6 vols. Portland: Maine Historical Society, 1928–75.

Moody, Robert E., and Richard C. Simmons, eds. *The Glorious Revolution in Massachusetts: Selected Documents, 1689–1692.* Publications of the Colonial Society of Massachusetts 64. Boston: Colonial Society of Massachusetts, 1988.

Noble, John, ed. *Records of the Court of Assistants of the Colony of the Massachusetts Bay, 1630–1692.* 3 vols. Boston: Suffolk County, 1901–28. Reprint, New York: Arno, 1973.

Pierce, Richard D., ed. *Records of the First Church in Boston, 1630–1868.* Publications of the Colonial Society of Massachusetts 39–41. Boston: Colonial Society of Massachusetts, 1961.

———. *The Records of the First Church in Salem, Massachusetts, 1629–1736.* Salem, Mass.: Essex Institute, 1974.

Probate Records of Essex County. 3 vols. Salem, Mass.: Essex Institute, 1920.

Records of the Boston Selectmen, 1701–1715. Reports of the Records Commissioners 11. Boston: Rockwell and Churchill, 1884.

Records of the Suffolk County Court, 1671–1680. Publications of the Colonial Society of Massachusetts 29, 30. Boston: Colonial Society of Massachusetts, 1933.

Records of the Town of Cambridge, Massachusetts, 1603–1703. Cambridge, Mass.: Cambridge City Council, 1901.

Records of the Town Meetings of Lyn. 2 vols. Lynn, Mass.: Lynn Historical Society, 1949–56.

Roxbury Land and Church Records. Reports of the Records Commissioners 6. 2d ed. Boston: Rockwell and Churchill, 1884.

"Scotch Prisoners Sent to Massachusetts in 1652, by Order of the English Government." *New England Historical and Genealogical Register* 1 (1847): 377–80.

Scots' Charitable Society. *Constitution and By-laws of the Scots' Charitable Society of Boston.* Cambridge, Mass.: Scots' Charitable Society, 1878.

Sewall, Samuel. "Letter-Book of Samuel Sewall." *Collections of the Massachusetts Historical Society.* 2 vols. Boston: Massachusetts Historical Society, 1886–88.

Shurtleff, Nathaniel B., ed. *Records of the Governor and Company of the Massachusetts Bay in New England.* 5 vols. Boston: William White, 1853. Reprint, New York: Arno, 1968.

Tepper, Michael, ed. *Passengers to America: A Consolidation of Ship Passenger Lists.* Baltimore: Genealogical Publishing, 1980.

Thomas, M. Halsey, ed. *Diary of Samuel Sewell.* 2 vols. New York: Farrar, Straus and Giroux, 1973.

Town Records of Salem, Massachusetts. 3 vols. Salem, Mass.: Essex Institute, 1911–34.

Town Records of Topsfield, Massachusetts, 1659–1739. Topsfield, Mass.: Topsfield Historical Society, 1917.

Trask, William Blake. "Records of the Congregational Church in Wenham, Mass." *New England Historical and Genealogical Register* 61 (October 1907): 330–38.

————. "Records of the Congregational Church in Wenham, Mass." *New England Historical and Genealogical Register* 62 (January 1908): 34–48.

View of the Merchants House of Glasgow. Glasgow: Bell and Bain, 1871.

Vital Records of Ipswich, Massachusetts, to 1849. 3 vols. Salem, Mass.: Essex Institute, 1910–19.

Vital Records of Lynn, Massachusetts, to 1849. 2 vols. Salem, Mass.: Essex Institute, 1905–6.

Vital Records of Marblehead, Massachusetts, to 1849. 3 vols. Salem, Mass.: Essex Institute, 1903.

Vital Records of Reading to 1850. Boston: Wright and Polter Printing, 1912.

Vital Records of Rowley, Massachusetts, to 1849. 2 vols. Salem, Mass.: Essex Institute, 1928–1931.

Vital Records of Salem, Massachusetts. 6 vols. Salem, Mass.: Essex Institute, 1916.

Vital Records of Topsfield, Massachusetts, to the End of the Year 1849. Topsfield, Mass.: Topsfield Historical Society, 1903.

Vital Records of Wenham, Massachusetts, to the End of the Year 1849. Salem, Mass.: Essex Institute, 1904.

Whitmore, W. H., ed. *Andros Tracts.* 3 vols. Boston: Prince Society, 1868. Reprint, New York: Burt Franklin, 1968.

Winslow, Edward. *Hypocrisie Unmasked.* London, 1646. Reprint, New York: Burt Franklin, 1968.

Winthrop Papers. 5 vols. Boston: Massachusetts Historical Society, 1943–47.

Wood, William. *New England's Prospect.* London, 1634. Reprint, Boston: Prince Society, 1865.

SECONDARY MATERIALS

Akenson, Donald H. "Why the Accepted Estimates of the Ethnicity of the American People, 1790, Are Unacceptable." *William and Mary Quarterly* 41, no. 1 (1984): 102–19.

Allen, David Grayson. *In English Ways: The Movement of Societies and the Transferal of English Local Law and Custom to Massachusetts Bay in the Seventeenth Century.* Chapel Hill: University of North Carolina Press, 1981.

American National Biography. Oxford: Oxford University Press, 1999. S.v. "Andrew Hamilton."

Anderson, Benedict. *Imagined Communities: Reflections on the Origins and Spread of Nationalism.* London: New Left Books, 1983.

Anderson, Terry L., and Robert Paul Thomas. "White Population, Labor Force, and Extensive Growth of the New England Economy in the Seventeenth Century." *Journal of Economic History* 33, no. 3 (1973): 634–67.

Anderson, Virginia DeJohn. *New England's Generation: The Great Migration and the Formation of Society and Culture in the Seventeenth Century.* Cambridge: Cambridge University Press, 1991.

Appleby, J. C. "Neutrality, Trade, and Privateering, 1500–1689." In *A People of the Sea: A Maritime History of the Channel Islands,* edited by A. G. Jamieson. London: Methuen, 1986.

Archer, Richard. *Fissures in the Rock: New England in the Seventeenth Century.* Hanover: University Press of New England, 2001.

————. "New England Mosaic: A Demographic Analysis for the Seventeenth Century." *William and Mary Quarterly* 47, no. 4 (1990): 477–502.

Armitage, David. "The Darien Venture." In *Scotland and the Americas, 1600–1800,* edited by Michael Fry. Providence: John Carter Brown Library, 1995.

Babson, John J. *History of the Town of Gloucester, Cape Ann, Including the Town of Rockport.* Gloucester, Mass.: Procter Brothers, 1860.

Bailyn, Bernard. "The Apologia of Robert Keayne." *William and Mary Quarterly* 7, no. 4 (1950): 568–87.

———. *The New England Merchants in the Seventeenth Century.* Cambridge: Harvard University Press, 1955.

———. *Voyagers to the West: A Passage in the Peopling of America on the Eve of the Revolution.* New York: Knopf, 1986.

Bailyn, Bernard, and Philip D. Morgan, eds. *Strangers Within the Realm: Cultural Margins of the First British Empire.* Chapel Hill: University of North Carolina Press, 1991.

Baird, Charles. *History of the Huguenot Emigration to America.* 2 vols. New York: Dodd, Mead, 1885.

Baker, Emerson W., and John G. Reid. *The New England Knight: Sir William Phipps, 1651–1695.* Toronto: University of Toronto Press, 1998.

Bancroft, George. *History of the United States of America.* New York: D. Appleton, 1886.

Banks, Charles Edward. *History of York, Maine.* 2 vols. Boston: C. E. Banks, 1931–35. Reprint, Baltimore: Regional Publishing, 1967.

———. "Scotch Prisoners Deported to New England by Cromwell, 1651–1652." *Proceedings of the Massachusetts Historical Society* 61 (1927–28): 4–29.

Barbour, James Samuel. *A History of William Paterson and the Darien Company.* Edinburgh: W. Blackwood and Sons, 1907.

Barnard, T. C. *Cromwellian Ireland: English Government and Reform in Ireland, 1649–1660.* Oxford: Oxford University Press, 1975. Reprint, 2000.

Barnard, T. C., Dáibhí Ó Cróinín, and Katherine Simms, eds. *"A Miracle of Learning": Studies in Manuscripts and Irish Learning: Essays in Honour of William O'Sullivan.* Aldershot, U.K.: Ashgate, 1998.

Battis, Emery. *Saints and Sectaries: Anne Hutchinson and the Antinomian Controversy in the Massachusetts Bay Colony.* Chapel Hill: University of North Carolina Press, 1962.

Beckles, Hilary McD. "The 'Hub of Empire': The Caribbean and Britain in the Seventeenth Century." In *The Origins of Empire: British Overseas Expansion to the Close of the Seventeenth Century,* edited by Nicholas Canny. Oxford: Oxford University Press, 1998.

Belknap, Henry Wyckoff. *Trades and Tradesmen of Essex County, Massachusetts.* Salem, Mass.: Essex Institute, 1929.

Bender, Thomas. *Community and Social Change in America.* New Brunswick: Rutgers University Press, 1978. Reprint, Baltimore: Johns Hopkins University Press, 1982.

Berlin, Ira. *Many Thousands Gone: The First Two Centuries of Slavery in North America.* Cambridge: Harvard University Press, 1998.

Bidwell, Percy Wells, and John I. Falconer. *History of Agriculture in the Northern United States, 1620–1860.* Washington, D.C.: Carnegie Institute of Washington, 1925. Reprint, New York: Peter Smith, 1941.

Billias, George Athan, ed. *Law and Authority in Colonial America.* Barre, Mass.: Barre Publishers, 1965.

Black, Robert C. *The Younger John Winthrop.* New York: Columbia University Press, 1966.

Blaikie, Alexander. *History of Presbyterianism in New England.* Boston: Alexander Moore, 1882.

Blake, John. "Transportation from Ireland to America, 1653–1660." *Irish Historical Studies* 3 (1942–43): 267–81.

Bodge, George Madison. *Soldiers of King Philip's War*. Boston: George Madison Bodge, 1906. Reprint, Baltimore: Genealogical Publishing, 1967.

Bosher, J. F. "Huguenot Merchants and the Protestant International in the Seventeenth Century." *William and Mary Quarterly* 52, no. 1 (1995): 77–102.

Bottigheimer, Karl. *Ireland and the Irish: A Short History*. New York: Columbia University Press, 1982.

Boyer, Paul, and Stephen Nissenbaum. *Salem Possessed: The Social Origins of Witchcraft*. Cambridge: Harvard University Press, 1974.

Bradshaw, Brendan, and John Morrill, eds. *The British Problem, 1534–1707: State Formation in the Atlantic Archipelago*. New York: St. Martin's Press, 1996.

Breen, Louise A. *Transgressing the Bounds: Subversive Enterprises Among the Puritan Elite in Massachusetts, 1630–1692*. Oxford: Oxford University Press, 2001.

Breen, T. H. "Creative Adaptations: Peoples and Cultures." In *Colonial British America: Essays in the New History of the Early Modern Era*, edited by Jack P. Greene and J. R. Pole. Baltimore: Johns Hopkins University Press, 1984.

———. "Who Governs: The Town Franchise in Seventeenth-Century Massachusetts." *William and Mary Quarterly* 27, no. 3 (1970): 460–74.

Breen, T. H., and Stephen Foster. "The Puritans' Greatest Achievement: A Study of Social Cohesion in Seventeenth-Century Massachusetts." *Journal of American History* 40, no. 1 (1973): 5–22.

Bremer, Francis J. *Congregational Communion: Clerical Friendship in the Anglo-American Puritan Community, 1610–1692*. Boston: Northeastern University Press, 1994.

———. *John Winthrop: America's Forgotten Founding Father*. Oxford: Oxford University Press, 2003.

Bremer, Francis J., and Lynn A. Botelho, eds. *The World of John Winthrop: Essays on England and New England, 1588–1649*. Boston: Massachusetts Historical Society, 2005.

Bridenbaugh, Carl. *Cities in the Wilderness: The First Century of Urban Life in America, 1625–1742*. 2d ed. New York: Knopf, 1960.

Brock, William R. *Scotus Americanus: A Survey of Sources for Links Between Scotland and America in the Eighteenth Century*. Edinburgh: Edinburgh University Press, 1982.

Brooke, John L. *The Heart of the Commonwealth: Society and Political Culture in Worcester County, Massachusetts, 1713–1861*. Amherst: University of Massachusetts Press, 1992.

———. *The Refiner's Fire: The Making of Mormon Cosmology, 1644–1844*. Cambridge: Cambridge University Press, 1996.

Buckroyd, Julia. *Church and State in Scotland*. Edinburgh: John Donald, 1980.

Budde, William. "The Scots' Charitable Society of Boston, Massachusetts." In *A Cup of Kindness: The History of the Royal Scottish Corporation, a London Charity, 1603–2003*, by Justine Taylor. East Lothian, U.K.: Tuckwell, 2003.

Bush, Sargent, Jr., ed. *The Correspondence of John Cotton*. Chapel Hill: University of North Carolina Press, 2001.

Bushman, Richard. *From Puritan to Yankee: Character and Social Order in Connecticut, 1690–1765*. Cambridge: Harvard University Press, 1967.

Butler, Jon. *The Huguenots in America: A Refugee People in New World Society*. Cambridge: Harvard University Press, 1983.

Butlin, R. A. "Land and People, c. 1600." In *A New History of Ireland*. Vol. 3, *Early Modern Ireland, 1534–1691*, edited by T. W. Moody, F. X. Martin, and F. J. Byrne. Oxford: Oxford University Press, 1976.

Byers, Edward. *The Nation of Nantucket: Society and Politics in an Early American Commercial Center, 1660–1820*. Boston: Northeastern University Press, 1987.

Canny, Nicholas. "Fashioning 'British' Worlds in the Seventeenth Century." In *Empire, Society, and Labor: Essays in Honor of Richard S. Dunn*, edited by Nicholas Canny, Gary B. Nash, Joe Illick, and William Pencak. University Park: Pennsylvania History, 1997.

———. *Making Ireland British, 1580–1650*. Oxford: Oxford University Press, 2001.

———. "The Origins of Empire: An Introduction." In *The Origins of Empire: British Overseas Empire to the Close of the Seventeenth Century*, edited by Nicholas Canny. Oxford: Oxford University Press, 1998.

———, ed. *The Origins of Empire: British Overseas Enterprise to the Close of the Seventeenth Century*. Oxford: Oxford University Press, 1998.

Canny, Nicholas, and Anthony Pagden, eds. *Colonial Identity in the Atlantic World, 1500–1800*. Princeton: Princeton University Press, 1987.

Canup, John. *Out of the Wilderness: The Emergence of an American Identity in Colonial New England*. Middletown: Wesleyan University Press, 1990.

Colley, Linda. *Britons: Forging the Nation, 1707–1837*. New Haven: Yale University Press, 1992.

———. *Captives*. New York: Pantheon Books, 2002.

Conforti, Joseph A. *Imagining New England: Explorations of Regional Identity from the Pilgrims to the Mid-Twentieth Century*. Chapel Hill: University of North Carolina Press, 2001.

———. *Saints and Strangers: New England in British North America*. Baltimore: Johns Hopkins University Press, 2006.

Conroy, David. *In Public Houses: Drink and the Revolution of Authority in Colonial Massachusetts*. Chapel Hill: University of North Carolina Press, 1995.

Cook, Edward M., Jr. *The Fathers of the Towns: Leadership and Community Structure in Eighteenth-Century New England*. Baltimore: Johns Hopkins University Press, 1976.

Cook, S. F. *The Indian Population of New England in the Seventeenth Century*. Berkeley and Los Angeles: University of California Press, 1976.

Cooper, James F., Jr. *Tenacious of Their Liberties: The Congregationalists in Colonial Massachusetts*. Oxford: Oxford University Press, 1999.

Cornish, Patrick J. "The Cromwellian Regime, 1650–1660." In *A New History of Ireland*. Vol. 3, *Early Modern Ireland, 1534–1691*, edited by T. W. Moody, F. X. Martin, and F. J. Byrne. Oxford: Oxford University Press, 1976.

Cowan, Ian B. *The Scottish Covenanters, 1660–1688*. London: Victor Gollancz, 1976.

Creager, Angela N. H., and William Chester Jordan, eds. *The Animal/Human Boundary: Historical Perspectives*. Rochester: University of Rochester Press, 2002.

Cressy, David. *Coming Over: Migration and Communication Between England and New England in the Seventeenth Century*. Cambridge: Cambridge University Press, 1987.

Cullen, James Bernard. *The Story of the Irish in Boston*. Boston: James B. Cullen, 1889.

Deane, Charles. "The Irish Donation in 1676." *New England Historical and Genealogical Register* 2 (July 1848): 245–50.

Demos, John. *Entertaining Satan: Witchcraft and the Culture of Early New England*. Oxford: Oxford University Press, 1982.

Dempsey, Jack. *Thomas Morton of Merrymount: The Life and Renaissance of an Early American Poet.* Stoneham, Mass.: Jack Dempsey, 2000.

Devine, T. M. *Scotland's Empire, 1600–1815.* London: Penguin, 2003.

Devine, T. M., and Gordon Jackson, eds. *Glasgow.* Vol. 1, *Beginnings to 1830.* Manchester: University of Manchester Press, 1995.

Dobson, David. *Directory of Scottish Settlers in North America, 1625–1825.* 7 vols. Baltimore: Genealogical Publishing, 1984–86.

———. *Scottish Emigration to Colonial America, 1607–1785.* Athens: University of Georgia Press, 1994.

Doreski, Carole, ed. *Massachusetts Officers and Soldiers in the Seventeenth-Century Conflicts.* Boston: New England Historical Genealogical Society and the Society of Colonial Wars in the Commonwealth of Massachusetts, 1982.

Dow, F. D. *Cromwellian Scotland, 1651–1660.* Edinburgh: John Donald, 1979.

Dow, George Francis. *History of Topsfield, Massachusetts.* Topsfield, Mass.: Topsfield Historical Society, 1940.

Drake, Samuel Adams. *Old Boston Taverns and Tavern Clubs.* Boston: W. A. Butterfield, 1917.

Dunn, Richard S. *Puritans and Yankees: The Winthrop Dynasty of New England, 1630–1717.* Princeton: Princeton University Press, 1962.

———. "Servants and Slaves: The Recruitment and Employment of Labor." In *Colonial British America: Essays in the New History of the Early Modern Era,* edited by Jack P. Greene and J. R. Pole. Baltimore: Johns Hopkins University Press, 1984.

Edmonds, John H. "'Dorman Mahoone Alias Mathews': An Early Boston Irishman." *Proceedings of the Bostonian Society* (January 1917): 44–71.

Ernest, Carl Wilhelm. *Postal Service in Boston, 1639–1893.* Boston: Boston Public Library, 1975.

Fischer, David Hackett. *Albion's Seed: Four British Folkways in America.* Oxford: Oxford University Press, 1989.

Foote, Henry Wilder. *Annals of King's Chapel.* 2 vols. Boston: Little, Brown, 1882.

Foster, R. F. *Modern Ireland, 1600–1972.* London: Penguin, 1988.

———, ed. *The Oxford History of Ireland.* Oxford: Oxford University Press, 1989.

Foster, Stephen. *The Long Argument: English Puritanism and the Shaping of New England Culture, 1570–1700.* Chapel Hill: University of North Carolina Press, 1991.

———. "The Massachusetts Franchise in the Seventeenth Century." *William and Mary Quarterly* 24, no. 4 (1967): 613–23.

Franklin, Benjamin, ed. *Boston Printers, Publishers, and Booksellers, 1640–1800.* Boston: G. K. Hall, 1980.

Frothingham, Richard, Jr. *History of Charlestown, Massachusetts.* Boston: Charles C. Little and James Brown, 1845.

Fry, Michael, ed. *Scotland and the Americas, 1600 to 1800.* Providence: Brown University Press, 1995.

Galenson, David W. *White Servitude in Colonial America: An Economic Analysis.* Cambridge: Cambridge University Press, 1981.

Galvin, William Francis. *Historical Data Relating to Counties, Cities, and Towns in Massachusetts.* Boston: Secretary of the Commonwealth and the New England Historic Genealogical Society, 1997.

Games, Alison. *Migration and the Origins of the English Atlantic World.* Cambridge: Harvard University Press, 1999.

Gardiner, Ginny. "A Haven for Intrigue: The Scottish Exile Community in the Netherlands, 1660–1690." In *Scottish Communities Abroad in the Early Modern Period,* edited by Alexia Grosjean and Steve Murdoch. Leiden: Brill, 2005.

Gemery, Henry A. "Emigration from the British Isles to the New World, 1630–1700: Inferences from Colonial Populations." *Research in Economic History* 5 (1980): 179–231.

Gildrie, Richard P. *The Profane, the Civil, and the Godly: The Reformation of Manners in Orthodox New England.* University Park: Pennsylvania State University Press, 1994.

———. *Salem, Massachusetts, 1626–1683: A Covenant Community.* Charlottesville: University Press of Virginia, 1975.

———. "Salem Society and Politics in the 1680s." *Essex Institute Historical Collections* 114, no. 4 (1978): 185–206.

Godbeer, Richard. *Escaping Salem: The Other Witch Hunt of 1692.* Oxford: Oxford University Press, 2005.

———. *Sexual Revolution in Early America.* Baltimore: Johns Hopkins University Press, 2002.

Goodfriend, Joyce D. *Before the Melting Pot: Society and Culture in Colonial New York City, 1664–1730.* Princeton: Princeton University Press, 1992.

Granger, John D. *Cromwell Against the Scots: The Last Anglo-Scots War, 1650–1652.* East Linton, U.K.: Tuckwell, 1997.

Greene, Evarts B., and Virginia D. Harrington. *American Population Before the Federal Census of 1790.* New York: Columbia University Press, 1932. Reprint, Gloucester, Mass.: Peter Smith, 1966.

Greene, Jack P. *Pursuits of Happiness: The Social Development of Early Modern British Colonies and the Formation of American Culture.* Chapel Hill: University of North Carolina Press, 1988.

Greene, Jack P., and J. R. Pole, eds. *Colonial British America: Essays in the New History of the Early Modern Era.* Baltimore: Johns Hopkins University Press, 1984.

Greene, Lorenzo J. *The Negro in Colonial New England, 1620–1776.* New York: Columbia University Press, 1942. Reprint, Port Washington, N.Y.: Kennikat, 1966.

Greven, Philip. *Four Generations: Population, Land, and Family in Colonial Andover.* Ithaca: Cornell University Press, 1970.

Griffin, Patrick. *The People with No Name: Ireland's Ulster Scots, America's Scots Irish, and the Creation of a British Atlantic World, 1689–1764.* Princeton: Princeton University Press, 2001.

Grosjean, Alexia, and Steve Murdoch, eds. *Scottish Communities Abroad in the Early Modern Period.* Leiden: Brill, 2005.

Gura, Philip F. "'The Contagion of Corrupt Opinions' in Puritan Massachusetts: The Case of William Pynchon." *William and Mary Quarterly* 39, no. 3 (1982): 469–91.

———. *A Glimpse of Sion's Glory: Puritan Radicalism in New England, 1620–1660.* Middletown: Wesleyan University Press, 1984.

———. "The Radical Ideology of Samuel Gorton: New Light on the Relation of English to American Puritanism." *William and Mary Quarterly* 36, no. 1 (1979): 78–100.

Guy, John. *Tudor England.* Oxford: Oxford University Press, 1988.

Haines, Michael R., and Richard H. Steckel, eds. *A Population History of North America.* Cambridge: Cambridge University Press, 2000.

Hall, David D., and David Grayson Allen, eds. *Seventeenth-Century New England.* Boston: Colonial Society of Massachusetts, 1984.

Hall, David D., John M. Murrin, and Thad W. Tate, eds. *Saints and Revolutionaries: Essays on Early American History.* New York: Norton, 1984.

Hall, Michael Garibaldi. *Edward Randolph and the American Colonies, 1676–1703.* Chapel Hill: University of North Carolina Press, 1960.

Hamilton, Marsha L. "'As Good Englishmen': 'Strangers' in Seventeenth-Century Massachusetts." Ph.D. diss., SUNY Stony Brook, 2001.

Hancock, David. *Citizens of the World: London Merchants and the Integration of the British Atlantic Community, 1735–1785.* Cambridge: Cambridge University Press, 1995.

Harris, Ralph Bertram. "Philip English." *Essex Institute Historical Collections* 67 (1930): 273–90.

Hart, James S., and Richard J. Ross. "The Ancient Constitution in the Old World and the New." In *The World of John Winthrop: Essays on England and New England, 1588–1649,* edited by Francis J. Bremer and Lynn A. Botelho. Boston: Massachusetts Historical Society, 2005.

Hartley, E. N. *Ironworks on the Saugus.* Norman: University of Oklahoma Press, 1957.

Haskins, George Lee. *Law and Authority in Early Massachusetts: A Study in Tradition and Design.* New York: Macmillan, 1960.

Hatfield, April Lee. *Atlantic Virginia: Intercolonial Relations in the Seventeenth Century.* Philadelphia: University of Pennsylvania Press, 2004.

Henretta, James A. "Economic Development and Social Structure in Colonial Boston." In *Colonial America: Essays in Politics and Social Development,* edited by Stanley A. Katz. 2d ed. Boston: Little, Brown, 1971.

Herndon, Ruth Wallis. *Unwelcome Americans: Living on the Margins in Early New England.* Philadelphia: University of Pennsylvania Press, 2001.

Heyrman, Christine Leigh. *Commerce and Culture: The Maritime Communities of Colonial Massachusetts, 1690–1750.* New York: Norton, 1984.

———. "Specters of Subversion, Societies of Friends: Dissent and the Devil in Provincial Essex County, Massachusetts." In *Saints and Revolutionaries: Essays on Early American History,* edited by David D. Hall, John M. Murrin, and Thad W. Tate. New York: Norton, 1984.

Higginbotham, A. Leon. *In the Matter of Color: Race and the American Legal Process: The Colonial Period.* Oxford: Oxford University Press, 1978.

Hill, Christopher. *God's Englishman: Oliver Cromwell and the English Revolution.* London: Dial, 1970.

Hill, Hamilton Andrews. *History of the Old South Church (Third Church), Boston, 1669–1884.* Boston: Houghton Mifflin, 1890.

Hoffer, Peter Charles. *Law and People in Colonial America.* Rev. ed. Baltimore: Johns Hopkins University Press, 1998.

Hoffer, Peter Charles, and N. E. H. Hull, eds. *Murdering Mothers: Infanticide in England and New England, 1558–1803.* New York: New York University Press, 1981.

Holmes, A. "Memoir of the French Protestants Who Settled at Oxford, Massachusetts, A.D. 1686." *Collections of the Massachusetts Historical Society,* 3d ser., 2 (1830): 1–83.

Houston, R. A., and I. D. Whyte, eds. *Scottish Society, 1500–1800.* Cambridge: Cambridge University Press, 1989.

Howe, Mark DeWolfe. "The Sources and Nature of Law in Colonial Massachusetts." In *Law and Authority in Colonial America,* edited by George Athan Billias. Barre, Mass.: Barre Publishers, 1965.

Hunter, Phyllis Whitman. *Purchasing Identity in the Atlantic World: Massachusetts Merchants, 1670–1780.* Ithaca: Cornell University Press, 2001.

Hurd, D. Hamilton. *History of Essex County, Massachusetts.* 2 vols. Philadelphia: J. W. Lewis, 1888.

Hutchinson, Thomas. *The History of the Colony and Province of Massachusetts Bay.* Edited by Lawrence Shaw Mayo. 3 vols. Cambridge: Harvard University Press, 1936.

Hyman, Elizabeth Hannan. "A Church Militant: Scotland, 1661–1690." *The Sixteenth Century Journal* 26, no. 1 (1995): 49–74.

Ingram, J. H. *The Islands of England: A Survey of the Islands Around England and Wales and the Channel Islands.* London: Batsford, 1932.

Innes, Stephen. *Creating the Commonwealth: The Economic Culture of Puritan New England.* New York: Norton, 1995.

———. *Labor in a New Land: Economy and Society in Seventeenth-Century Springfield.* Princeton: Princeton University Press, 1983.

———, ed. *Work and Labor in Early America.* Chapel Hill: University of North Carolina Press, 1988.

Insh, George Pratt. *The Company of Scotland Trading to Africa and the Indies.* London: Charles Scribner's Sons, 1932.

Isaac, Rhys. *The Transformation of Virginia, 1740–1790.* Chapel Hill: University of North Carolina Press, 1982.

Jackson, Gordon. "Glasgow in Transition, c. 1660–c. 1740." In *Glasgow.* Vol. 1, *Beginnings to 1830,* edited by T. M. Devine and Gordon Jackson. Manchester: University of Manchester Press, 1995.

Jamieson, A. G. "The Channel Islands and Overseas Settlement, 1600–1900." In *A People of the Sea: The Maritime History of the Channel Islands,* edited by A. G. Jamieson. London: Methuen, 1986.

———, ed. *A People of the Sea: The Maritime History of the Channel Islands.* London: Methuen, 1986.

Johnson, Richard R. *Adjustment to Empire: The New England Colonies, 1675–1715.* New Brunswick: Rutgers University Press, 1981.

Jones, Douglas Lamar. "The Strolling Poor: Transiency in Eighteenth-Century Massachusetts." *Journal of Social History* 8, no. 3 (Spring 1975): 28–54.

———. *Village and Seaport: Migration and Society in Eighteenth-Century Massachusetts.* Hanover: University Press of New England, 1981.

Jordan, Winthrop D. *White over Black: American Attitudes Toward the Negro, 1550–1812.* Chapel Hill: University of North Carolina Press, 1968.

Kamensky, Jane. *Governing the Tongue: The Politics of Speech in Early New England.* Oxford: Oxford University Press, 1997.

Kamil, Neil. *Fortress of the Soul: Violence, Metaphysics, and Material Life in the Huguenots' New World, 1517–1751.* Baltimore: Johns Hopkins University Press, 2005.

Karlsen, Carol. *The Devil in the Shape of a Woman: Witchcraft in Colonial New England.* New York: Norton, 1987.

Katkin, Wendy F., Ned C. Landsman, and Andrea Taylor, eds. *Beyond Pluralism: The Conception of Group Identities in America.* Urbana: University of Illinois Press, 1998.

Kettner, James H. *The Development of American Citizenship, 1608–1870.* Chapel Hill: University of North Carolina Press, 1978.

Kidd, Colin. *British Identities Before Nationalism: Ethnicity and Nationhood in the Atlantic World, 1600–1800.* Cambridge: Cambridge University Press, 1999.

Kierner, Cynthia A. *Traders and Gentlefolk: The Livingstons of New York, 1675–1790.* Ithaca: Cornell University Press, 1992.

Kishlansky, Mark. *A Monarchy Transformed: Britain, 1603–1714.* London: Penguin, 1996.

Knight, Janice. *Orthodoxies in Massachusetts: Rereading American Puritanism.* Cambridge: Harvard University Press, 1994.

Konig, David Thomas. *Law and Society in Puritan Massachusetts: Essex County, 1629–1692.* Chapel Hill: University of North Carolina Press, 1979.

———. "A New Look at the Essex 'French': Ethnic Frictions and Community Tensions in Seventeenth-Century Essex County, Massachusetts." *Essex Institute Historical Collections* 110, no. 3 (1974): 167–80.

Kupperman, Karen Ordahl. *Providence Island, 1630–1641: The Other Puritan Colony.* Cambridge: Cambridge University Press, 1993.

———. "Thomas Morton, Historian." *New England Quarterly* 50, no. 4 (1977): 660–64.

Kussmaul, Ann. *Servants in Husbandry in Early Modern England.* Cambridge: Cambridge University Press, 1981.

Landsman, Ned C. *From Colonials to Provincials: American Thought and Culture, 1680–1760.* New York: Twayne, 1997.

———. "Immigration and Settlement." In *Scotland and the Americas, 1600 to 1800,* edited by Michael Fry. Providence: John Carter Brown Library, 1995.

———. "Nation, Migration, and the Province in the First British Empire: Scotland and the Americas, 1600–1800." *American Historical Review* 104, no. 2 (1999): 463–75.

———. "Pluralism, Protestantism, and Prosperity: Crèvecoeur's American Farmer and the Foundations of American Pluralism." In *Beyond Pluralism: The Conception of Groups and Group Identities in America,* edited by Wendy F. Katkin, Ned C. Landsman, and Andrea Tyree. Urbana: University of Illinois Press, 1998.

———. *Scotland and Its First American Colony, 1683–1765.* Princeton: Princeton University Press, 1985.

Leder, Lawrence H. *Robert Livingston and the Politics of Colonial New York.* Chapel Hill: University of North Carolina Press, 1961.

Lepore, Jill. *The Name of War: King Philip's War and the Origins of American Identity.* New York: Knopf, 1999.

Levack, Brian P. *The Formation of the British State: England, Scotland, and the Union, 1603–1707.* Oxford: Oxford University Press, 1987.

Lewis, Alonzo, and James Newhall. *History of Lynn.* Lynn, Mass.: By the authors, 1865. Reprint, Lynn, Mass.: G. C. Herbert, 1890.

Lockridge, Kenneth. *A New England Town: The First Hundred Years.* Expanded ed. New York: Norton, 1985.

Loeber, Rolf. "Preliminaries to the Massachusetts Bay Colony: The Irish Ventures of Emanuel Downing and John Winthrop, Sr." In *"A Miracle of Learning": Studies in Manuscripts and Irish Learning: Essays in Honour of William O'Sullivan,* edited by T. C. Barnard, Dáibhí Ó Cróinín, and Katharine Sims. Aldershot, U.K.: Ashgate, 1998.

Loetscher, Lefferts A. *A Brief History of the Presbyterians.* 4th ed. Philadelphia: Westminster, 1978.

Lovejoy, David S. *The Glorious Revolution in America.* Middletown: Wesleyan University Press, 1972.

Lucas, Paul R. "Colony or Commonwealth: Massachusetts Bay, 1661–1666." *William and Mary Quarterly* 24, no. 1 (1967): 88–107.

Lynch, M. "Continuity and Change in Urban Society, 1500–1700." In *Scottish Society, 1500–1800,* edited by R. A. Houston and I. D. Whyte. Cambridge: Cambridge University Press, 1989.

Macfarlane, Alan. *The Family Life of Ralph Josselin: A Seventeenth-Century Clergyman.* Cambridge: Cambridge University Press, 1970.

Marcus, Gail Sussman. "'Due Execution of the Generall Rules of Righteousnesse': Criminal Procedure in New Haven Town and Colony." In *Saints and Revolutionaries: Essays on Early American History,* edited by David D. Hall, John M. Murrin, and Thad W. Tate. New York: Norton, 1984.

Martin, John Frederick. *Profits in the Wilderness: Entrepreneurship and the Founding of New England Towns in the Seventeenth Century.* Chapel Hill: University of North Carolina Press, 1991.

McCusker, John J. "Colonial Statistics." In *Historical Statistics of the United States: Earliest Times to the Present.* Vol. 5, *Governance and International Relations,* edited by Susan B. Carter et al. Cambridge: Cambridge University Press, 2006.

McDonald, Forrest, and Ellen Shapiro McDonald. "The Ethnic Origins of the American People, 1790." *William and Mary Quarterly* 37, no. 2 (1980): 179–99.

McWilliams, James E. *Building the Bay Colony: Local Economy and Culture in Early Massachusetts.* Charlottesville: University of Virginia Press, 2007.

Melish, Joann. *Disowning Slavery: Gradual Emancipation and "Race" in New England, 1780–1860.* Ithaca: Cornell University Press, 1998.

Merritt, Percival. "The French Protestant Church in Boston." *Transactions of the Colonial Society of Massachusetts* 26 (1924–26): 323–48.

Miller, Kerby A. "Class, Culture, and Immigrant Group Identity in the United States: The Case of Irish-American Ethnicity." In *Immigration Reconsidered: History, Sociology, and Politics,* edited by Virginia Yans-McLaughlin. Oxford: Oxford University Press, 1990.

———. *Emigrants and Exiles: Ireland and the Irish Exodus to North America.* Oxford: Oxford University Press, 1985.

Miller, Perry. *The New England Mind: From Colony to Province.* Cambridge: Harvard University Press, 1953.

———. *The New England Mind: The Seventeenth Century.* Cambridge: Harvard University Press, 1938.

Moody, T. W., F. X. Martin, and F. J. Byrne, eds. *A New History of Ireland.* 9 vols. Oxford: Oxford University Press, 1976.

Moore, Susan Hardman. *Pilgrims: New World Settlers and the Call of Home.* New Haven: Yale University Press, 2007.

Morison, Samuel Eliot. *The Maritime History of Massachusetts, 1783–1860.* Boston: Houghton Mifflin, 1921. Reprint, Cambridge, Mass.: Riverside, 1961.

Morris, Richard B. *Government and Labor in Early America.* New York: Octagon Books, 1965.

Murdoch, Steve. *Network North: Scottish Kin, Commercial, and Covert Associations in Northern Europe, 1603–1746.* Leiden: Brill, 2006.

Murrin, John M. "The Legal Transformation: The Bench and Bar of Eighteenth-Century Massachusetts." In *Colonial America: Essays in Political and Social Development*, 2d ed., edited by Stanley A. Katz. Boston: Little, Brown, 1971.

———. "Magistrates, Sinners, and a Precarious Liberty: Trial by Jury in Seventeenth-Century New England." In *Saints and Revolutionaries: Essays on Early American History*, edited by David D. Hall, John M. Murrin, and Thad W. Tate. New York: Norton, 1984.

———. "Review Essay." *History and Theory* 11, no. 2 (1972): 226–75.

———. "'Things Fearful to Name': Bestiality in Early America." In *The Animal/Human Boundary: Historical Perspectives*, edited by Angela N. H. Creager and William Chester Jordan. Rochester: University of Rochester Press, 2002.

Nash, R. C. "Irish Atlantic Trade in the Seventeenth and Eighteenth Centuries." *William and Mary Quarterly* 42, no. 3 (1985): 329–56.

Nelson, William E. *Americanization of the Common Law: The Impact of Legal Change on Massachusetts Society, 1760–1830*. Cambridge: Harvard University Press, 1975.

Newell, Margaret E. *From Dependency to Independence: Economic Revolution in Colonial New England*. Ithaca: Cornell University Press, 1998.

———. "Robert Child and the Entrepreneurial Vision: Economy and Ideology in Early New England," *New England Quarterly* 68, no. 2 (1995): 223–56.

Nissenbaum, Stephen. *The Battle for Christmas*. New York: Knopf, 1997.

———. "New England as Region and Nation." In *All over the Map: Rethinking American Regions*, edited by Edward L. Ayres, Patricia Nelson Limerick, Stephen Nissenbaum, and Peter S. Onuf. Baltimore: Johns Hopkins University Press, 1996.

Norton, Mary Beth. *Founding Mothers and Fathers: Gendered Power and the Forming of American Society*. New York: Knopf, 1996.

———. *In the Devil's Snare: The Salem Witchcraft Crisis of 1692*. New York: Knopf, 2002.

O'Brien, Jean M. *Dispossession by Degrees: Indian Land and Identity in Natick, Massachusetts, 1650–1790*. Cambridge: Cambridge University Press, 1997.

Olsen, Alison. "The English Reception of the Huguenots, Palatines, and Salzburgers, 1680–1734: A Comparative Perspective." In *From Strangers to Citizens: The Integration of Immigrant Communities in Britain, Ireland, and Colonial America, 1550–1750*, edited by Randolph Vigne and Charles Littleton. Brighton, U.K.: Sussex Academic Press, 2001.

O'Neill, William L., ed. *Insights and Parallels: Problems and Issues of American Social History*. Minneapolis: Burgess Publishing, 1973.

Ormrod, David. "The Atlantic Economy and the 'Protestant Capitalist International,' 1651–1775." *Historical Research* 66, no. 160 (1993): 197–208.

Palfrey, John Gorham. *History of New England*. 3 vols. Boston: Little, Brown, 1858. Reprint, New York: AMS, 1966.

Perley, Sidney. *The History of Salem, Massachusetts*. 3 vols. Salem, Mass.: Sidney Perley, 1926.

Pestana, Carla Gardina. *Quakers and Baptists in Colonial Massachusetts*. Cambridge: Cambridge University Press, 1991.

———. "The Social World of Salem: William King's 1681 Blasphemy Trial." *American Quarterly* 41, no. 2 (1989): 308–27.

Piersen, William D. *Black Yankees: The Development of an Afro-American Subculture in Eighteenth-Century New England*. Amherst: University of Massachusetts Press, 1988.

Plane, Ann Marie. *Colonial Intimacies: Indian Marriage in Early New England.* Ithaca: Cornell University Press, 2000.

———. "Colonizing the Family: Marriage, Household, and Racial Boundaries in Southeastern New England to 1730." Ph.D. diss., Brandeis University, 1995.

Powell, Sumner Chilton. *Puritan Village: The Formation of a New England Town.* Middletown: Wesleyan University Press, 1963.

Powers, Edwin. *Crime and Punishment in Early America, 1620–1692.* Boston: Beacon, 1966.

Pulsipher, Jenny Hale. *Subjects unto the Same King: Indians, English, and the Contest for Authority in Colonial New England.* Philadelphia: University of Pennsylvania Press, 2005.

Purvis, Thomas L. "The European Ancestry of the United States Population, 1790." *William and Mary Quarterly* 41, no. 1 (1984): 85–101.

Purvis, Thomas L., Donald H. Akenson, Forest McDonald, and Ellen Shapiro McDonald. "Commentary." *William and Mary Quarterly* 41, no. 1 (1984): 119–35.

Rapaport, Diane. "Scots for Sale: The Fate of the Scottish Prisoners in Seventeenth-Century Massachusetts." *New England Ancestors* (Winter 2003): 30–32.

———. "Scots For Sale, Part II: Scottish Prisoners in Seventeenth-Century Maine and New Hampshire." *New England Ancestors* (Holiday 2004): 26–28.

———. "Scottish Slavery in Seventeenth-Century New England." *History Scotland* 5, no. 1 (2005): 44–52.

———. "Scottish Slaves in Colonial New England, Part I: 'Disposed of . . . For Our Best Advantage.'" *The Highlander* 42, no. 5 (2004): 10–18, 71.

———. "Scottish Slaves in Colonial New England, Part II: 'A Pore Man . . . That Hath Nothing to Live by But His Labor.'" *The Highlander* 42, no. 6 (2004): 10–17.

Rediker, Marcus. *Between the Devil and the Deep Blue Sea: Merchant Seamen, Pirates, and the Anglo-Atlantic Maritime World, 1700–1750.* Cambridge: Cambridge University Press, 1987.

Reid, John G. *Acadia, Maine and New Scotland: Marginal Colonies in the Seventeenth Century.* Toronto: University of Toronto Press, 1981.

Robbins, Chandler. *History of the Second Church, or Old North, in Boston.* Boston: John Wilson and Son, 1852.

Roberts, Oliver Ayer. *History of the Military Company of the Massachusetts, Now Called the Ancient and Honorable Artillery Company of Massachusetts, 1637–1888.* 5 vols. Boston: Alfred Mudge and Son, 1895.

Russell, Conrad. *The Causes of the English Civil War.* Oxford: Oxford University Press, 1990.

———. *The Fall of the British Monarchies, 1637–1642.* Oxford: Oxford University Press, 1991.

Rutman, Darrett B. "The Mirror of Puritan Authority." In *Law and Authority in Colonial America,* edited by George Athan Billias. Barre, Mass.: Barre Publishers, 1965.

———. "The Social Web: A Prospectus for the Study of Early American Community." In *Insights and Parallels: Problems and Issues of American Social History,* edited by William L. O'Neill. Minneapolis: Burgess Publishing, 1973.

———. *Winthrop's Boston: A Portrait of a Puritan Town, 1630–1649.* Chapel Hill: University of North Carolina Press, 1965. Reprint, New York: Norton, 1972.

Salisbury, Neal. *Manitou and Providence: Indians, Europeans, and the Making of New England, 1500–1643.* Oxford: Oxford University Press, 1982.

———. "Red Puritans: The 'Praying Indians' of Massachusetts Bay and John Eliot." *William and Mary Quarterly* 31, no. 1 (1974): 27–54.

Saunders, A. C. *Jersey in the Seventeenth Century.* Channel Islands, U.K.: J. T. Bigwood, 1931.

Schutz, John A. *Legislators of the Massachusetts General Court, 1691–1780.* Boston: Northeastern University Press, 1997.

Seybolt, Robert Francis. *The Town Officials of Colonial Boston, 1634–1775.* Cambridge: Harvard University Press, 1939.

Sheridan, Richard. *Sugar and Slavery: An Economic History of the British West Indies, 1625–1775.* Baltimore: Johns Hopkins University Press, 1973.

Shipton, Clifford K. *Biographical Sketches of Those Who Attended Harvard College.* Cambridge: Harvard University Press, 1933.

———. "Immigration to New England, 1680–1740." *Journal of Political Economy* 44, no. 2 (1936): 225–39.

———. "The Locus of Authority in Colonial Massachusetts." In *Law and Authority in Colonial America*, edited by George Athan Billias. Barre, Mass.: Barre Publishers, 1965.

Sibley, John Langdon. *Biographical Sketches of Graduates of Harvard University.* 3 vols. Cambridge, Mass.: Charles Wilson Sever, 1873–85.

Siminoff, Faren R. *Crossing the Sound: The Rise of Atlantic American Communities in Seventeenth-Century Eastern Long Island.* New York: New York University Press, 2004.

Simmons, William S. "Conversion from Indian to Puritan." In *New England Encounters: Indians and Euroamericans, c. 1600–1850*, edited by Alden T. Vaughan. Boston: Northeastern University Press, 1999.

Smith, Abbott Emerson. *Colonists in Bondage: White Servitude and Convict Labor in America, 1607–1776.* Chapel Hill: University of North Carolina Press, 1947. Reprint, Gloucester, Mass.: Peter Smith, 1965.

Smith, Daniel Scott. "The Demographic History of Colonial New England." *Journal of Economic History* 32, no. 2 (1972): 165–83.

Smout, T. C. "The Development and Enterprise of Glasgow, 1556–1707." *Scottish Journal of Political Economy* 7 (1967): 194–212.

———. "The Early Scottish Sugar Houses, 1660–1720." *Economic History Review* 2d ser., 14 (1961–62): 240–53.

———. "The Glasgow Merchant Community in the Seventeenth Century." *Scottish Historical Review* 47, no. 1 (1968): 53–71.

———. *History of the Scottish People, 1560–1830.* Glasgow: Collins, 1969.

———. *Scottish Trade on the Eve of Union, 1660–1707.* Edinburgh: Oliver and Boyd, 1963.

Solow, Barbara. *Slavery and the Rise of the Atlantic System.* Cambridge: Cambridge University Press, 1991.

Sosin, J. M. *English America and the Restoration Monarchy of Charles II: Transatlantic Politics, Commerce, and Kinship.* Lincoln: University of Nebraska Press, 1980.

Sprague, William B. *Annals of the American Pulpit.* 9 vols. New York: Arno, 1969.

Staloff, Darren. *The Making of an American Thinking Class: Intellectuals and Intelligentsia in Puritan Massachusetts.* Oxford: Oxford University Press, 1998.

Steele, Ian K. *The English Atlantic, 1675–1740.* Oxford: Oxford University Press, 1986.

Stevenson, David. *Scottish Covenanters and Irish Confederates: Scottish-Irish Relations in the Mid-Seventeenth Century.* Belfast: Ulster Historical Foundation, 1981.

Stout, Harry. *The New England Soul: Preaching and Religious Culture in Colonial New England.* Oxford: Oxford University Press, 1986.

Tarule, Robert. *The Artisan of Ipswich: Craftsmanship and Community in Colonial New England.* Baltimore: Johns Hopkins University Press, 2004.

Taylor, Justine. *A Cup of Kindness: The History of the Royal Scottish Corporation, a London Charity, 1603–2003.* East Linton, U.K.: Tuckwell, 2003.

Thomas, Isaiah. *History of Printing in America.* New York: Weathervane Books, 1970.

Thompson, Roger. *Sex in Middlesex: Popular Mores in a Massachusetts County, 1649–1699.* Amherst: University of Massachusetts Press, 1986.

Towner, Lawrence W. "'A Fondness for Freedom': Servant Protest in Puritan Society." *William and Mary Quarterly* 19, no. 2 (1962): 201–19.

———. "A Good Master Well Served: A Social History of Servitude in Massachusetts, 1620–1750." Ph.D. diss., Northwestern University, 1955.

Trinterud, Leonard J. *The Forming of an American Tradition: A Re-examination of Colonial Presbyterianism.* Philadelphia: Westminster, 1949.

Truxes, Thomas M. *Irish-American Trade, 1660–1783.* Cambridge: Cambridge University Press, 1988.

Twombly, Robert C., and Robert H. Moore. "Black Puritan: The Negro in Seventeenth-Century Massachusetts." *William and Mary Quarterly* 24, no. 2 (April 1967): 224–42.

Vaughan, Alden T., ed. *New England Encounters: Indians and Euroamericans, c. 1600–1850.* Boston: Northeastern University Press, 1999.

Vaughan, Alden T., and Virginia Mason Vaughan. "England's 'Others' in the Old and New Worlds." In *The World of John Winthrop: Essays on England and New England, 1588–1649,* edited by Francis J. Bremer and Lynn A. Botelho. Boston: Massachusetts Historical Society, 2005.

Vickers, Daniel. "Competency and Competition: Economic Culture in Early America." *William and Mary Quarterly* 47, no. 1 (1990): 3–29.

———. *Farmers and Fishermen: Two Centuries of Work in Essex County, Massachusetts, 1630–1850.* Chapel Hill: University of North Carolina Press, 1994.

———. "Work and Life on the Fishing Periphery of Essex County, Massachusetts, 1630–1675." In *Seventeenth-Century New England,* edited by David D. Hall and David Grayson Allen. Boston: Colonial Society of Massachusetts, 1984.

———. "Working the Fields in a Developing Economy." In *Work and Labor in Early America,* edited by Stephen Innes. Chapel Hill: University of North Carolina Press, 1988.

Vigne, Randolph, and Charles Littleton, eds. *From Strangers to Citizens: The Integration of Immigrant Communities in Britain, Ireland, and Colonial America, 1550–1750.* Brighton, U.K.: Sussex Academic Press, 2001.

Virgadamo, Peter R. "Colonial Charity and the American Character: Boston, 1630–1775." Ph.D. diss., University of Southern California, 1982.

———. "Urban Poverty and Church Charity in Colonial Boston." Institute for the Research on Poverty. Discussion Paper 896–89. Madison: University of Wisconsin, Madison, 1989.

Wall, Robert Emmet, Jr. "The Decline of the Massachusetts Franchise: 1647–1666." *Journal of American History* 59, no. 2 (1972): 303–10.

Walsh, Lorena S. "The African American Population of the Colonial United States." In *A Population History of North America,* edited by Michael R. Haines and Richard H. Steckel. Cambridge: Cambridge University Press, 2000.

Waters, John J. "Hingham, Massachusetts, 1631–1661: An East Anglian Oligarchy in the New World." *Journal of Social History* 1, no. 4 (1968): 351–70.

Waters, Thomas Franklin. *Ipswich in the Massachusetts Bay Colony.* 2 vols. Ipswich, Mass.: Ipswich Historical Society, 1905.

Weis, Frederick Lewis. *The Colonial Clergy and the Colonial Churches of New England.* Lancaster, Mass.: Society of the Descendants of the Colonial Clergy, 1936.

Whyte, Ian D. *Scotland Before the Industrial Revolution: An Economic and Social History, 1050–1750.* London: Longman, 1995.

Wilson, Kathleen. *The Island Race: Englishness, Empire, and Gender in the Eighteenth Century.* London: Routledge, 2002.

Windsor, Justin. *Memorial History of Boston.* Boston: James R. Osgood, 1881.

Winship, Michael P. *The Times and Trials of Anne Hutchinson.* Lawrence: University Press of Kansas, 2005.

Wood, Joseph. *The New England Village.* Baltimore: Johns Hopkins University Press, 1997.

Woodward, Walter William. "Prospero's America: John Winthrop, Jr., Alchemy, and the Creation of New England Culture, 1606–1676." Ph.D. diss., University of Connecticut, 2001.

Wormald, Jenny. "James VI, James I, and the Identity of Britain." In *The British Problem, c. 1534–1707: State Formation in the Atlantic Archipelago*, edited by Brendan Bradshaw and John Morrill. New York: St. Martin's Press, 1996.

Wright, Conrad Edick. *The Transformation of Charity in Postrevolutionary New England.* Boston: Northeastern University Press, 1992.

Wrightson, Keith. *English Society, 1580–1680.* New Brunswick: Rutgers University Press, 1982.

Wroth, L. Kinvin. "The Massachusetts Vice-admiralty Court." In *Law and Authority in Colonial America*, edited by George Athan Billias. Barre, Mass.: Barre Publishers, 1965.

Yans-McLaughlin, Virginia, ed. *Immigration Reconsidered: History, Sociology, and Politics.* Oxford: Oxford University Press, 1990.

Zahedieh, Nuala. "Overseas Expansion and Trade in the Seventeenth Century." In *The Origins of Empire: British Overseas Enterprise to the Close of the Seventeenth Century*, edited by Nicholas Canny. Oxford: Oxford University Press, 1998.

Zelner, Kyle. "Essex County's Two Militias: The Social Composition of Offensive and Defensive Units During King Philip's War, 1675–1676." *New England Quarterly* 72, no. 4 (1999): 577–93.

Zuckerman, Michael. *Peaceable Kingdoms: New England Towns in the Eighteenth Century.* New York: Knopf, 1980.

Index

Entries in *italics* refer to ships.